What People are saying about *Experiencing the Psalms*

"This **in-depth study of the Psalms** took me deeper not only into the word of God, but caused me to go deeper into myself and found a place that opened up a well of words and gave me insight that **caused me to worship in a whole new way**." – Cindy Johnson

"I appreciate Dr. Wilson's application to the true Word of God, the research into the roots of the original language(s), and his helpful insights that enable putting God's Word into practical living, not just study and knowledge. **Each lesson continues to draw me closer to God in a deeper personal relationship, which is vital to every believer!**" – Paul Klein

"If you've only thought of the Psalms as a book of songs or as peak moments in Davidic history as I did, think again. This study will grip your whole being as it **makes application of the Psalms to your daily life a real possibility**." – Veronica Heabler

"I like the **focus on discipleship** in these studies and the personal way in which they are written. The question often both summarize and put the finger on things." – Judith Korsgren

"The Psalm study **took you inside the mind of David as he bared his soul** to the Lord in anguish and praise. It is as modern as tomorrow!" – Don Miller

Experiencing the Psalms

Bible Study Commentary for Personal Devotional Use, Small Groups or Sunday School Classes, and Sermon Preparation for Pastors and Teachers

JesusWalk® Bible Study Series

by Dr. Ralph F. Wilson

Additional books and reprint licenses are available at:
www.jesuswalk.com/books/psalms.htm

Free Participant Guide handout sheets are available at:
www.jesuswalk.com/psalms/psalms-lesson-handouts.pdf

JesusWalk® Publications
Loomis, California

Paperback

ISBN-13: 978-0-9819721-0-7

ISBN-10: 0981972101

Library of Congress Control Number: 2010902569

Library of Congress subject headings:

Bible – O.T. – Psalms – Commentaries

Bible – O.T. – Psalms – Criticism, interpretation. etc.

Bible – O.T. – Psalms – Study and teaching

Bible – O.T. – Psalms – Devotional literature

Suggested Classifications:

Library of Congress BS1430.3

Dewey: 223.2

Published by JesusWalk® Publications, P.O. Box 565, Loomis, CA 95650-0565, USA. www.jesuswalk.com/books/

JesusWalk is a registered trademark and Joyful Heart is a trademark of Joyful Heart Renewal Ministries.

Unless otherwise noted, all the Bible verses quoted are from the New International Version (International Bible Society, 1973, 1978), used by permission.

100301

Preface

The Book of Psalms represents a rich tapestry of prayer and praise. Some psalms reflect a texture of deep despair, other glow with a deep peace in the Lord's strength, still others bubble with an exuberant exaltation of the Most High God. They cover the range of human emotion and experience. What they all have in common is prayer, a reaching out to God from every imaginable experience.

Marc Chagall, "David with His Harp" (1956) Color lithograph.

In this 12-week study we'll attempt to enter into the experience of the psalms. Yes, we'll explore the meanings of words and learn to appreciate the high art of these poetic masterpieces. We will study thoughtfully, carefully. But more than that we will find out how to pray. We will know how to find peace in the midst of turmoil. We will learn to be thankful. We will begin to follow the pattern of the psalmists as we begin to praise. In short, with the psalms that we study as our guide, we will grow deeper in our walk with the Lord and more able to offer worthy praise to the King. We will experience the Psalms.

I must say that narrowing down the psalms we'll study to just a few has been difficult. For more than forty years I have been reading the Psalms through at least twice a year. So many of the psalms have become my friends, my companions. When I come to them in my reading I am delighted to read their faith-filled words once again. As I surveyed the Psalms in preparation for this study I listed 70 psalms as my "favorites," and even that list of nearly half of the total of 150 psalms had to leave out some that I loved. But how can I narrow down the number to perhaps three dozen without leaving out some of the gems of the Psalter? I can't. At best the 13 lessons in this study can serve only as an introduction to the rich collection of psalms that speak to us so profoundly.

My prayer is that you will purpose in this study to grow in your heart even more than you grow in your mind. That you will embrace these psalms and make them your own. That as you journey through this life you walk with these psalms as your guides and companions as you travel to your final destination – an eternity in fellowship with the Father and the Son and the Holy Spirit.

Yours in Christ,
Dr. Ralph F. Wilson
Loomis, California
August 31, 2007

Table of Contents

References and Abbreviations

Allen   Leslie C. Allen, *Psalms 101-150* (Word Biblical Commentary 21; Word, 1983), ISBN 0849902207

BDB   Francis Brown, S.R. Driver, and Charles A. Briggs, *A Hebrew and English Lexicon of the Old Testament* (Clarendon Press: Oxford, originally published 1907, reprinted with corrections 1953). ISBN 0198643012. I am using an electronic version.

Craigie   Peter C. Craigie, *Psalms 1-50* (Word Biblical Commentary 19; Word, 1983), ISBN 0849902185

Firth and Johnson   David Firth and Philip S. Johnson, *Interpreting the Psalms* (IVP Academic, 2005). ISBN 0830828338. Includes chapters by 15 evangelical Old Testament scholars on recent advances in the study of the Psalms. Recommended for pastors and serious students if you want to dig deeper.

Harrison   Roland Kenneth Harrison, *Introduction to the Old Testament* (Eerdmans, 1969). ISBN 0802831079. Contains a traditional introduction to the Psalms.

Holladay   William L. Holladay, *A Concise Hebrew and Aramaic Lexicon of the Old Testament*, based on the Lexical work of Ludwig Koehler and Walter Baumbartner (Grand Rapids: Eerdmans / Leiden: E. J. Brill, 1988). ISBN 0802834132

ISBE   *The International Standard Bible Encyclopedia*, Geoffrey W. Bromiley (general editor), (Eerdmans, 1979-1988; fully revised from the 1915 edition). ISBN: 0802837859. Excellent 4-volume scholarly, evangelical Bible dictionary.

KB   *Lexicon in Veteris Testamenti Libros*, edited by Ludwig Koehler and Walter Baumgartner (Leiden: E.J. Brill, 1958). ISBN: 9004076395. Newer

	Hebrew/Aramaic-German-English lexicon, though it doesn't fully displace BDB
KD	*Commentary on the Old Testament*, Carl Friedrich Keil and Franz Delitzsch (Eerdmans, reprinted 1976). Vol 1 (Pentateuch) was written by Carl Friedrich Keil (Johann Friedrich Karl Keil, 1807-1888), published in German in 1861 and translated by James Martin from German. Current ISBN 0913573884
Kidner	Derek Kidner, *Psalms 1-72* and *Psalms 73-150* (Tyndale Old Testament Commentaries; InterVarsity Press/Tyndale Press, 1973) ISBN 0877842647 and ISBN 0877842655. An affordable and very useful commentary on the Psalms. Recommended as your first commentary.
Kirkpatrick	A.F. Kirkpatrick, *The Book of Psalms* (The Cambridge Bible; Cambridge University Press, first edition 1902)
KJV	*King James Version* (Authorized Version, 1611)
Lewis	C.S. Lewis, *Reflections on the Psalms* (Harcourt, Brace and Company, 1958). ISBN 015676248X.
Longman	Tremper Longman III, *How to Read the Psalms* (InterVarsity Press, 1998). ISBN 0877849412. A really well-written, easy-to-understand introduction to the Psalms that includes recent advances in Psalms study. Strongly recommended.
NASB	*New American Standard Bible* (Lockman Foundation, 1971, 1977)
NIV	*New International Version* (International Bible Society, 1973, 1978)
NJB	*New Jerusalem Bible* (Darton, Longman & Todd Ltd., 1985)
NRSV	*New Revised Standard Version* (Division of Christian Education of the National Council of Churches of Christ USA, 1989)
Spurgeon	C.H. Spurgeon, *A Treasury of David: An Exposition of the Psalms* (Cornerstone, n.d., originally published 1869), 3 volumes.

Tate   Marvin E. Tate, *Psalms 51-100* (Word Biblical Commentary 20; Word, 1990), ISBN 0849902193

TDNT   *Theological Dictionary of the New Testament*, Gerhard Kittel and Gerhard Friedrich (editors), Geoffrey W. Bromiley (translator and editor), (Eerdmans, 1964-1976; translated from Theologisches Wörterbuch zum Neuen Testament, ten volume edition). CD-ROM, ISBN 1577990994. Standard for many years, mixture of conservative and liberal treatments of NT Greek words.

TWOT   R. Laird Harris, Gleason L. Archer, Jr., and Bruce K. Waltke, *Theological Wordbook of the Old Testament* (Moody Press, 1980), 2 volumes. ISBN 0802486312. An electronic version is available for iExalt WordSearch.

Reprint Guidelines

You are free to print out a copy of this book for your own use in this study.

Copying the Handouts. In some cases, small groups or Sunday school classes would like to use these notes to study this material. That's great. An appendix provides copies of handouts designed for classes and small groups. There is no charge whatsoever to print out as many copies of the handouts as you need for participants.

All charts and notes are copyrighted and must bear the line: "Copyright © 2010, Ralph F. Wilson. All rights reserved. Reprinted by permission."

You may not resell these notes to other groups or individuals outside your congregation. You may, however, charge people in your group enough to cover your copying costs.

Copying the book (or the majority of it) in your congregation or group, you are requested to purchase a reprint license for each book. A Reprint License, $2.50 for each copy, is available for purchase at:

www.jesuswalk.com/books/psalms.htm

Or you may send a check to:

> Dr. Ralph F. Wilson
> JesusWalk Publications
> PO Box 565
> Loomis, CA 95650, USA

The Scripture says,

> "The laborer is worthy of his hire" (Luke 10:7) and "Anyone who receives instruction in the word must share all good things with his instructor" (Galatians 6:6).

However, if you are from a third world country or an area where it is difficult to transmit money, please make a small contribution to help the poor in your community instead.

Online Bible Study Forum

Each chapter in this study contains four or five questions to help you learn and process what you've been studying. As you engage your mind in the attempt to frame an answer, you'll begin to understand the issues raised in the Scripture text and the implications of applying the principles in your own life.

But learning is better with others. This book began as an interactive e-mail Bible study. One component of this learning approach has been to give students a chance to post their answers to the questions in an online Forum and read how others answered the questions as a way of deepening their understanding. You'll find that each of the questions in the chapters contains a web address where you, too, can take advantage of the Forum.

However, if you want to participate in the Forum, you'll need to agree to some basic guidelines (www.jesuswalk.com/admin/pu_forum_guidelines.htm). In short:

- No denomination or religion bashing.
- Practice a loving spirit.
- Comments may be removed in the future.
- Stay on topic.
- Be discrete. Don't give out your e-mail address or share things too personal.

If you haven't participated in the Forum before, you'll need to register first. To keep from getting confused, why don't you read the Instructions for the Forum. They will explain exactly how to register (www.joyfulheart.com/forums/instructions.htm).

Once you've registered for the Forum you can introduce yourself to others in this study (www.joyfulheart.com/forums/index.php?showtopic=650) and get started with the questions posed in each chapter.

Table of Psalms Referenced

Psalm	page	Psalm	page
Psalm 1	62	Psalm 61	108
2	174	63	57
3	132	69	90
8	34	80	103
15	67	91	111
16	131	95	81
19	38	96	143
22	181	98	84
23	127	100	205
24	151	103	157
27	47	107	208
31	133	110	178
32	188	117	169
34	213	118	209
40	98	119	224
42	52	121	118
43	52	126	147
46	134	131	125
47	223	133	72
51	193	139	43
57	139	145	163
		150	78

Introduction to the Psalms

David, the shepherd boy of the Bethlehem hills, loved to sing, sang to his sheep. Over the years he grew into a gifted songwriter, a poet. And then, when he was but a teenager, the Prophet Samuel came to his family's farm and poured oil over his head, anointing David King of Israel. From that moment the Holy Spirit of God poured over him as well. His gift of song and poetry took on a new level of inspiration.

Over the next 600 years other God-inspired poets gave voice to psalms, completing the collection of psalms that we know today as the Book of Psalms, the Psalter – 150 poetic songs that lie at the heart of our Bibles. The Psalms express the entire spectrum of human emotion – fear, despair, longing, love, hope, joy, and exultation. They also instruct us in how we can voice our own prayers and praise to God.

James J. Tissot (1836-1902, French artist and illustrator), "David Singing" (1896-1900), watercolor. Psalms 57:7.

What Is a Psalm?

The word Psalm (Greek *psalmos*) translates the Hebrew noun *mizmôr*, "song, instrumental music," from the verb *zāmar*, "sing, sing praise, make music." It reminds us that the Book of Psalms was – and is – intended for singing. This was the church's first song book. Though we have lost the original tunes, individual psalms have been put to music many times since. The ancient songwriters were devout poets who put their heartfelt devotion toward God into verse.

The Psalms are meant to be sung – and accompanied by musical instruments. David, the author of many of the psalms, was a skilled player of the "harp," more accurately perhaps, the "lyre" (*kinnôr*), "a musical instrument having strings and a wooden frame," and commonly associated in the Bible with joy and gladness.[1]

Hebrew Poetry

Hebrew poetry differs from most Western poetry in that it doesn't rhyme. There seem to be two primary elements that distinguish Hebrew Poetry:

1. Thought parallelism
2. Imagery

In western poetry we use both rhyme and rhythm in traditional poems. But in Hebrew poetry the rhythm may be in terms of units per line. However, the exact nature of this is still debated and some recent scholars have concluded that the Psalms are not metrical, that this is an idea imported from Western poetical forms. Longman recommends caution about any interpretation based primarily on a verse's supposed meter.[2]

1. Thought Parallelism

However, the element of thought parallelism in Hebrew poetry is quite apparent and has become better understood in recent decades. Unlike poetry that relies on rhyme, parallelism can be translated into other languages without losing its distinct flavor. The two basic types of parallelism are:

Synonymous Parallelism is the most common form of parallelism. Here the idea of the first line is reinforced in the second line.

> "He does not treat us as our sins deserve
> or repay us according to our iniquities." (Psalm 103:10)

You can find parallelism in Jesus' teaching, too (for example, Matthew 5:43-45). But scholars have realized rather recently that synonymous parallelism is something of a misnomer. The lines are not strictly synonymous. You might describe it as "A, what's more B." The second line always seems to carry forward the thought found in the first phrase in some way. This progression is sometimes subtle, but often quite obvious. The second – or sometimes third line – reinforces and extends the meaning of the first, like a second wave that mounts higher than the first, and a third even higher yet (for example, Psalms 92:9; 93:3; 145:18).

---

[1] Longman, *How to Read the Psalms*, pp. 97-98.
[2] Longman, *How to Read the Psalms*, p. 108. He cites his article, "A Critique of Two Recent Metrical Systems," *Biblica* 63 (1982):230-254.

When interpreting Hebrew poetry however, it's important not to overemphasize the nuances between the similar words, for example, between "man" and "Son of man" in 8:4 or "my soul" and "my flesh" in Psalm 63:1. As Kidner puts it, "They are in double harness, rather than in competition."[3] Rather look for the ways that second idea builds upon the first.

Antithetic Parallelism is also common. The idea in the first line is contrasted or negated in the second line as a means of reinforcing it. It is found most commonly in the Proverbs and in the didactic psalms.

> "The wicked borrow and do not repay,
> but the righteous give generously." (Psalm 37:21)

In addition to these two common forms of Hebrew parallelism, scholars have found a number of other less prominent varieties. Hebrew poetry was a fine art that we are just beginning to appreciate more fully.

2. Imagery

A second common characteristic of Hebrew poetry is its use of imagery, comparing one thing to another. Of course, imagery can be found in prose sections of the Old Testament and it is not found in every psalm, but it is especially rich in Hebrew poetry. Imagery has a way of fixing an idea in our minds with clarity.

Think about the images in the familiar 23rd Psalm. In prose we might say with some accuracy: "God meets all our needs and protects us." It is true, but not particularly memorable. The power and beauty of the 23rd Psalm is the way that it communicates these ideas through images: shepherd/sheep, green pastures/still waters, the valley of the shadow of death, a table, an anointing, and an overflowing cup. These images in our minds with the thoughts and emotions they evoke contribute to make this psalm an all-time favorite.

There are two kinds of images used in the Psalms:

1. **Simile** is a comparison which is made explicit by the presence of the word "like" or "as." For example:

   > "As the deer pants for streams of water,
   > So my soul pants for you, O God." (Psalm 42:1)

2. **Metaphor** is a comparison that is implicit, that is, a comparison without the mention of "like" or "as." For example:

   > "The LORD is my shepherd, I shall not want." (Psalm 23:1)

---

[3] Kidner, *Psalms 1-72*, p. 2.

A metaphor communicates a more vivid image than a simile because it is implicit and draws the comparison more closely.

As you study the Psalms, be aware of the images that are used and the thoughts and emotions that they are intended to evoke in us, the readers.

A few psalms (9, 10, 25, 34, 37, 111, 112, 119, 145) are structured as an acrostic, each verse or section beginning with a successive letter of the Hebrew alphabet. Exactly the function acrostics serve, we're not sure. But the acrostics may be a way of reflecting the order of God in creation. They may be an aid to memorization, or simply aesthetically pleasing because of their intricacy.[4]

Categories of Psalms

The twentieth century saw various attempts to classify psalms by their structure and form, a discipline known as Form Criticism. Hermann Gunkel, comparing the Psalms with parallels in other ancient Near Eastern cultures, saw five major groups or genre of psalms: hymns, community laments, individual laments, royal psalms, and individual thanksgivings, plus some subcategories.[5] Gunkel's categories have sparked intense debate. Since a number of psalms fit into more than one category, these categories can't be seen as rigid. A psalm genre is a kind of template, but the author is free to improvise or alter the template as necessary. Tremper Longman III suggests the following genre of psalms:

- **The Hymn**, recognized by its exuberant praise of the Lord. Examples are abundant, such as, Psalms 8, 19, 29, 33, 47, 48, 92, 96, 103.
- **The Lament**, the polar opposite of the hymn on the emotional spectrum. Lamentations begin with a complaint, but often conclude with praise. Within a lament you may find several of the following elements: (a) invocation, (2) plea to God for help, (3) complaints, (4) confession of sin or assertion of innocence, (5) curse of enemies (imprecation), (6) confidence in God's response, and (7) hymn or blessing. Examples include: Psalm 3, 7, 13, 25, 22, 42-43, 44, 51, 74, 79, 80 and many others.
- **Thanksgiving Psalms**. These are similar to hymns, but particularly recount what God has done. They are closely related to laments, in that a thanksgiving psalm is often an answer to a lament. Examples include: Psalms 18, 30, 32, 34
- **Psalms of Confidence**, an expression of the psalmist's trust in God's goodness and power. Examples include Psalms 11, 16, 23, 27, 62, 91, 121, 125, 131.

---

[4] Longman, *How to Read the Psalms*, pp. 107-108.
[5] For a helpful examination of prayers in neighboring cultures, see Tremper Longman III, "Ancient Near Eastern Prayer Genres," in Firth and Johnston, *Interpreting the Psalms*, pp. 41-59.

- **Psalms of Remembrance** make reference to the great redemptive acts of the past, particularly the Exodus (Psalm 77:16) and the establishment of the Davidic covenant and dynasty (Psalms 89, 132). Examples are found in Psalms 78, 105, 106, 135, 136.
- **Wisdom Psalms** tell us in concrete ways how God wants us to live our lives. This kind of literature is found in Proverbs, Job, and Ecclesiastes. But it is also found in several psalms, such as Psalms 1, 19, 37, 49, 119.
- **Kingship Psalms** focus on two kings: (1) the human king of Israel (Psalms 18, 20, 21, 45, 72, 101, 132) and (2) God as king (Psalms 47, 98). There is also a messianic theme throughout the Psalms collection that looks forward to the coming Davidic king, especially in Psalms 2 and 110.[6]

Authorship

Of the 150 psalms, 116 include an extended title or an ascription that is part of verse 1 in the Hebrew text. While not part of the original text, they were probably inserted by editors fairly early – certainly long before the second or third century when they were translated into Greek.

The titles at the beginning of many of the psalms, such as "of David," use a Hebrew preposition l^e. It can carry the ideas "of, for, from, at, in reference to, belonging to." Thus "of David" could mean "belonging to David" or "(dedicated) to David."[7] In the ascription to Psalm 18 it is quite clear that authorship was intended:

> "For (l^e) the director of music. Of (l^e) David the servant of the LORD. He
> sang to the LORD the words of this song when the LORD delivered him from
> the hand of all his enemies and from the hand of Saul. He said...."

We do know that David was closely identified with worship music. He sang to calm King Saul (1 Samuel 16:14-23; 18:10-11), accompanying himself on a lyre or harp. He is called "the sweet psalmist of Israel" (2 Samuel 23:1), and is named as an inventor of musical instruments (Amos 6:5).

While realizing that it is not entirely certain, I am taking the preposition l^e in the ascription of psalms as primarily ascribing authorship.[8] If this is indeed the case, named authors include:

---

[6] Longman, *How to Read the Psalms*, chapter 19.
[7] Craigie, *Psalms 1-50*, p. 35.
[8] Kidner, *Psalms 1-72*, p. 33.

David	Named as author of nearly half the collection		73 psalms
Asaph	Called "Asaph the Seer" (2 Chronicles 29:30), and was from a Levitical family. He founded the temple choir as chief musician (1 Chronicles 15;17-19; chapter 16).	Psalms 50, 73-83	12 psalms
Sons of Korah	A Levitical family, singers and musicians of the temple choir founded by Heman the Ezrahite (1 Chronicles 6:31-46).	Psalms 42-49, 84-85, 87-88	12 psalms
Ethan the Ezrahite = Juduthun	From a Levitical family and founded one of the temple choirs (1 Chronicles 16:41; 25:1-6).	Psalm 89, 39, 62, 77	4 psalms
Heman the Ezrahite	Called "Heman the Musician" (1 Chronicles 6:33) and was founder of a temple choir.	Psalm 88	1 psalm
Solomon	Third king of Israel	Psalms 72, 127	2 psalms
Moses	Leader during the Exodus	Psalm 90	1 psalm
No title at all			34 psalms

Date of the Psalms

While there has been considerable debate about the dating of the Psalms as rather late, the following points should be considered in defense of an earlier dating:

1. Egypt, Babylon, and Canaan all had developed psalmody before and during Israel's residence in Palestine.

2. Psalmody was known from the earliest times in Israel, such as the Song of Deborah (Judges 5) from about 1150 BC. It is even possible that some of the psalms in our Psalter predated David. Some of the allusions to the temple could possible refer to the tabernacle at Shiloh, known as the "holy place" (Exodus 28:43; 29:30), "the house of the Lord" (Joshua 6:24; 1 Samuel 1:7ff; 3:3; cf. 2 Samuel 12:20).

3. It is difficult to imagine that psalms mentioning the king or the ark could have been first composed after the exile.

4. The traces of Aramaic found in some of the psalms are no reason to date them late, since Aramaic was known in Jerusalem as early as the eighth century BC. The presence of Ugaritic language affinities are witness to the early date of many of the psalms.

Elizabeth Jane Gardner (1837–1922), "The Shepherd David, " (ca. 1895), oil on canvas; 61 1/2 x 42 3/8 in. (156.2 x 107.6 cm), National Museum of Women in the Arts.

5. The Psalms could have been written no later than the translation of the Greek Septuagint 300-200 BC.

Thus it is likely that the Psalms were composed during the period of the Kings and before the Maccabean period, that is, a 600 year period between about 1000 and 400 BC.[9] The dating of the Psalms can be divided into three groups:

1. **Pre-Exilic**, written during the period of the Kings prior to the Exile (1000-600 BC). This would include the royal psalms, those which mention the existence of the northern kingdom, and those with greater affinity to Ugaritic language and syntax. David who reigned approximately 1010-970 BC was by all accounts the most prolific author of psalms.

2. **Exilic**, those written during the exile (605-537 BC). This would include some of the dirge or lament psalms and perhaps those mentioning the betrayal of Judah by her

---

[9] This section draws on material from Harrison, *Introduction*, pp. 983-985 and lecture notes from David J. Cline.

enemies. Psalm 137 recalls this period: "By the rivers of Babylon we sat and wept when we remembered Zion...."

3. **Post-Exilic**, written after the Exile (537 to about 400 BC). This probably includes psalms about the righteous sufferer, how the Torah should be observed, wisdom, and cautions against atheism.

Structure of the Psalter

While the dating of the Psalms seems to be between 1000 and 400 BC, editing took place somewhat later, but by the time the Septuagint was translated.

Recently, scholars have taken much more seriously the composition of the Book of Psalms as a whole, as an editor put it into final form. The Book of Psalms in our Bibles is divided into five books, probably to echo the five books of the Pentateuch. Book 1, chapters 1-41; Book 2, chapters 42-72; Book 3, chapters 73-89; Book 4, chapters 90-106; and Book 5, chapters 107-150. Each of the books concludes with a doxology, such as the last verse of Book 1:

> "Praise be to the LORD, the God of Israel,
> from everlasting to everlasting.
> Amen and Amen." (Psalm 41:13)

Psalms begins deliberately with a psalm designed to urge the reader to study the Psalms with the same diligence as one studied the Torah.

> "His delight is in the law of the LORD,
> and on his law he meditates day and night." (Psalm 1:2)

In his careful survey of the Psalter, Gerald H. Wilson also observes "frames" – a Royal Covenantal Frame (Psalms 2, 72, 89, 144) and a Final Wisdom Frame (Psalms 1, 73, 90, 107, 145).[10] The Psalter is much more than a haphazard compilation of individual psalms. It is "the end result of a process of purposeful editorial arrangement of psalms and collections of psalms producing a unified whole."[11]

Canonicity of the Psalms

As the Hebrew Bible developed, it was divided into three sections: The Law (the Pentateuch, Torah, first five books of the Bible), the Prophets (the historical books, and the major and minor prophets), and the Writings (Job, Psalms, Proverbs, Ecclesiastes, Song of Solomon). Some psalms scrolls found at Qumran contain both psalms that appear in our Bibles and psalms that "didn't make the cut." However, the canon of accepted psalms in the

---

[10] David M. Howard, Jr., "The Psalms and Current Study," in Firth and Johnston, *Interpreting the Psalms*, pp. 25-29; and Gerald H. Wilson, "The Structure of the Psalter," *Ibid.*, pp. 229-246.

[11] Gerald H. Wilson, *Ibid.*, p. 229.

Hebrew Bible seems to have been fixed by the time of the translation of the Septuagint in the third and second centuries BC, since it is very similar to the Book of Psalms in the Masoretic Hebrew text that forms the basis of our modern Bibles.

Chapter and Verse Confusions

The chapter numbers were added much later in the 13th century AD. Up until that point, individual psalms would be referred to by their first line rather than their chapter number. When Jesus from the cross quoted Psalm 22:1 with the words, "My God, my God, why have you forsaken me?" he was probably calling the whole psalm to mind, which included the phrase "they have pierced my hands and my feet...." (22:16b).

Adding chapter numbers and verses should have clarified things, but in some ways they've confused matters. For example, while the Hebrew numbering counts a psalm's inscription as verse 1, our English versions number from the verse *following* any inscription. Another confusion comes from slight discrepancies between the numbering of the Hebrew and Greek versions of Psalms. Modern Protestant and Roman Catholic translations are based on the Hebrew numbering, while the Catholic lectionary and Eastern Orthodox translations are based on the Greek numbering.

Technical Terms

Some of the intriguing aspects of the psalms are technical terms which often appear in the ascription. Unfortunately, there's lots of speculation but not much firm knowledge about most of these.

a. Interjections.

- **Selah** occurs 71 times. It is probably a signal for an interlude or change of musical accompaniment, probably from the root *sll*, "to lift up" or perhaps an Aramaic verb "to bend.[12]
- **Higgaion**, found in 9:16 in a note with Selah and in the text of 19:14; and 92:3. It seems to derive from *hāgā*, "meditate, devise, plot." It may mean "meditation, whispering melody." As a musical direction it may perhaps indicate the quieter instruments.[13]

---

[12] Kidner, *Psalms 1-72*, pp. 36-37.
[13] Kidner, *Psalms 1-72*, p. 37. Herbert Wolf, *hāgā*, TWOT #467c.

b. Classifications

- **Psalm** (*mizmôr*) and **Song** (*shîr*) can't be completely distinguished, but psalm probably implies that it was sung to an instrumental accompaniment.[14]
- **Shiggaion** (Psalm 7) seems to derive from *shāgā*, "to err, wander." Perhaps it means "wild and ecstatic" or denotes a stirring of the emotions.[15]
- **Maskil** (*maskîl*) designates 13 psalms. The root *śkl*, denotes "insight" or "wisdom," so a maskil might be an "efficacious psalm" or "skillful psalm," but we don't really know the meaning.[16]

c. Liturgical Notes

There are a number of designations that we can only speculate about their actual meanings. The following two, however, seem fairly well established.

- **To the Choirmaster** (*nāṣaḥ*), "chief musician" (KJV), "leader" (NRSV), "director of music" (NIV) occurs in 55 psalms. The Hebrew root (*nāṣaḥ*) means "to excel," thus "to superintend," so "choirmaster" seems like a reasonable translation.[17] Again, we're not sure what it means.
- **A Song of Ascents** (Psalms 120-134), ascribed to 15 psalms, probably referring to the pilgrimage up to Jerusalem, or the processional ascent of "the hill of the Lord" (Isaiah 30:29).[18] They were used particularly during the Feast of Tabernacles.

Two other groups of psalms should also be noted:

- **Egyptian Hallel Psalms** (Psalms 113-118) are traditionally associated with the feast of Passover and deliverance from Egypt. Hallel means "praise." The first half of the Hallel (Psalms 113-114) was sung earlier in the Passover. The "hymn" that Jesus and his disciples sang after the Last Supper (Mark 14:26; Matthew 26:30) was, no doubt, the second half of the Hallel (Psalms 114-118 or 115-118), sung at the end of the Passover meal.[19]
- **Hallel Psalms** (Psalms 146-150) were for more general use in worship.

---

[14] Kidner, *Psalms 1-72*, p. 37.
[15] *Ibid.*
[16] Kidner, *Psalms 1-72*, p. 37; Herbert Wolf, *śākal*, TWOT 2263b.
[17] Kidner, *Psalms 1-72*, pp. 40; Milton C. Fisher, *nāṣaḥ*, TWOT 1402.
[18] Kidner, *Psalms 1-72*, p. 43.
[19] Joachim Jeremias, *The Eucharistic Words of Jesus* (Oxford: Basil Blackwood, 1955), pp. 30-31, especially fn. 1 on page 31.

A Phantom New Year Festival

Before we conclude our introduction to the Psalms, it's important to mention a wrong turn in twentieth century Psalms studies. As mentioned above, Gunkel's categories of Psalm forms came out of a study of literature of other Near Eastern cultures and, as a whole, has been helpful in better understanding the Psalms as literature. However, this comparative religions approach led several leading scholars, beginning with Gunkel and Mowinckel, to argue that a high percentage of Israel's psalms must be related to an Israelite New Year Festival, celebrated in the autumn, in which the Lord's kingship was annually reaffirmed over the forces of chaos. This hypotheses relies on the existence of an Israelite festival corresponding to the Babylonian *Akitu* festival. However, there is nothing in the Psalms or the Old Testament that suggests celebration of such a festival in Israel.[20] Arthur Weiser later modified this hypothesis to the celebration of an autumn covenant festival, but the evidence of such a festival just isn't there.

The unfortunate result is that the commentaries that adopted these hypotheses are much less useful than they would have been if they had limited their search for a life-setting within the history and culture of Israel itself. The emphasis on determining the life setting (*Sitz im Leben*) of a psalm is good, but the fact is that most of the psalms just don't provide much context to the reasons for their composition and we must accept that limitation rather than import speculative theories to "guide" our interpretation.

Authority of the Psalms

The New Testament quotes the Psalms extensively. But note the reverent way in which the author of Hebrews quoted passages from Psalms:

- "God says... He says" (Hebrews 1:7-8)
- "The Holy Spirit says..." (Hebrews 1:7)

Jesus, too, regarded the Psalms as inspired Scripture.

- "This is what I told you while I was still with you: Everything must be fulfilled that is written about me in the Law of Moses, the Prophets and the Psalms." (Luke 24:44)
- "David himself, speaking by the Holy Spirit, declared.... (Mark 12:35, regarding Psalm 110:1)
- "This is to fulfill the scripture...." (John 13:18 regarding Psalm 41:9)
- Jesus interpreted Psalm 118:22 as predictive prophecy concerning himself (Matthew 21:42-43).

[20] Harrison, *Introduction*, p. 995-996.

Hopefully this rather academic introduction doesn't ruin the Psalms for you. Ultimately they find their highest use in inspiring believers to trust in God in spite of the tough times we may go through in our lives. And in that role of inspiring us humans, some of the psalms in our Bibles are old enough to have done admirably for a full three thousand years. How about that for enduring value!

1. Marveling at God's Majesty in Creation (Psalms 8, 19, 139)

In this chapter we are examining three psalms – Psalms 8, 19, and 139 – that marvel at the wonder of God's creation, but in the subsequent meditation on creation go three different directions in applying that knowledge. These psalms are full of awe in God's greatness and minuteness of care.

Before you begin your study of these psalms, I hope you'll re-read the section on Hebrew poetry in the Introduction above. Also, take time to read this psalm – and every psalm we come to – out loud from your favorite Bible

Probably the most famous painting of the creation is Michelangelo's huge "Creation of Adam" fresco (1510) on the ceiling of the Sistine Chapel in the Vatican, 280 x 570 cm. The detail above shows God's hand on the right touching Adam's hand on the left..

translation before beginning the study, and perhaps after you've studied the material here. As you speak it out loud, you are "praying" it in your own voice. The more you understand the psalmist's words, the more you can invest them with your own prayers and longings.

I'm not trying to be exhaustive in these notes. There are excellent commentaries mentioned among the references that analyze each psalm in great detail. Rather, my purpose here is to help you quickly understand important details that will help you get the gist of what the psalmist is saying. I'll define only the Hebrew words where the definition is important in rounding out your understanding of the concepts being discussed, and try to resist the temptation to get too detailed. If we get bogged down in the details, it'll be hard to be caught up in the sweep of prayer that is our goal here.

Psalm 8 – How Majestic Is Your Name in All the Earth

"For the director of music. According to gittith. A psalm of David."

Notice that this psalm is meant to be sung. Here it is noted as "of" or "for" the choirmaster or director of music. We can only guess at the meaning of "gittith." The psalm is attributed to David.

After you've read the psalm out loud, step back a moment and see the overall flow of the ideas:

1. Beginning praise in earth and heavens (8:1-2)
2. The wonder of contrasting the Creator of the infinite universe with finite man (8:3-8)
3. Ending praise which echoes the first line (8:9)

How Majestic Is Your Name (8:1-2)

"O LORD, our Lord,
how majestic is your name in all the earth!
You have set your glory
above the heavens." (8:1)

In our English translations we often miss the impact of the first line, since "LORD" in small caps designates the unique name of Israel's God, Yahweh. The NJB catches it with "Yahweh our Lord, how majestic...."

Verse one consists of two parallel phrases. The first speaks of God's majesty in the earth; the second points to his glory above the heavens. If God's glory in his earthly creation isn't enough, just look at his glory even beyond the heavens! Two words describe Yahweh in verse 1:

- "Majestic" (NIV, NRSV) or "excellent" (KJV) is the adjective 'addîr, "mighty, majestic, noble, principal, stately," from a root that connotes that which is superior to something else, and therefore, that which is majestic.[1]
- "Glory" (hôd) refers here to God's "splendor, majesty, vigor, glory, honor."[2]

God's "name" refers to his revealed name, Yahweh (Exodus 3:14). But the concept of "name" (shēm) also extends to ideas of existence, character, and reputation.[3] Perhaps it also suggests: Your "reputation" is considered majestic in the world you have created.

Praising such a sublime God is fitting, but the next verse is curious at first glance:

"From the lips of children and infants
you have ordained praise

---

[1] Leonard J. Coppes, 'ādar, TWOT #28b.
[2] Victor P. Hamilton, hwd, TWOT #482a.
[3] Walter C. Kaiser, shēm, TWOT #2405.

because of your enemies,
to silence the foe and the avenger." (8:2)

What do praising children have to do with enemies? Though the translation is a bit difficult, the psalmist seems to be contrasting the supposed weakness of children and infants with the supposed power of God's enemies. The point seems to be that even the weakest have abundant strength when they take the name of God on their lips. See 1 Corinthians 1:27-29; 2 Chronicles 20, especially verses 21-23.

Contrasting the Infinite Universe with Finite Man (8:3-8)

Now the psalmist looks to the night sky, as David must have done countless times in the sheepfields:

"3When I consider your heavens,
the work of your fingers,
the moon and the stars,
which you have set in place,
4what is man that you are mindful of him,
the son of man that you care for him?
5You made him a little lower than the heavenly beings
and crowned him with glory and honor." (8:3-5)

I can remember driving across the Arizona desert about 2 o'clock in the morning. Everyone else in the car was asleep, but I just had to pull over and look at the brilliant stars above. I felt the smallness that David alludes to. We are so infinitesimal compared to the vastness of God's creation. How can he even be bothered to know about or care for a mere human being? The majesty and wonder of God is that he *does* care about us!

Now the psalmist recounts the responsibility that God gave to Adam and Eve over his creation:

"Be fruitful and increase in number; fill the earth and subdue it. Rule over the fish of the sea and the birds of the air and over every living creature that moves on the ground." (Genesis 1:28)

David puts it poetically:

"6You made him ruler over the works of your hands;
you put everything under his feet:
7all flocks and herds,
and the beasts of the field,
8the birds of the air,

and the fish of the sea,
all that swim the paths of the seas." (8:6-8)

Now he closes the psalm as he began it:

"O LORD, our Lord,
how majestic is your name in all the earth!" (8:9)

His majesty is in the greatness of creation, on earth and extending to the farthest heavens. And yet he wants to know *us* and include *us* in his plan. The glory of his infinite creation is seen in his particular care for lowly man. Oh, yes, Lord, how majestic you are!

A Christological Application

The author of Hebrews carries this even farther (Hebrews 2:6-9). He sees a Christological application in "the son of man" of Psalm 8:4, which was Jesus' primary self-designation in the Gospels. The boundless God of creation so cares for us that his Son humbles himself to become lower than the heavenly beings that he might become a man, and then goes farther yet to humble himself to die a shameful death, "even death on a cross" (Philippians 2:8), that he might restore his rebellious creation to fellowship again with their Creator.

"For God so loved the world that he gave his one and only Son, that whoever believes in him shall not perish but have eternal life." (John 3:16)

Psalm 8 is about the infinite creation of God contrasted with the weakness of man. But to man he gives an opportunity to take a role in the creation. The psalm helps me gain:

1. **Perspective** – our minuteness contrasted with God's majesty as shown in his humongous creation, and
2. **Purpose** – To serve God by ruling responsibly over his creation, the work of God's hands. Our rule is never independent of God, but in submission to God.

Q1. (Psalm 8). What does this psalm teach about God? What does it teach about human beings? What does it teach us about Christ? What does it teach about our responsibilities?
http://www.joyfulheart.com/forums/index.php?showtopic=651

Psalm 19 – The Heavens Proclaim the Glory of God

Our second creation song is found in Psalm 19. Here again, David is amazed by the infinite expanse of the heavens, and what it says about the Creator. It also is a sung psalm – "For the director of music" – and is attributed to David. The psalm has several parts.

1. The Unspoken Word Expressed in the Heavens (19:1)
    a. The Heavens Express God's Word Wordlessly (19:2-4a)
    b. The Glory of the Sun (19:4b-6)
2. The Perfection of God's Written Word (19:7-9)
    a. The Value and Sweetness of God's Word (19:10)
    b. The Word Exposes and Protects Against Sin (19:11-13)
3. A Prayer for a Pure Heart (19:14)

On first glance, you wonder how the parts fit together. But on reflection they make wondrous sense. C.S. Lewis, an Oxford professor of medieval English and a Christian apologist, wrote of Psalm 19, "I take this to be the greatest poem in the Psalter and one of the greatest lyrics in the world."[4]

God's Glory Proclaimed by the Heavens (19:1)

"The heavens declare the glory of God;
the skies proclaim the work of his hands." (19:1)

The first couplet of parallel lines considers two descriptions of the expanse of outer space:

"Heavens" is *shāmayim*, "heaven, heavens, sky."[5]

"Skies" (NIV) or "firmament" (NRSV, KJV) is *rāqīa'*, literally, "expanse" (NASB). The basic idea of the root is "stamping, as with the foot, and what results, i.e. a spreading out or stretching forth." Here the word identifies "God's heavenly expanse."[6]

The word in verse 1 for "glory" (*kābōd*) is different from the word (*hôd*) we saw in 8:1b above. *Kābōd* is by far the most common word for glory in the Old Testament, from a root with the basic idea of "to be heavy, weighty." From this figurative usage it is an easy step to the concept of a "weighty" person in society, someone who is honorable, impressive, worthy of respect. When referring to God it expresses "the unchanging beauty of the manifest God,"

---

[4] C.S. Lewis, *Psalms*, p. 63.

[5] Hermann J. Austel, *shmh*, TWOT #2407a.

[6] J. Barton Payne, *rāqa'*, TWOT 2217b. Our English word "firmament" means literally "the vault or arch of the sky" from Latin *firmare*, "support."

sometimes of a visible manifestation. Here, it is not only God's reputation which fills the earth, but it is the very reality, the splendor of his presence.[7]

The Heavens Express God's Word Wordlessly (19:2-4a)

"²Day after day they pour forth speech;
night after night they display knowledge.
³There is no speech or language
where their voice is not heard.
⁴Their voice goes out into all the earth,
their words to the ends of the world." (19:2-4a)

What an amazing insight! Each time someone looks up at the heavens – day and night – they receive a wordless but powerful message of God's greatness and glory. The Apostle Paul expressed it this way:

"For since the creation of the world God's invisible qualities – his eternal power and divine nature – have been clearly seen, being understood from what has been made, so that men are without excuse." (Romans 1:20).

The Glory of the Sun (19:4b-6)

Now the psalmist considers the amazing glory of the sun God created:

"In the heavens he has pitched a tent for the sun,
⁵ which is like a bridegroom coming forth from his pavilion,
like a champion rejoicing to run his course.
⁶ It rises at one end of the heavens
and makes its circuit to the other;
nothing is hidden from its heat." (19:4b-6)

David paints the vigor and power of the sun with word images:

- A **tent** represents the darkness of the night when the sun is hidden.
- A **bridegroom** coming forth from his pavilion, expresses the enthusiasm of the bridegroom emerging from either the tent in which the ceremony was conducted or from the wedding chamber the morning after the wedding.
- A **mighty man of valor**, a renowned runner who takes great pleasure in the race.[8]

---

[7] John N. Oswalt, *kābēd*, TWOT #943e.

[8] "Champion" (NIV) or "strong man" (NRSV, KJV) is *gibbôr*, "mighty man." The word is used particularly of the heroes or champions of the armed forces, such as David's mighty men of valor (John N. Oswalt, *gābar*, TWOT #310b).

The Perfection of God's Written Word (19:7-9)

While it may seem like an abrupt shift from the heavens to the Torah, the shift is quite natural. The psalmist has been relating how God speaks wordlessly through creation. Now he shifts to how Yahweh speaks through his written Word:

> "7The law of the LORD is perfect,
> reviving the soul.
> The statutes of the LORD are trustworthy,
> making wise the simple.
> 8The precepts of the LORD are right,
> giving joy to the heart.
> The commands of the LORD are radiant,
> giving light to the eyes.
> 9The fear of the LORD is pure,
> enduring forever.
> The ordinances of the LORD are sure
> and altogether righteous." (19:7-9)

Notice the obvious parallelism of verses 7-9. Each line uses a synonym for the law, adds "of Yahweh," follows with a descriptive adjective, and concludes with a benefit. It's a brief meditation on God's Word and the wonders David finds in it.

For the Jew, "the law of the Lord" would refer to the Torah, the commands contained in the first five books of the Bible. For the Christian, "the law of the Lord" refers to the whole Word of God, especially the teachings and commands of Jesus our Lord and supreme Teacher sent from God.

Consider the imagery of verses 7-9, reviving, giving joy, giving light. "Reviving" (NIV, NRSV) or "converting" (KJV) is *shûb*, "turn, return." Here it is used in a covenantal sense, returning to God, being restored to full fellowship.[9] Look at the benefits of meditation on the Word: the inner life of the soul is revived, the ignorant are made wise, the heart is gladdened, one's spiritual eyes are enlightened, reverence for God is extended forever, and their righteousness is readily apparent.

The Value and Sweetness of God's Word (19:10)

Having considered the benefits of meditation on God's word, David now turns to value and sweetness of his Word:

> "They are more precious than gold,
> than much pure gold;

---

[9] Victor P. Hamilton, *shûb*, TWOT #2340.

they are sweeter than honey,
than honey from the comb." (19:10)

Two new images are invoked to suggest the value (gold, the most precious metal) and sweetness (honey, the sweetest food) of God's Word in verse 10.

The Word Exposes and Protects Against Sin (19:11-13)

"[11]By them is your servant warned;
in keeping them there is great reward.
[12] Who can discern his errors?
Forgive my hidden faults.
[13] Keep your servant also from willful sins;
may they not rule over me.
Then will I be blameless,
innocent of great transgression." (19:11-13)

When faced with the glory of God in the creation and the awesome requirement of God in his Word, the psalmist is suddenly conscious of his own sins. The psalm has begun with all creation, narrowed to those who honor God's Word, and now narrowed again to David himself – and the reader. What about me? How do I fit in all of this? How about my sins?

The psalmist rightly observes that by ourselves we often cannot discern our own errors. We have blind spots that keep us from seeing ourselves as others see us – and especially as God sees us. "Discern" (NIV), "detect" (NRSV), "understand" (KJV) in verse 12 is *bîn*, "understand, consider, perceive." The background idea of the verb is to "discern."[10] That's why God's Word is so important to us as a mirror (James 1:22-25), and as a "discerner of the thoughts and intentions of the heart" (Hebrews 4:12-13, KJV).

Notice how the parallel phrases of verses 12 and 13 progress from "errors" to "great transgression."

- **"Errors"** is *shegîâ*, from the verb *shāgā*, "go astray, stray, err." The primary emphasis is on sin done inadvertently.[11]
- **"Hidden faults"** (NIV, NRSV) or "secret faults" (KJV) is from *sātar*, "hide, conceal."[12]
- **"Willful sins"** (NIV), "presumptuous sins"(KJV) renders the adjective *zēd*, "proud, arrogant," from *zîd, zûd*, "act proudly, presumptuously, rebelliously."[13] It could be a

---

[10] Louis Goldberg, *bîn*, TWOT #239.
[11] Victor P. Hamilton, *shāgā*, TWOT #2325a.
[12] R. D. Patterson, *sātar*, TWOT #1551.
[13] Leon J. Wood, *zîd, zûd*, TWOT #547.

prayer for God to deliver from "the insolent" (NRSV), "presumptuous persons"[14] who would lead us astray. Unwitting errors are one thing; the psalmist prays that overt, willful, arrogant rebelliousness might not take hold in his life and turn him from God. The Word helps us see that for what it is; it helps us call sin "sin" instead of excusing it.

- **"Great transgression"** is the final culmination of sin's progress. May God help us nip our sins in the bud when they are small and have little hold over us, long before they begin to manifest themselves in great and open transgression.

A Prayer for a Pure Heart (19:14)

The psalm concludes with a very humble and personal prayer:

"May the words of my mouth and the meditation of my heart
be pleasing in your sight,
O LORD, my Rock and my Redeemer." (19:14)

David prays for both his outer life, "the words of my mouth" that others will hear, as well as his inner life, "the meditation of my heart," to be pleasing before God. "Meditation" is *higgāyōn* from *hāgā*, that has the basic meaning of a low sound, such as the cooing of a dove.[15] Here it refers to the whisperings of the heart. We are instructed to meditate on the Word of God (Joshua 1:8; Psalm 1:2), the works of God (Psalm 77:12; 143:5), and God himself (Psalm 63:6).

"Pleasing" (NIV), "acceptable" (KJV, NRSV) is *rāṣōn*, "pleasure, delight, favor." In a ritual sense *rāṣōn* can describe the "permissibility" or "acceptance" of a gift or sacrifice (Leviticus 1:3; 22:20; Isaiah 56:7).[16] We want our thoughts to be acceptable before God. But even more we want him to take delight in our thoughts and actions – not to earn points that we might cash in on Judgment Day, but because we are loving children of our heavenly Father and make it our aim to please him (2 Corinthians 5:9; 2 Timothy 2:4).

Yahweh our Rock and Kinsman-Redeemer (19:14b)

David concludes the psalm with twin names for Yahweh: "my Rock and my Redeemer."

"Rock" (NIV, NRSV) or **"strength"** (KJV) is *ṣûr*, "rock." Yahweh is often referred to as a Rock because he is a sure source of strength and endures throughout every generation.[17]

---

[14] Craigie, *Psalms*, p. 178.

[15] Herbert Wolf, *hāgā*, TWOT #467b.

[16] William White, *rāṣā*, TWOT 2207a. Craigie follows Dahood, in rendering this, "be according to your will" (Craigie, *Psalms*, pp. 178-179).

[17] John E. Hartley, *ṣwr*, TWOT #1901a.

"Redeemer" is *gā'al*, "redeem, avenge, revenge, ransom, do the part of a kinsman."[18] In Hebrew culture, the redeemer was a kinsman who had responsibility to help members of his extended family. If someone's property had to be sold, he would "redeem" it buy buying it back into the family. If a cousin or uncle owed so much that he had to be sold as a slave to pay his debt, the kinsman-redeemer would pay the ransom price to redeem him. The story of Ruth and Boaz (Ruth 1-4) gives us the picture of Boaz as the kinsman-redeemer who marries a kinsman's widow (Ruth) and redeems his property to carry on his name. The psalmist's point here is that God is to us our Kinsman-Redeemer who will rescue us in trouble and redeem us from slavery of any kind.[19]

Q2. (Psalm 19) Verses 1 to 6 seem very different from verses 7 to 13, but there is a common thread that relates the first part to the second part. What is it? In what way does the psalmist seem to bask in God's Word? Have you ever felt that way? How does the psalmist's wonder in creation seem to affect him in this psalm? In the classic prayer of verse 14, what is David asking God to do?
http://www.joyfulheart.com/forums/index.php?showtopic=652

Psalm 139 – The Creator and Searcher of My Inmost Being

Since I have covered Psalm 139 in much greater detail as "David's Psalm of Surrender" in the *Great Prayers of the Bible* series, I'll want to skip directly to the portion of the psalm which speaks of God's creation. However, I encourage you to open your Bible and read the entire psalm out loud right now before going on.

---

[18] R. Laird Harris, *gā'al*, TWOT #300.
[19] For more on names of God, see my book *Names and Titles of God* (JesusWalk Publications, 2010). www.jesuswalk.com/books/names-god.htm

Though earlier in the psalm David has complained that God has searched him out, almost hounded him, here he begins to relax and reflect on God's love expressed in the intricacy of his own personal creation in his mother's womb.

> "13For you created my inmost being;
> you knit me together in my mother's womb.
> 14I praise you because I am fearfully and wonderfully made;
> your works are wonderful,
> I know that full well.
> 15My frame was not hidden from you
> when I was made in the secret place.
> When I was woven together in the depths of the earth,
> 16your eyes saw my unformed body.
> All the days ordained for me
> were written in your book
> before one of them came to be." (139:13-16)

If you've ever wondered about the trivial value of human life – your life, perhaps – this psalm makes it clear that God values each of us with a love and intimacy. "Created" (NIV), "possessed" (KJV), and "formed" (NRSV) in verse 13 is *qānā*, which here (and 5 other places in the Old Testament) appears to mean "create."[20] God has made the heavens and the earth by his great power, but also the tiniest parts of a tiny human while still an embryo, a fetus. God's awesome power extends to the smallest detail. "Inmost being" (NIV), "inward parts" (NRSV), and "reins" (KJV) is *kilyâ*, "kidney," then a symbol of the innermost being.[21]

"... You knit me together in my mother's womb." (139:13b)

The psalmist uses a fascinating word, here translated "knit together" (NIV, NRSV) and "covered" (KJV). The verb is *śākak* (also in Job 10:11) which probably means "weave together," parallel to "woven together" in verse 15, an allusion to cloth woven with different colored threads.[17] Imagine a weaver, an artist in cloth, weaving an intricate pattern, and you see God's love and care.

David realizes that along with intricate, intimate formation, God's creation means that God knows his whole life from its very beginning to its very end. The Creator is both omnipotent (all-powerful), but also omniscient (all-knowing). We might feel that God's foreordination might be imposing on our supposed freedom, but his full knowledge of us is just a fact of life.

---

[20] Leonard J. Coppes, *qānā*, TWOT #2039.
[21] John N. Oswalt, *klh*, TWOT #983a.

This is the third creation psalm we've considered. Look at how meditating on God's creation affects the psalmist on this occasion:

> "[23]Search me, O God, and know my heart;
> test me and know my anxious thoughts.
> [24]See if there is any offensive way in me,
> and lead me in the way everlasting." (139:23-24)

His prayer is a prayer of surrender to God the Creator, the Searcher. Search me, know my heart, test me, check out my worries. And God, if you find anything in me that needs your help – and you will – cleanse my heart. Lead me back to the path that I might experience your everlasting life.

Q3. (Psalm 139). In what way does the wonder of creation in the psalm seem to affect the psalmist? In his concluding prayer in verses 23-24, what does he ask God to do?
http://www.joyfulheart.com/forums/index.php?showtopic=653

The wonder of creation is at many levels:

- Awe at the magnitude and scale of the heavens and the earth,
- Realization that God has created human beings for a particular role within his creation, and finally,
- Acute awareness that God has created me, you, very deliberately, very specifically. We don't just matter, we have a particular mission in God's world.

Exercise. For one of the psalms in this lesson – or another psalm with a similar theme – do one of the suggested exercises to help you experience the Psalms in Appendix 1. These include such things as praying a psalm, meditating, reading to a shut-in, paraphrasing, writing your own psalm, singing, preparing a liturgy, and memorizing. Then report to the forum what the exercise meant to you personally or share what you've written with others.
http://www.joyfulheart.com/forums/index.php?showtopic=654

Prayer

Creator of the Universe, God and Father of mankind, we come to you with awe and wonder, worship and rededication. Help us relate to you as is appropriate to our status as created beings. Help us to learn to approach you as beloved children. Reform us in your image. In Jesus' name, we pray. Amen.

Songs

- **"How Majestic Is Your Name,"** words and music by Michael W. Smith (© 1981 Meadowgreen Music Company, Admin. by EMI Christian Music Publishing). Psalm 8.
- **"O Lord, Our Lord, How Excellent Your Name Is,"** words and music by Peter Jacobs (© 1984, Maranatha Praise, Inc., Admin. by Music Services)
- **"Search Me, O Lord, and try this heart of mine,"** words: (1875) by Fanny Crosby, music: ("Ellers," 1869) by Edward J. Hopkins (1869).
- **"Search Me, O God, and know my heart today,"** words (1936) by J. Edwin Orr (1912-1987), music, Maori tune
- **"The Law of the Lord Is Perfect,"** by J.J. Williams (© 1978, Living Way Ministries). Psalm 19.
- **"Let the Words of My Mouth,"** words and music by Warren W. Wiersbe (© 1989, Hope Publishing Co.), Chalice Hymnal #301. Psalm 19:14.

2. Thirsting for God (Psalms 27, 42-43, 63)

When I read the Psalms I am often shocked by how very personal some of these psalms are. Most are not framed as national prayers, but as personal pleas, the song of a heart hungry and thirsty to know God better. As we examine this theme, let's consider four psalms: 27, 42-43, and 63. As before, please take the time to read each psalm *out loud* from your favorite translation before studying the comments below.

James J. Tissot (1836-1902, French artist and illustrator), "David Praying in the Night," OT watercolor series. Jewish Museum, New York.

Psalm 27 – Your face, Lord, I Will Seek

This psalm doesn't seem to be forged in the heart of a crisis. Rather it looks back reflectively upon the strength David has experienced in the past. It is certainly a psalm that celebrates the protection of the Lord in times of trouble.

Confident in Yahweh I Do Not Fear Trouble (27:1-3)

"¹The LORD is my light and my salvation –
whom shall I fear?
The LORD is the stronghold of my life –
of whom shall I be afraid?
²When evil men advance against me
to devour my flesh,
when my enemies and my foes attack me,
they will stumble and fall.
³Though an army besiege me,
my heart will not fear;
though war break out against me,
even then will I be confident." (27:1-3)

These first few verses celebrate the utter lack of fear with which David's faith in Yahweh strengthens his heart. Notice the imagery of Yahweh that David begins with in verse 1:

- My light
- My salvation
- My stronghold

Since Yahweh is his light, salvation, and fortress, he walks with a certain confidence, even in trouble.

Safe in the House of the Lord (27:4-6)

The next section focuses on the confidence David feels in "the house of the Lord."

> "⁴One thing I ask of the LORD,
> this is what I seek:
> that I may dwell in **the house of the LORD**
> all the days of my life,
> to gaze upon the beauty of the LORD
> and to seek him in **his temple**.
> ⁵For in the day of trouble
> he will keep me safe in **his dwelling**;
> he will hide me in the shelter of **his tabernacle**
> and set me high upon a rock.
> ⁶Then my head will be exalted
> above the enemies who surround me;
> at **his tabernacle** will I sacrifice with shouts of joy;
> I will sing and make music to the LORD." (27:4-6)

The terms "house" (*bayît*[1]), "temple" (*hêkāl*[2]), "dwelling/shelter/pavilion" (*sōk*[3]), and "tabernacle" (*'ōhel*[4]) are all used synonymously. Even though Solomon's Temple wasn't built until after David's time – the tabernacle was at Shiloh then – the expression "temple" is a

---

[1] *Bayît* is the generic word for "house, household," and can also be used of a palace or temple. You often see this in place names, such as Beth-lehem ("house of bread"), Beth-el ("house of God"), etc. (Louis Goldberg, bayît, TWOT #241).

[2] *Hêkāl* is sometimes used of a king's dwelling quarters, that is, a palace, a luxurious dwelling place. In the Bible it used primarily of God's house (Leonard J. Coppes, hêkāl, TWOT #493).

[3] *Sōk, sūkkā* has the idea of "covering." In a physical sense it is used in the building activities relative to the sacred places of worship. In a figurative sense it pictures God's protection for one who comes to him for refuge (R. D. Patterson, sōk, sūkkā, TWOT #1492).

[4] *'Ōhel* is used of a dwelling, home, especially a tabernacle or tent. It was used of the Tabernacle in the Wilderness and the Tent of Meeting (Jack P. Lewis, 'ōhel, TWOT #32a).

generic term that means "palace, a king's dwelling quarters," and was used of the tabernacle itself (1 Samuel 1:9).

There are many references in the Psalms to dwelling in God's house, beginning with the familiar Psalm 23:6, "and I shall dwell in the house of the Lord forever." Others include:

> "Happy are those whom you choose and bring near
> to live in your courts.
> We shall be satisfied with the goodness of your house,
> your holy temple." (Psalm 65:4)

> "How lovely is your dwelling place,
> O Lord Almighty!
> My soul yearns, even faints,
> for the courts of the Lord;
> my heart and my flesh cry out
> for the living God....
>
> Better is one day in your courts
> than a thousand elsewhere;
> I would rather be a doorkeeper
> in the house of my God
> than dwell in the tents of the wicked."
> (Psalm 84:1-2, 10)

One such verse I learned as a boy:

> "I was glad when they said to me,
> 'Let us go to the house of the Lord!'" (Psalm 122.1, NRSV)

Priests and Levites might occasionally actually "dwell" in the tabernacle or temple during their period of duty – Samuel did as a boy (1 Samuel 3). Moreover, the Israelites were well aware that the temple couldn't confine God to a single place (1 Kings 8:27). But in the psalms, to "dwell in the house of the Lord" is a metaphor for being close to the Lord at all times. It expresses the longing of the psalmist to draw near to God. It is also the psalmist's place of safety and rejoicing.

Your Face, Lord, I Will Seek (27:7-12)

> "Hear my voice when I call, O Lord;
> be merciful to me and answer me.
> My heart says of you, 'Seek his face!'
> Your face, Lord, I will seek." (27:7-8)

Now we see another expression of devotion, to "seek the face" of the Lord. "Seek" (*bāqash*) comes from a root that connotes a person's earnest seeking of something or someone. Its intention is that its object be found or acquired (Deuteronomy 4:29; Jeremiah 29:13; Malachi 3:1).[5] The expression "seek the face (*peñê*) of" means (of a human ruler) to seek an audience with, (of God), it means to seek his presence, that is, to be face to face with him (Hosea 5:15; 1 Chronicles 16:11= Psalm 105:4; 2 Chronicles 7:14; 2 Samuel 21:1; Psalm 24:6).[6] It speaks of desiring, a yearning for personal intimacy with the Almighty, seeking a personal hearing before the Lord himself. We see this same kind of flat-out, earnest seeking in the Apostle Paul:

> "I want to know Christ and the power of his resurrection and the fellowship of sharing in his sufferings, becoming like him in his death, and so, somehow, to attain to the resurrection from the dead." (Philippians 3:10-11)

The expression in verse 9, "hide one's face," means to refuse to allow one into his presence, to refuse to answer one's petition. The psalmist calls on God not to reject him, even as his parents may have (verse 10), and he is confident that the Lord will "receive" him.

> "⁹Do not hide your face from me,
> do not turn your servant away in anger;
> you have been my helper.
> Do not reject me or forsake me,
> O God my Savior.
> ¹⁰Though my father and mother forsake me,
> the Lᴏʀᴅ will receive me." (27:9-10)

He calls on God to instruct him, to lead him "in a straight path," since his way is perilous with enemies all around.

> "¹¹Teach me your way, O Lᴏʀᴅ;
> lead me in a straight path
> because of my oppressors.
> ¹²Do not turn me over to the desire of my foes,
> for false witnesses rise up against me,
> breathing out violence." (27:11-12)

---

[5] Leonard J. Coppes, *bāqash*, TWOT #276. BDB p. 135.

[6] *Peñê*, "face," is used here in the sense of presence. With a preposition, the word signifies "in the presence of, before" (Victor P. Hamilton, *pānâ*, TWOT #1782a).

I Will See the Goodness of the Lord in the Land of the Living (27:13-14)

This has been a lament, but like many laments, it ends on the upswing, a word of hope and confidence:

> "¹³I am still confident of this:
> I will see the goodness of the LORD
> in the land of the living.
> ¹⁴Wait for the LORD;
> be strong and take heart
> and wait for the LORD." (27:13-14)

Verses 13 and 14 describe the psalmist's attitude in the midst of his trial and struggle. "The land of the living" means this life, rather than in the afterlife. I will see the Lord provide deliverance in my lifetime! In verse 14 he counsels both himself and others to develop both strength and perseverance. Look at the interesting kind of parallelism:

- Wait for/expect (*qāwā*) the Lord
- Be strong (*hāzaq*)7 [7]
- Take heart8 [8]
- Wait for/expect the Lord

"Wait for the LORD" (NIV, NRSV), "wait on the LORD" (KJV), is well translated by the NJB as, "Put your hope in Yahweh." The verb *qāwā* means "to wait or look for with eager expectation."[9]

This command to "wait for the LORD" both precedes and follows the commands to be strong. It wraps them with a commitment to wait expectantly until Yahweh comes through with the answer, the help needed. It doesn't give up. It reminds me of some of my favorite New Testament verses:

> "Therefore, my beloved brethren, be steadfast, immovable, always abounding in the work of the Lord, knowing that in the Lord your labor is not in vain." (1 Corinthians 15:58, RSV)

> "And so after waiting patiently, Abraham received what was promised." (Hebrews 6:15)

---

[7] "Be strong" (NIV, NRSV) or "be of good courage" (KJV) is *hāzaq*, that has the basic meaning in the Qal stem of "be(come) strong" (Carl Philip Weber, *hāzaq*, TWOT #636) It is so easy to become weak; we are commanded to do the opposite.

[8] "Take heart" (NIV), "let your heart take courage" (NRSV), "let your heart be bold" (NJB), "he shall strengthen thine heart (KJV) uses the verb *'āmēs*, "be stout, strong." In the Hiphil stem as here it has the force of "exhibit strength, feel strong ... the strength of faith and hope"(Charles L. Feinberg, *'āmēs*, TWOT #117).

[9] John E. Hartley, *qāwā*, TWOT #1994.

"So do not throw away your confidence; it will be richly rewarded. You need to perse-
vere so that when you have done the will of God, you will receive what he has promised. (Hebrews 10:35-36)

Q1. (Psalm 27) What does it mean that David desires to "dwell in the house of the
Lord"? What does it mean to "seek his face"? How does David provide hope at the
end of this Psalm?
http://www.joyfulheart.com/forums/index.php?showtopic=655

Psalm 42-43 – Combating Depression with Faith

Our second psalm in this chapter is really two psalms – Psalms 42 and 43, which belong
as a single psalm. This is surely a lament of one who is sore pressed but is seeking God.
While the psalmist pours out his soul to the Lord in complaint, at the end of the psalm you
see a characteristic upswing of hope that usually, but not always, concludes this type of
psalm. The structure falls naturally into three parts, each ending with the same repeated
refrain:

1.   42:1-5   a. Lament (verses 1-4)
                    b. *Refrain* (verse 5)

2.   42:6-11   a. Lament (verses 6-10)
                    b. *Refrain* (verse 11)

3.   43:1-5   a. Lament (verses 1-4)
                    b. *Refrain* (verse 5)

From the title we can see that it is intended to be sung, since it is addressed "For the director of music." It is titled "a maskil," a word which designates 13 psalms. It may mean an "efficacious psalm" or "skillful psalm," but we don't really know the meaning.[10] It seems to be a companion to Psalm 43, though the two psalms can be sung independently of each other.

The title also tells us the author, "the Sons of Korah." They were a Levitical family, singers and musicians of the temple choir founded by Heman the Ezrahite (1 Chronicles 6:31-46). It seems to be the anguished cry of one who is exile far from Jerusalem – whether the exile was in the mountainous headwaters of the Jordan (42:6) or beyond that in Babylon, we don't know.

A Thirst of a Parched Soul for God (42:1-2)

Wherever he writes from, this former temple musician expresses in the most graphic image his thirst for God:

"[1]As the deer pants for streams of water,
so my soul pants for you, O God.
[2]My soul thirsts (*ṣāmē'*[11]) for God,
for the living God.
When can I go and meet with God?" (42:1-2)

We're given the word picture or simile of a wild animal in a parched, unrelenting wilderness craving water, in this case, of a stag or hart[12] literally on his last legs from dehydration. The verb is a rare one, *'ārag*, "pant for, long for," used only here and in Joel 1:20.[13] The psalmist compares his spiritual thirst to the physical thirst of the deer.

---

[10] Kidner, *Psalms 1-72*, p. 37; Herbert Wolf, *śākal*, TWOT 2263b.
[11] *Ṣāmē'*, "be thirsty" (John E. Hartley, TWOT #1926).
[12] *'Ayyāl*, "stag, male deer," Herbert Wolf, *'wl*, TWOT #45k.
[13] *'Ārag*, Holladay 282; BDB 788.

Psalm 63, "A psalm of David, when he was in the Desert of Judah," uses a similar image of spiritual thirst.

"O God, you are my God,
earnestly I seek you;
my soul thirsts (*ṣāmē'*) for you,
my body longs[14] for you,
in a dry and weary[15] land
where there is no water." (63:1)

At the time he wrote this psalm, David himself was living in the desert in order to escape capture by his enemy. He experienced the extreme dryness of the desert, the plant life stunted from lack of moisture. The parched land, he realized, is much like his own dry soul that thirsts to be refreshed from God himself. A third psalm, again from David, bears this same image:

"I spread out my hands to you;
my soul thirsts for you
like a parched[16] land. (143:6)

Spreading out one's hands is a sign of prayer.

Doubt and Longing for Past Joy (42:3-4)

Back to Psalm 42, this temple musician in exile continues his lament, plagued by doubt and remembrance:

"[3]My tears have been my food
day and night,
while men say to me all day long,
'Where is your God?'
[4]These things I remember
as I pour out my soul:
how I used to go with the multitude,
leading the procession to the house of God,
with shouts of joy and thanksgiving
among the festive throng." (42:3-4)

---

[14] *Kāmah*, "faint (with longing)" (BDB 484).

[15] *'Āyēp*, "faint, exhausted, weary." It can also be used to describe the condition of extreme thirst. It is used figuratively. "The psalmist, wandering in the desert land of Judah, realizes that his soul is in much the same parched condition as the land in which he wanders." The adjective is also used in 143:6 (Carl Schultz, *'îp*, TWOT #1614a).

[16] *'Āyēp* again.

Once our author had been a key participant in the joyous festival processions up to the temple in Jerusalem, punctuated by shouts of joy, singing, and praise. Now he is far from the temple courts that remind him of God. His erstwhile friends stab doubts into his heart, "Where is your God now?" and it is taking its toll on his spirit.

Combating Depression with Self-Talk, Remembrance, and Praise (42:5-8)

But he is not content to grovel in his misery. He addresses himself, his soul, his innermost being (*nephesh*):

"⁵Why are you downcast, O my soul?
Why so disturbed within me?
Put your hope in God,
for I will yet praise him,
my Savior and ⁶my God.

My soul is downcast within me;
therefore I will remember you
from the land of the Jordan,
the heights of Hermon – from Mount Mizar.
⁷Deep calls to deep
in the roar of your waterfalls;
all your waves and breakers
have swept over me.

⁸By day the LORD directs his love,
at night his song is with me--
a prayer to the God of my life. (42:5-8)

At the risk of being too analytical in this context of spiritual and poetic feeling, I can see three approaches that the psalmist uses to combat his doubt and depression.

1. **Self-talk**, words addressed to himself, of hope, that he will eventually have cause to rejoice in God again. (42:5)
2. **Deliberate remembrance,** recalling God to mind, (42:6-7)
3. **Singing and praying** to God night and day (42:8)

Deep Calls to Deep (42:7)

I've often wondered what the phrase "Deep calls to deep" means in verse 7. The noun is *tehôm*, "deep, depths, deep places," usually used of the ocean depths, but sometimes of surface springs coming from subterranean waters far below (Deuteronomy 8:7; Psalm 78:15).

Synonymns[17] are used figuratively in Psalms 69:2 ("I have come into the deep waters....") and 130:1 ("Out of the depths I cry to you, O LORD....").

I think in the context, by "deep calls to deep," the psalmist means that the deep waters in the waterfall pool before him remind him of the depth of pain in his spirit. Along a similar vein, the violent waterfalls of the Jordan in the rainy season remind him of the breakers and waves of the ocean deep. Instead of providing solace, they remind him of his turmoil of soul.

Continuing to Combat Depression with Hope (42:9-11)

The struggle continues – doubts, physical aching, and scoffers don't cease.

"[9]I say to God my Rock,
"Why have you forgotten me?
Why must I go about mourning,
oppressed by the enemy?"
[10]My bones suffer mortal agony
as my foes taunt me,
saying to me all day long,
"Where is your God?" (42:9-10)

But the psalmist doesn't let up his resistance. His self-talk of hope reappears in verse 11.

"Why are you downcast, O my soul?
Why so disturbed within me?
Put your hope in God,
for I will yet praise him,
my Savior and my God." (42:11)

Send Forth Your Light and Guide Me (Psalm 43:1-5)

As the psalm continues in chapter 43, the psalmist begins to come out of his depression. He calls:

"[3]Send forth your light and your truth,
let them guide me;
let them bring me to your holy mountain,
to the place where you dwell.
[4]Then will I go to the altar of God,
to God, my joy and my delight.
I will praise you with the harp,
O God, my God." (43:3-4)

---

[17] *Ma'ămaqqîm*, "deep, depths," and *meṣûlâ*, "depth, deep."

Now in his heart God is leading him back to the temple mount in Jerusalem. He takes out his harp and is worshipping and praising with joy and delight. Now the final refrain seems to take hold in his spirit. His hope is firmly reestablished in the Lord:

"... For I will yet praise him,
  my Savior and my God." (43:5b)

Psalms 42 and 43 are a lament, but a lament in which the author struggles to praise. I suppose it is one of my favorites because it expresses so well an honest but determined seeking of God in the face of the spiritual struggles that I face – and probably you. Why don't you let these twin psalms mold your prayers, in times of trial.

Q2. (Psalms 42-43). What is the psalmist feeling during this spiritual struggle? How does he combat his spiritual depression? Have you ever felt this way? How did you reach out to God at this time?

http://www.joyfulheart.com/forums/index.php?showtopic=656

Psalm 63 – Earnestly I Seek You

Psalm 63 is the final psalm we'll consider in this series. We already looked at verse 1 earlier in this chapter when we examined the powerful image of the soul's dryness and thirst:

"A psalm of David. When he was in the Desert of Judah.

O God, you are my God,
earnestly I seek you;
my soul thirsts for you,
my body longs for you,
in a dry and weary land
where there is no water."

"Seek earnestly" (NIV, NASB) or "early will I seek" (KJV) is *shāhar*, "be intent on, inquire for, seek."[18] The word for dawn comes from this root,[19] so the word suggests an eagerness that is willing to rise early to continue the quest with earnestness. In my experience of more than five decades as a Christian I've observed that a passive person seldom connects with God in any satisfying or authentic manner. The Scripture says:

> "From there you will seek the LORD your God, and you will find him if you search after him with all your heart and soul." (Deuteronomy 4:29, NRSV)

> "You will seek me and find me when you seek me with all your heart." (Jeremiah 29:13)

I Will Lift Up My Hands in Your Name (63:2-8)

Like the descendent of Korah in Psalms 42-43 above, here David remembers his precious times of worship in the sanctuary and it fills him with joy!

> "²I have seen you in the sanctuary
> and beheld your power and your glory.
> ³Because your love is better than life,
> my lips will glorify you.
> ⁴I will praise you as long as I live,
> and in your name I will lift up my hands.
> ⁵My soul will be satisfied as with the richest of foods;
> with singing lips my mouth will praise you.
> ⁶On my bed I remember you;
> I think of you through the watches of the night.
> ⁷Because you are my help,
> I sing in the shadow of your wings.
> ⁸My soul clings to you;
> your right hand upholds me." (63:2-8)

David's memory of God's love stimulates praise. "Love" (NIV), "lovingkindness" (KJV), "steadfast love" (NRSV) is *hesed*. It means more than obligatory loyalty within a covenant relationship, as some have suggested. It is a love that includes acts of kindness and mercy. The images of the KJV's "lovingkindness" are not far from the fullness of meaning of the word.[20] Notice the result of David's recognition of this firm and lasting love, expressed in this wonderful parallelism:

1.   Lips that glorify (3b),

---

[18] *Shāhar*, Holladay 366.
[19] Victor P. Hamilton, *shāhar*, TWOT #2369.
[20] R. Laird Harris, *hsd*, TWOT #698a.

2. Lifelong praise (4a),
3. Prayer (signified by the lifting of hands, 4b),
4. Fullness in one's inner being, "my soul will be satisfied" (5a),
5. Singing praise (5b),
6. A memory of God in the night-time hours (6),
7. A singing in the refuge provided by God's strong presence (7),
8. An mutual holding of one another – the soul clasps God tight, God's hand securely grasps[21] David (8).

As I think of this psalm I recall the song made famous by Debbie Boone decades ago, "You Light Up My Life,"[22] applying it to God's presence. Yes, an assurance of God's love is life-changing!

God Will Deliver David from His Enemies (63:9-11)

The psalm concludes with David's confidence in God's ultimate deliverance:

"⁹They who seek my life will be destroyed;
they will go down to the depths of the earth.
¹⁰They will be given over to the sword
and become food for jackals.

¹¹But the king will rejoice in God;
all who swear by God's name will praise him,
while the mouths of liars will be silenced."

Consider the emotional course of the psalm:

1. Earnest seeking in a period of dryness of soul and hiding from one's enemies (verse 1)
2. A remembrance of God's presence and especially His steadfast and merciful love. (verses 2-3a)
3. The outflow of praise, prayer, and faith resulting in a fullness of soul (verses (3b-8)
4. A confidence that God will bring ultimate deliverance to him, the king (verses (9-11)

---

[21] "Upholds" is *tāmak*, "grasp, lay hold of, hold fast, support," from a West Semitic root that means "grasping securely" (R. D. Patterson, *tāmak*, TWOT 2520.
[22] "You Light Up My Life," words and music by Joe Brooks (©1976, 1977, Bigg Hill Music Corp.).

Q3. (Psalm 63) Why is recognition that God loves you the basis of all faith? What does this realization bring about in your life?
http://www.joyfulheart.com/forums/index.php?showtopic=657

What do *you* do? How do *you* respond when you recognize the dryness of your soul? Do you earnestly seek or are you passive? In these psalms we see a course not only for the psalmist, but for ourselves to seek afresh the face of God and find fullness for our souls.

Exercise. For one of the psalms in this lesson – or another psalm with a similar theme – do one of the suggested exercises to help you experience the Psalms in Appendix 1. These include such things as praying a psalm, meditating, reading to a shut-in, paraphrasing, writing your own psalm, singing, preparing a liturgy, and memorizing. Then report to the forum what the exercise meant to you personally or share what you've written with others.
http://www.joyfulheart.com/forums/index.php?showtopic=658

Prayer

Lord, sometimes we do feel dry and parched in our souls. I pray that you would put within me and within my brothers and sisters the same kind of earnestness to seek you that is required of true followers. Help me, help us, to seek you with all our hearts and find the fullness of soul that you have for us. In Jesus' name, I pray. Amen.

Songs

- **"As the Deer,"** words and music by Martin Nystrom (© 1894, Maranatha! Music). Psalm 42:1.
- **"As Pants the Hart for Streams,"** words unknown paraphrase, music, "Consolation" by Felix Mendelssohn (1809-1847). Psalm 42.

- **"As Thirsts the Hart for Water Brooks,"** words unknown paraphrase, music by William B. Bradbury (c. 1858). Psalm 42.
- **"As Pants the Hart for Cooling Streams,"** words by Nahum Tate and Nicholas Brady (1696), music by Ludwig Spohr (1835). Psalm 42.
- **"Beautiful,"** words and music by Dennis Cleveland (© 1982, Maranatha! Music). Psalm 27:4
- **"Early, My God, without Delay,"** words by Isaac Watts (1719), music: "St. Mark," by Henry J. Gauntlett (1805-1876), and other composers. Psalm 63:1-2
- **"I Hunger and I Thirst,"** words by John S. B. Monsell (1866), music: "Eccles," by Bertram Luard-Selby (1904). Psalm 63:1
- **"I Will Bless Thee, O Lord,"** words and music by Esther Watanabe (© 1970, Esther Watanabe). Psalm 63:4
- **"Isn't He Beautiful?"** words and music by John Wimber (© 1980, Mercy Publishing). Psalm 27:4.
- **"One Thing Have I Desired,"** words and music by Stuart Scott (© 1984, Maranatha! Music). Psalm 27:4
- **"Psalm 27,"** by John Michael Talbot (© 1990, Birdwing Music). Psalm 27.
- **"Psalm 27:1,"** words and music by Pauline Michael Mills (© 1966, Fred Bock Music Company). Psalm 27:1.
- **"Send the Light"** (the blessed Gospel light), words and music by Charles H. Gabriel (1890). Psalm 43:3
- **"Thy Lovingkindness"** (Is Better than Life), words and music by Hugh Mitchell (© 1956, New Spring). Psalm 63:3-4.
- **"The Lord Is My Light"** (and my salvation, Whom shall I fear?), words and music by Pauline Michael Mills (© 1966, Fred Bock Music Company). Psalm 27:1, 3.
- **"We Must Wait on the Lord,"** words and music by Randy Thomas (© 1979, Maranatha! Music). Psalm 27:14.

3. Choosing the Right Path (Psalms 1, 15, and 133)

Our next group of psalms – Wisdom Psalms 1, 15, and 133 – seem to share some characteristics with the Bible's Wisdom Literature, such as Proverbs. They urge believers to righteous living, provide warnings to avoid evil, and exalt the beauty of right relationships.

Psalm 1 compares the righteous person to a tree planted by the water. Vincent van Gogh, "Olive Trees with the Alpilles in the Background" (Saint-Rémy: June, 1889). Oil on canvas, 72.5 x 92.0 cm, New York Museum of Modern Art.

Psalm 1 – The Two Ways: Righteousness and Unrighteousness

It is no accident that this psalm was placed first in the Book of Psalms. By doing so the editor is suggesting that the Psalter is a book of wisdom, containing Yahweh's instruction for the faithful. David Howard suggests, "Psalm 1, with its instructions about studying the Torah, can be seen as directing readers to study the Psalter in the same way."[1] In some ancient manuscripts of the Psalms, the first psalm seems to be treated as a preface to the entire collection.[2]

Blessed is ... (1:1a)

The psalm begins with a statement of blessedness:

"Blessed is the man
who does not walk in the counsel of the wicked...." (1:1)

"Blessed" (*'āshār*), is the adjective "happiness, blessedness." There are two verbs that mean "to bless" in Hebrew, *bārak* and *'āshar*. *Bārak* is used more of God's blessing that comes

---

[1] David M. Howard, Jr., "The Psalms in Current Study," in *Interpreting the Psalms*, p. 25.
[2] Gerald H. Wilson, "The Structure of the Psalter," in *Interpreting the Psalms*, p. 232-233.

undeserved, while *'āshar* expresses more the idea of the natural blessing that comes from right living.[3]

Āshar isn't a bad word or an inferior blessing, it just has a different connotation than *bārak*. This isn't an extraordinary, miraculous blessing of Yahweh – though God is fully capable of miraculous blessing. It is the normal result of a life lived for God. Missionaries have observed a phenomenon of "redemption and lift." The first generation of Christians in a new area may be dirt poor. But the second generation of Christians – the children of the first generation – are quite likely to be more prosperous than the dirt-poor non-Christians in the community. Since they've adopted a godly lifestyle, stopped getting drunk, doing drugs, and gambling they've been able to see the prosperity that comes naturally from a life well lived.

Happy, to be congratulated, is the person who ... delights in the law of the Lord, rather than be under the influence of sinners and sinful ways.

Separating from Sin, Delighting in God (1:1-2)

Observe the three-fold parallelism that describes what a believer *doesn't* do in verse 1b:

walk	in the counsel of the wicked
stand	in the way of sinners
sit	in the seat of mockers

That's the negative part. The positive is found in verse 2. Look at the verbs that describe the godly person's actions:

"But his **delight** is in the law of the LORD,
and on his law he **meditates** day and night." (1:2)

The righteous person cherishes the Torah, and by extension, all of God's Word.

"Delight" (*hēpes*) functions as a verb in this sentence. The basic meaning of the root is to feel great favor towards something. The object solicits favor by its own intrinsic qualities. The verb means "to experience emotional delight."[4] In our verse then, the righteous man takes emotional delight in the law of the Lord.

---

[3] There are three distinctions between the use of *bārak* and *āshar*: (1) *Bārak* is never used to bless God or in God's mouth to bless people. It may be that *'āshar* is reserved for man as a word of envious desire, "to be envied with desire is the man who trusts in the Lord." (2) *Bārak* can be a blessing from God that man doesn't deserve, but to be blessed (*'ashrê*), man has to do something. (3) *Bārak* is a benediction, *'āshar* more of a congratulation (Victor P. Hamilton, *bārak*, TWOT #183a).

[4] Leonard J. Wood, *ḥāpēs*, TWOT #712b.

"Meditates" is *hāgā*, "meditate, utter, mutter." The basic meaning is a low sound, characteristic of the moaning of a dove. It can be used negatively "to plot, whisper," or positively, "to meditate, ponder." Perhaps the Scripture was read half out loud in the process of meditation.[5] The NJB renders this line, "and murmurs his law day and night," which may catch the idea here. The verb is also used in Psalms 63:6; 77:12; and 143:5. In God's word to Joshua, meditation results in prosperity:

> "Do not let this Book of the Law depart from your mouth; meditate on it day and night, so that you may be careful to do everything written in it. Then you will be prosperous and successful." (Joshua 1:8)

That also is the result of the righteous man in our psalm:

> "Whatever he does prospers." (verse 3d)

"Prospers" is *ṣālēah*, "prosper, succeed, be profitable." The root means to accomplish satisfactorily what is intended.[6]

The Lord's Watch-Care over the Believer (1:6)

After the imagery of the fruit-bearing tree and the chaff, which we'll consider in a moment, we see the conclusion of this short psalm, the punch line:

> "For the LORD watches over the way of the righteous,
> but the way of the wicked will perish." (1:6)

It is the "way" that is the focus of this verse. *Derek*, "way, road," is a very common Hebrew noun. Beyond a literal path worn by constant walking, it is commonly used figuratively to refer to the customary actions or behavior of a person.[7] A dynamic translation here might be "lifestyle."

The promise of this verse is that Yahweh "watches over" (NIV, NRSV, NJB) or "knoweth" (KJV, NASB) the path of the believer. The verb is *yāda'*, "know," here with the specific meaning of "protect, guard."[8] This verse has several parallels in the Bible, in particular:

> "In all thy ways acknowledge him, and he shall direct thy paths." (Proverbs 3:6, KJV)

> "Enter through the narrow gate. For wide is the gate and broad is the road that leads to destruction, and many enter through it. But small is the gate and narrow the road that leads to life, and only a few find it." (Matthew 7:13-14)

---

[5] Herbert Wolf, *hāgā*, TWOT 467.

[6] John E. Hartley, *ṣālēah*, TWOT #1917.

[7] Herbert Wolf, *dārak*, TWOT #453a

[8] On this special use of *yāda'*, Craigie (*Psalms* 1-50, p. 58) cites Dahood, *Psalms*, I, 5. "Care about, be concerned about" ... "take care of, take up the cause of" (*Yāda'*, Holladay, p. 129, meaning 7a.).

Poetic Structure

Let's look for a moment at the poetic elements of this remarkable psalm – its parallel structure along with its imagery, the major elements of Hebrew poetry. So far in our study of the Psalms we've seen mainly synonymous parallelism. Psalm 1 contains a mixture of synonymous and antithetic parallelism, which is characteristic of Wisdom literature, such as the Book of Proverbs. The simplest example in our psalm is in verse 6:

> "For the LORD watches over the way of the righteous,
> but the way of the wicked will perish." (1:6)

As typical of antithetic parallelism, the first line states the positive, reinforced by the second line which states the negative. Here's an example from Proverbs:

> "Hear, my child, your father's instruction,
> and do not reject your mother's teaching." (Proverbs 1:8)

Once you learn to recognize parallelism in the Bible, you'll begin to appreciate the poetic beauty of a psalm as well as its teaching. Psalm 1, however, doesn't show simple antithetic parallelism, but whole verses that are positive followed by others that are negative, a intricate interweaving that enhances the beauty and power of this psalm.

Above you can see the clear positive/negative structure of this psalm. The positive is highlighted in green, the negative in red.

A Fruit-Bearing Tree Planted by the Water (1:3)

The second powerful poetic element in Hebrew poetry is imagery – and the imagery in Psalm 1 is simple, but very powerful indeed:

Fruit-bearing tree

vs.

Chaff

> "He is like a tree planted by streams of water,
> which yields its fruit in season
> and whose leaf does not wither.
> Whatever he does prospers." (1:3)

In the arid climate of Israel, consider the beauty and calm pictured by a vigorous tree planted next to a water-channel,[9] that bears fruit regularly and not a bit of withering of its

---

[9] *Peleg,* means "artificial water-channel, canal" (Holladay 292).

leaves, no matter how dry the summer. Its roots go down deep. So long as the water keeps flowing, it will be healthy. The water in this figure would probably be God's word, or the Lord himself.

This is a powerful, enduring image expressed by the words of the familiar African American spiritual:

> "I shall not be, I shall not be moved,
> I shall not be, I shall not be moved,
> Just like a tree planted by the water, Lord,
> I shall not be moved."

Psalm 92 gives a similar word picture of the righteous:

> "The righteous will flourish like a palm tree,
> they will grow like a cedar of Lebanon;
> planted in the house of the LORD,
> they will flourish in the courts of our God.
> They will still bear fruit in old age,
> they will stay fresh and green...." (Psalm 92:12-14)

Chaff that the Wind Blows Away (1:4)

The second image in our psalm is of chaff being blown in the wind.

> "Not so the wicked!
> They are like chaff
> that the wind blows away." (1:4)

Chaff is the paper-thin membrane surrounding the grain. It is removed before the grain is ground to make flour. The ancient Hebrews would gather the cut and dried wheat stalks into a flat area, best in a breezy area, and physically remove the chaff from the wheat by driving a donkey over it pulling a sled or log. Now the grain and chaff would lie together on the threshing floor. To separate the two, the farmer would use a pitchfork, called a winnowing fork, to throw the straw into the air. The breeze would blow away the light straw and the paper-thin chaff, while the grain would fall back to the ground by itself, where it would be collected and stored.

In this simile, the wicked are identified as the chaff – light, insubstantial, and transitory. The heavier, substantial, valuable grain which is not mentioned in this brief image, would represent the believer. Winnowing is a symbol of judgment in verses 4 and 5. John the Baptist picks up a similar image as he declares the coming of the Messiah who will bring judgment:

"His winnowing fork is in his hand to clear his threshing floor and to gather the wheat into his barn, but he will burn up the chaff with unquenchable fire." (Luke 3:17)

The chaff, if any remains, will be burned up by the farmer. Our psalm concludes fittingly:

"For the LORD watches over the way of the righteous,
but the way of the wicked will perish." (1:6)

Q1. (Psalm 1). This short psalm seems to reaffirm what we already know: the righteous will succeed and the wicked will perish. Why do we need to be reminded of this? From an emotional standpoint, what lines in this psalm stand out to you. Why do you think you like them?
http://www.joyfulheart.com/forums/index.php?showtopic=659

Psalm 15 – Characteristics of a Righteous Person

Sometimes Christians are afraid to talk about righteousness. They are either too judgmental and self-righteous that they can't see straight or they are so quick to talk about grace not works so that righteous living doesn't seem to matter much.

But the Bible has a lot to say about righteous living. Why? Because in our world – as in the ancient world – there are far too many people who live for themselves, shade the truth, cut corners where they can – and call themselves Christians. Just what is a righteous person? This psalm of David considers the question.

Dwelling with God (15:1)

"LORD, who may dwell in your sanctuary?
Who may live on your holy hill?" (15:1)

The real question here is: Who can dwell in God's presence? The answer is, someone who is conscientiously trying to live as God commands. Is that too much for us to handle?

Yes, we are imperfect and need forgiveness. There are other psalms that explore grace and forgiveness, but this psalm is talking about the lifestyle of one who claims to be a believer.

This "sanctuary" (NIV), "tent" (NRSV), "tabernacle" (KJV) talked about in verse 1 (*'ōhel*) is God's "dwelling place, home, tabernacle, tent." Though it specifically refers to an animal-skin tent, it can be used generically as one's dwelling place, even long after the Israelites had adopted more permanent dwellings.[10] In the second line, the "holy hill" refers to Jerusalem, specifically the dwelling place of God in Jerusalem, where in Solomon's day the temple would be built (Psalm 2:6; 3:4; 43:3-4; 87:1-3). We see a similar question raised in Psalm 24 that we will consider in chapter 8:

> "Who may ascend the hill of the LORD?
> Who may stand in his holy place?" (Psalm 24:3)

Do you want to live in close proximity to God? I do. What is required? Jesus put it pretty bluntly when he said:

> "If anyone loves me, he will obey my teaching. My Father will love him, and we will come to him and make our home with him. He who does not love me will not obey my teaching." (John 14:23-24a)

What are those things? David doesn't give us an exhaustive list, but rather some earmarks, characteristics, of a person who is seeking to please God.

Poetic Structure

Before we continue, let's look at the fairly complex structure of the poem:

- An opening couplet (two parallel lines; verse 1)
- A closing single concluding line. (verse 5c)

Between these are

- Two triplets (verses 2 and 3) and
- Three doublets (verses 4 and 5)

---

[10] Jack P. Lewis, *'āhal*, TWOT #32a.

Another way to look at the structure is by alternating positive conditions vs. negative conditions:

A. Positive Conditions (verse 2)   **B. Negative Conditions** (verse 3)

- Walking blamelessly   - No falseness

- Doing right   - No evil

- Speaking truth   - No reproach

C. Positive Conditions (verse 4)   **D. Negative Conditions** (verse 5)

- Despise reprobates   - No usury

- Swear to do good   - No bribery

It may not be a coincidence that there are 10 of these conditions. While not corresponding directly to the 10 commandments, maybe they are meant to echo the idea of 10 conditions of a righteous person.[11]

The imagery in this psalm isn't complex. It is of a tent, a dwelling place on a hill where God lives. Who can live in the same tent with God day by day? Can you? Can I? What does it take to live with God?

Moral Integrity (15:2)

The first triplet or three parallel lines talk about inner integrity.

"He whose walk is blameless
and who does what is righteous,
who speaks the truth from his heart." (15:2)

I don't think that David is talking about complete moral perfection here – pure thoughts, pure motives, never getting angry inappropriately, etc. I think he is talking about living a law-abiding, upright life – abiding by God's law, that is. Notice that each of the verbs speak about actions: (1) "walk" or "live," (2) "do" or "work", and (3) "speak." Three words modify these verbs:

- **"Blameless"** (NIV, NRSV), "uprightly" (KJV) is *tāmîm*, from the verb *tāmam*, which carries the fundamental idea of completeness. Our word is used of animal sacrifices that are without blemish, as well as moral integrity, "whole, upright, perfect."[12]

---

[11] Craigie, *Psalms,* p. 150-151.

- **"Righteous"** (NIV, KJV) or "right" (NRSV) is ṣedeq, from a root that basically connotes conformity to an ethical or moral standard.[13]
- **"Truth"** ('ĕmet), from a root which denotes firmness or certainty. The noun means "truth, faithfulness, verity ... with an underlying sense of certainty, dependability."[14]

Fairness to Neighbors (15:3)

The second characteristic is a sense of fairness and even-handedness towards others. These are stated in the negative:

"... And has no slander on his tongue,
who does his neighbor no wrong
and casts no slur on his fellowman...." (15:3)

I've met a few people who act overtly to deceive, wrong, cheat, or ruin others. But the part of this which catches me and some people I know is the verb "slander" (NIV, NRSV) or "backbiteth" (KJV), rāgal, "slander, gossip," from a word that suggests roaming about, spying out, and telling secrets.[15] Too often we do wrong to our neighbor by talking casually about him or her, saying things that are unkind – that we would never think of saying to his or her face. One way to look at this is to, "Love your neighbor as yourself" (Leviticus 19:18; Matthew 22:39)

Clear Allegiance (15:4a)

Verse 4 may trouble Christians who have been taught by Jesus to love their enemies. It seems to suggest hate. Or does it?

"... Who despises a vile man
but honors those who fear the LORD." (15:4a)

"Despise" (NIV, NRSV) or "contemn" (KJV) is bāzā, which has the basic meaning "to accord little worth to something." It means "to despise, disdain, hold in contempt."[16] Here it is contrasted in antithetic parallelism with the word "honor."[17] A couple of other verses are appropriate here:

"Let those who love the LORD hate evil." (Psalm 97:10a)

---

[12] J. Barton Payne, tāmam, TWOT #2522d.
[13] Harold G. Sitgers, ṣādēq, TWOT 1879a.
[14] Our word "Amen" comes from the same root 'āman. Jack B. Scott, 'āman, TWOT #116k.
[15] Holladay, p. 332; Kidner, Psalms 1-72, p. 81.
[16] Bruce K. Waltke, bāzā, TWOT #244.
[17] The "vile person" (KJV, NIV) or "wicked" (NRSV) is mā'as, "refuse, reject." Holladay, p. 180b.

"To fear the LORD is to hate evil;
I hate pride and arrogance,
evil behavior and perverse speech." (Proverbs 8:13)

Again and again we see this idea in the Psalms: "Turn from evil and do good...." (Psalms 34:14; 36:4; 37:27; 101:3; 119:104, 163).

We live in a tolerant society that teaches us to overlook sin, to call evil "good" and good "evil." Intolerance in our society is considered an evil. Yes, there is a kind of proud judgmentalism that we must avoid. But we believers must *not* be tolerant of evil or regularly associate with evil people. We must stand clearly for the right. We are on God's side unashamedly! That doesn't mean that we can or should be complete separatists or hermits. We must live in society (1 Corinthians 5:1-13, especially 9-10). But we must be crystal clear about our allegiance.

Keeping One's Word (15:4b)

The next characteristic of a righteous person is keeping his word, even when it is difficult to do so.

"Who keeps his oath
even when it hurts." (15:4b)

All healthy human relationships are built on trust, require trust. We serve a God who is faithful to keep his word. It follows that a follower of the Lord will take pains to keep his promises, even though that later becomes costly.

Living without Greed (15:5)

Money is tempting; money is corrupting, that is, if our hearts desire it. "The love of money is a root of all kinds of evil" (1 Timothy 6:10). The last descriptor of a righteous person in our psalm is one who is not controlled or swayed by money:

"Who lends his money without usury
and does not accept a bribe against the innocent.
He who does these things
will never be shaken." (15:5)

Money-lending in ancient times wasn't thought of as funding for capital expenditures such as a house. Instead, it was a last resort for a poor person who didn't have any other choice. The Mosaic Law didn't forbid all money-lending at interest (Deuteronomy 23:20; Matthew 25:27), but in the strongest possible terms it condemned money-lending designed to take advantage of a poor brother's extremity. Thus the righteous person described in the psalm lends money as an act of charity, not business. Nor does he accept a bribe to act unjustly. Only a person who has money clearly submitted to God can walk righteously before him.

The psalm concludes with the promise of stability for the righteous:

"He who does these things
will never be shaken." (15:5b)

The final lines remind me again just a bit of the African American spiritual based on Psalm 1 that we just studied: "Like a tree planted by the water, I shall not be moved."

Q2. (Psalm 15) The Wisdom Psalms are meant to instruct us. How would you use this psalm in your family to instruct your children? What topics of right living does it cover?
http://www.joyfulheart.com/forums/index.php?showtopic=660

Psalm 133 – The Beauty of Unity

Our final psalm in this lesson doesn't speak of justice, but of the rightness and beauty of unity. It is a psalm "of David" and is called "a song of ascents," traditionally sung as pilgrims approached Jerusalem as they went up for a feast.

Begin by reading this short psalm out loud:

"¹How good and pleasant it is
when brothers live together in unity!
²It is like precious oil poured on the head,
running down on the beard,
running down on Aaron's beard,
down upon the collar of his robes.
³It is as if the dew of Hermon
were falling on Mount Zion.
For there the LORD bestows his blessing,
even life forevermore." (Psalm 133)

What stands out to me about this psalm is its startling imagery.

- Oil poured on the head
- Running down on the beard and clothing
- Dew

Brothers Living Together in Unity (133:1)

The key term here is "*yaḥad*, "unitedness, union, association, community."[18] Every other phrase in this short psalm amplifies and informs this word.

The single purpose of this psalm is to exalt the value and virtue of unity with brothers. That's it. Pure and simple. In a fractured world, unity gets a bad rap. We have separatist churches refusing to fellowship with others that might have some different understanding of the Bible, too often seeing doctrinal purity and separation from "worldly Christians" as their prime distinctives as a denomination. It is because of this attitude that the Protestant church is splintered into hundreds of self-righteous pieces. Jesus gave a higher command than separation:

> "A new command I give you: Love one another. As I have loved you, so you must love one another. By this all men will know that you are my disciples, if you love one another." (John 13:34-35)

This now is our "prime directive." So to reinforce this value in our hearts, let's consider Psalm 133 carefully, taking time to allow its words and images to settle in our hearts and affix themselves to our souls.

Good and Pleasant (133:1)

> "How good (*ṭôb*) and pleasant (*nā'îm*) it is
> when brothers live together in unity!

The first words we see are "good" and "pleasant." The root of "good" refers to "good" or "goodness" in its broadest senses. "Good" (*ṭôb*), depending on the context, can carry meanings such as, "good, pleasant, beautiful, delightful, glad, joyful, precious, correct, and righteous." Hebrew often uses *ṭôb* where in English we would say something like "beautiful" or "expensive." It may also include the ideas of superior quality or relative worth.[19]

The word "pleasant" (*nā'îm*) is a close synonym. It means "sweet, lovely, agreeable."[20] The root is used to describe David as the "sweet" psalmist of Israel (2 Samuel 23:1), the

---

[18] Paul R. Gilchrist, *yaḥad*, TWOT #858b; Holladay 132b.
[19] Andrew Bowling, *ṭôb*, TWOT #793a.
[20] Marvin R. Wilson, *nā'ēm*, TWOT #1384b.

physical beauty of two lovers in the Song of Solomon (1:16; 7:6), for the taste of bread (Proverbs 9:17) and the music of the lyre (Psalm 81:2).

The words themselves carry associations of beauty, joy, and loveliness. Unity is not evil compromise! Unity is love working itself out amidst the difficulties that otherwise tend to divide people. Unity is beautiful, a thing to behold. The Apostle Paul commands us:

> "Make every effort to keep the unity of the Spirit through the bond of peace. There is one body and one Spirit-- just as you were called to one hope when you were called – one Lord, one faith, one baptism; one God and Father of all, who is over all and through all and in all." (Ephesians 4:3-6)

Unity Is Like Perfumed Oil Generously Poured Out (133:2)

> "It is like precious oil poured on the head,
> running down on the beard,
> running down on Aaron's beard,
> down upon the collar of his robes." (133:2)

"Oil" (NIV, NRSV) or "ointment" (KJV) is the common word *shemen*, "oil," either of pure olive oil or prepared for various uses such as perfume or ointment. Kings and priests were anointed with oil and it became important in cosmetics and perfumery. Oil became a symbol of prosperity and blessing (Deuteronomy 32:13; 33:24; Psalm 92:10). It is referred to as "the oil of joy" (Isaiah 61:3; Psalm 45:7). An honored guest would be anointed with oil as an act of generous hospitality, as in the 23rd Psalm: "You anoint my head with oil; my cup overflows" (Psalm 23:5). In Jesus' day, putting oil on a guest's head was considered the act of a gracious host (Luke 7:46).

But in Psalm 133, this wasn't just olive oil. It was "precious" oil, probably perfumed. The adjective here is *ṭôb* which we saw in verse one, in the sense of "beautiful, expensive." The New Jerusalem Bible renders it "fine oil."

And it wasn't just "a little dab will do you." This oil is poured[21] until it begins to run off the hair and down onto the beard, and then even onto the recipient's robes.[22] I would worry about staining my clothes. But the figure here is used to suggest abundance, extravagance, overflowing blessing. Aaron is mentioned because he was anointed as high priest by Moses (Exodus 30:25-30; Leviticus 8:12).

---

[21] The word "poured" is implied. It isn't in the Hebrew text.

[22] "Skirts" (KJV) or "collar" (NRSV, NIV) is *peh*, "mouth," here used figuratively of the top opening of the robe (Victor P. Hamilton, *peh*, TWOT #1738).

3. Choosing the Right Path (Psalms 1, 15, and 133)

Unity Is Like Heavy Dew (133:3)

"It is as if the dew of Hermon
were falling on Mount Zion.
For there the LORD bestows his blessing,
even life forevermore." (133:3)

Mount Hermon is a high, snow-covered mountain on the border between Syria and Lebanon, the highest mountain in the lands of the Bible, 9,230 feet (2,814 meters). George Adam Smith observed, "The dews of Syrian nights are excessive; on many mornings it looks as if there had been heavy rain...."[23] The dew that falls on the slopes of Mt. Hermon is copious[24] Mount Zion, on the other hand, is a poetic term for the city of Jerusalem. The psalmist seems to be saying that unity of brothers can be compared to the proverbial heavy dew of Mount Hermon descending upon Jerusalem. Kirkpatrick expresses it this way:

"Dew is a symbol for what is refreshing, quickening, invigorating. The Psalmist compares the influence of brotherly unity upon the nation to the effect of dew on vegetation. From such dwelling together, individuals draw fresh energy; the life of the community, social and religious, is revived and quickened."[25]

Q3. (Psalm 133) What about this short psalm seems to attract you? Why is "dwelling together in unity" so difficult? What kinds of commitments does unity require of us? How do the principles of unity and purity seem to conflict with each other? Why are reconciliation and unity such high values in Jesus' teaching, do you think?
http://www.joyfulheart.com/forums/index.php?showtopic=661

---

[23] George Adam Smith, *The Historical Geography of the Holy Land* (Seventh Edition; New York: A.C. Armstrong and Son, 1900).
[24] Kirkpatrick, *Psalms*, p. 771.
[25] Ibid.

Exercise. For one of the psalms in this lesson – or another psalm with a similar theme – do one of the suggested exercises to help you experience the Psalms in Appendix 1. These include such things as praying a psalm, meditating, reading to a shut-in, paraphrasing, writing your own psalm, singing, preparing a liturgy, and memorizing. Then report to the forum what the exercise meant to you personally or share what you've written with others.
http://www.joyfulheart.com/forums/index.php?showtopic=662

Prayer

Dear Lord, we thank you for the encouragement to righteous living that you give us in these psalms. Help us to be diligent to obey you. Also help us to be diligent to seek unity, rather than just to judge, condemn, and separate. Teach us how to love – to love you and to love our neighbors. In Jesus' name, we pray. Amen.

Songs

- **"Can I Ascend,"** words and music by Matt Redman (© 1995 Thankyou Music). Psalm 24:3.
- **"Clean Hands and a Pure Heart,"** words and music by Dale Garratt (© 1980, Scripture in Song). Psalm 24:3-5; 2 Chronicles 16:9.
- **"I Shall Not Be Moved,"** African American spiritual. Psalm 1
- **"Give Us Clean Hands,"** words and music by Charlie Hall (© 2000, worshiptogether.com songs). Psalm 24:3-5.
- **"Micah 6:8,"** words and music by Bob Sklar (© 1978, 1980, Maranatha! Music)
- **"¡Miren Qué Bueno! (O Look and Wonder),"** words and music: Pablo Sosa (1979), translated by George Lockwood (© 1979 Cancionero Abierto, Buenos Aires). Psalm 133.
- **"Who May Ascend to the Hill of the Lord?"** words and music by Kirk Dearman (© 1989, Maranatha Praise, Inc.). Psalm 24:3-5.

4. Offering High Praises to God (Psalms 150, 95, 98)

What do Handel's "Hallelujah Chorus," Revelation, and the Psalms have in common? The word, "Hallelujah," that's what. The word rings throughout the Psalms in one mighty panoply of praise. Revelation reaches its climax with the triumphant cry:

> "Hallelujah!
> For our Lord God Almighty reigns." (Revelation 19:6)

But what does Hallelujah mean? It is a command, an imperative, made up of three parts:

Several instruments and high praise is shown in James J. Tissot's painting, "David Dancing before the Ark" (1896-1900), watercolor.

hālal	lu	Yah
Praise	you (plural)	short for Yahweh, "the LORD"

The verb *hālal* means "praise." "This root connotes being sincerely and deeply thankful for and/or satisfied in lauding a superior quality(ies) or great, great act(s) of the object." It can mean, "to brag," and be used to praise a man or woman. But its primary use in the Old Testament is directed toward God.[1]

In this lesson we're going to begin to examine the psalms of high praise to God, psalms of joy and celebration. This belongs at the end of the Psalter as the high point of the Hallel psalms. These belong to genre of Hebrew poetry known as "hymns," though they aren't like the traditional hymns you'll find in your hymnal. They tend to be exuberant rather than staid, emotional rather than restrained.

---

[1] In the cognate languages, *hālal* is related to the Akkadian root *alālu*, "to shout, brag, boast" and "to hail, acclaim, utter a cry, to generally express joy" (Leonard J. Coppes, *hālal*, TWOT #50)

Psalm 150 – Let Everything that Has Breath Praise the Lord!

The Psalter concludes with this short psalm, beginning and ending with "Hallelujah," wrapping the psalm fore and aft with praise. Read it out loud right now in your favorite translation:

> "¹*Praise the* LORD.
> Praise God in his sanctuary;
> praise him in his mighty heavens.
> ²Praise him for his acts of power;
> praise him for his surpassing greatness.
> ³Praise him with the sounding of the trumpet,
> praise him with the harp and lyre,
> ⁴praise him with tambourine and dancing,
> praise him with the strings and flute,
> ⁵praise him with the clash of cymbals,
> praise him with resounding cymbals.
> ⁶Let everything that has breath praise the LORD.
> *Praise the* LORD." (Psalm 150:1-6)

But the psalm doesn't just begin and end with praise. It has praise through and through, using the verb *hālal* a full thirteen times. There are many ways to look at this short psalm. One approach is to see it as answering various questions about praise:

- **What?** (verse 1a) – praise
- **Where?** (verse 1b) – in his holy place,[2] heavens
- **Why?** (verse 2) – for acts of power, for surpassing greatness
- **How?** (verse 3-5) – with instruments and dance
- **Who?** (verse 6a) – everyone that has breath

I doubt, however, that it is composed for us to analyze. Rather it is designed to catch us up in its all-out emotion of praise.

---

[2] "Sanctuary" is the noun *qōdesh*, "apartness, holiness, sacredness, hallowed, holy," from the root *qādash*, "the state of that which belongs to the sacred, distinct from the common or profane" (Thomas E. McComiskey, *qādash*, TWOT #1990a).

Instruments of Praise

Detail of Jewish kinnor player is found in the bas-relief in the palace of Assurbanipal (705-681 BC) at Nineveh, portraying the fall of the Judean city of Lachish.

We can't be exhaustive about this psalm, of course. But let's describe the instruments, most of which have a modern-day equivalent.

"Trumpet" (*shôpār*) was originally the ram's horn.[3] A metal trumpet (*ḥaṣōṣerā*) is also mentioned in the Old Testament. This trumpet was made of beaten silver (Numbers 10:2). Josephus describes it as "in length a little short of a cubit, it is a narrow tube, slightly thicker than a flute."[4]

"Harp" (NIV, NJB), "psaltery" (KJV), "lute" (NRSV), *nēbel*, is an instrument of 12 strings, plucked with the fingers.[5] It was larger than the *kinnôr* or "lyre," with a deeper tone. This lyre had two arms with a box-shaped body (a Canaanite version). David played such an instrument and it was the main instrument in

Captive musicians from the siege of Lachish sing praises to the conqueror. Detail of relief from SW Palace of Sennacherib at Nineveh, ca. 701 BC British Museum, London.

the second temple orchestra.[6] Psalm 98 declares:

"Make music to the LORD with the harp,
with the harp (*kinnôr*) and the sound of singing,
with trumpets (*ḥaṣōṣerā*) and the blast of the ram's horn (*shôpār*) –
shout for joy before the LORD, the King." (Psalm 98:5-6)

[3] Hermann J. Austel, *shāpar*, TWOT #2449c. Daniel A. Foxvog and Ann D. Kilmer, "Music," ISBE 3:436-449, especially p. 439.

[4] Josephus, *Antiquities* 3.12.6 (§291).

[5] Louis Goldberg, *nbl*, TWOT 1284b. See also the Introduction to Psalms above. Josephus, *Antiquities* 7.12.3.

[6] Foxvog and Kilmer, pp. 440-442, John N. Oswalt, *knr*, TWOT #1004a

"Tambourine" (NIV, NRSV, NJB), "timbrel"(KJV), *tōp*, is a general term for tambourines and small drums (the most common instruments of percussion in ancient times).[7] This was a hand drum, without the jingly metal plates we associate with a tambourine.

"Strings" (NIV, NRSV) or "stringed instruments" (KJV), *mēn*, is probably a collective term for stringed instruments.[8]

"Flute" (NIV), "organs" (KJV), pipes (NRSV, NJB), *'ûgāb*, " is probably an end-blown, vertical flute, a reed-pipe."[9]

"Cymbals" (*selṣelîm*) that have been found in various Near Eastern sites from the 14th to the 8th centuries BC are generally bronze round flat plates, 4 to 6 inches (10 to 15 cm.) in diameter, with central bowl-like depressions and fitted with iron finger rings. Verse 5 seems to describe two ways of playing the cymbals:

1. **Cymbals of pleasing sound**. "Clash" (NIV), "clanging" (NRSV), "loud" (KJV).[10]
2. **Cymbals of alarm**. "Resounding" (NIV), "loud clashing" (NRSV), "triumphant" (NJB), "high sounding" (KJV), *terû'â*, "alarm, signal, sound of the tempest."[11]

Everyone that Has Breath (150:6a)

The psalmist has encompassed all kinds of instrumentalists, all places, all reasons. Now he extends it the final step to "everyone who has breath." That's you and me. *We* are to praise Yahweh. We are! Praise *ye* the Lord!

Q1. (Psalm 150) What does this psalm teach us about praise? Where should praise occur? With what should praise be conducted? Who should praise? What does this psalm make you feel like after reading it out loud?
http://www.joyfulheart.com/forums/index.php?showtopic=663

---

[7] Ronald F. Youngblood, *tāpap*, TWOT #2536a.

[8] *Mēn*, Holladay 200a; Foxvog and Kilmer, p. 445.

[9] *'Ûgāb*, Holladay 266; TWOT #1559c; Foxvog and Kilmer, pp. 443-444.

[10] *Shema'*, "sounding cymbals. According to KB these are small tinkling cymbals as opposed to the loud, crashing cymbals" (Hermann J. Austel, *shāma'*, TWOT #2412b).

[11] William White, *rûa'* ("shout, raise a sound, cry out"), TWOT #2135b; Foxvog and Kilmer, p. 444.

Psalm 95 – Come, Let Us Worship and Bow Down

It's difficult to narrow down these high praise songs to just a few – there are so many wonderful psalms of this type! Psalm 95 is both a call to praise and thanksgiving. It is also an exhortation to obedience and faith.

Structure of Psalm 95

Look briefly at the structure:

1. A call to **exuberant praise** to the Lord (verses 1-2)
2. The reason to praise, **the Lord's greatness** as Creator and King (verses 3-5).
3. A call to **bow down** in humble worship before our God our Shepherd (verses 6-7c).
4. A warning and **exhortation to obey** the Lord (verses 7d-11).

Names and Titles of God

There are six names or metaphors for God in this psalm:

- LORD, Yahweh (1a)
- Rock of our salvation (1b)
- Great God (3a)
- Great King above all gods (3b)
- Our Maker (6b)
- Our Shepherd (7, implied)

Expressions of Worship

> "¹Come, let us sing for joy to the LORD;
> let us shout aloud to the Rock of our salvation.
> ²Let us come before him with thanksgiving
> and extol him with music and song." (95:1-2)

When I consider Psalm 95, I see several expressions of worship (in addition to *hālal*, "praise," which we examined above in Psalm 150). Since one of our purposes in the Psalms is to learn better to worship, let's examine the underlying Hebrew words:

- **"Sing "**(1a), *rānan*, means specifically, "cry out, shout for joy." The idea here is a shout of jubilation, a holy joy which is being celebrated by Israel's shouting. In Psalms the word appears in parallel poetry with nearly every term for joy, rejoicing, and praise, and a few times in parallel with "sing" (59:16; 98:4).[12]

---

[12] William White, *rānan*, TWOT #2179.

- **"Shout aloud"** (1b, NIV) or "make a joyful noise" (KJV, NRSV), is *rûa'*, "shout, raise a sound, cry out." The primary meaning is "to raise a noise" by shouting or with an instrument, especially a horn (Numbers 10:7; Joshua 6:5).[13] The word is repeated as "extol" (2b, NIV) in verse 2b. Kidner explains it as, "the spontaneous shout that might greet a king or a moment of victory."[14]
- **"Thanksgiving"** (2a) is *tôdâ*, "confession, praise" of God's character and works. The verb is used to express one's public proclamation or declaration (confession) of God's attributes and his works. It is most often translated "to thank" in English, though the Old Testament does not have our concept of thanks. The expression of thanks to God is included in praise, it is a way of praising.[15]

In verse 6 we see a particular kind of worship – kneeling, prostration, before the King.

> "Come, let us bow down in worship,
> let us kneel before the LORD our Maker." (95:6)

In this one verse are three words which indicate prostrating oneself, kneeling. Prostration was quite common as an act of self-abasement or submission performed before relatives, strangers, superiors, and especially before royalty. The Muslims practice it today in prayer, in which the forehead must touch the ground.[16]

God our Shepherd (95:7)

The next verse is a beautiful image of a flock of sheep in deep grass.

> "... For he is our God
> and we are the people of his pasture,
> the flock under his care." (95:7)

We worship, we bow down, because we recognize both God's ownership of us and his responsibility to care for us. As Jesus put it, he is not a hireling, but the owner of the sheep.

---

[13] William White, *rûa'*, TWOT #2135.

[14] Kidner, *Psalms 73-150*, pp. 352-353.

[15] Ralph H. Alexander, *yādā*, TWOT #847b

[16] "Bow down" (6a, NIV) or "worship" (KJV, NRSV) is now understood to be the Eshtaphal stem of *ḥāwā*. (Edwin Yamauchi, *shāḥā*, TWOT #2360). "The commonly occurring form *hishtaḥăwâ*, 'to prostrate oneself' or 'to worship,' which was analyzed as a Hithpael of *shāḥā*, is now regarded on the basis of Ugaritic evidence as an Eshtaphal stem (the only example) of *ḥāwā* (Edwin Yamauchi, TWOT #619). Holladay sees this as an hištafal stem (pp. 97a, 365b). "Worship" (6a, NIV) or "bow down" (KJV, NRSV), *kāra'*, "bow down, kneel, sink to one's knees, kneel in reverence, before God or a king" (R. Laird Harris, *kāra'*, TWOT #1044). "Kneel" (6b), is *bārak*, usually translated "bless," but here and in two other places rendered "kneel" (John N. Oswalt, *bārak*, TWOT #285).

Therefore, he is willing to lay down his life for the sheep – and did! He is the Shepherd, we are the sheep, the flock. He cares for us.

Obedience Must Follow Worship (95:7d-11)

The final verses of Psalm 95 seem different from the rest of the Psalm. But they follow on the theme of worship. Worship, exhorts this prophetic voice, requires a tender heart of obedience toward God, not the stubbornness shown by the Israelites in the wilderness.

"7dToday, if you hear his voice,
8do not harden your hearts as you did at Meribah,
as you did that day at Massah in the desert,
9where your fathers tested and tried me,
though they had seen what I did.
10For forty years I was angry with that generation;
I said, 'They are a people whose hearts go astray,
and they have not known my ways.'
11So I declared on oath in my anger,
'They shall never enter my rest.'" (95:7d-11)

The psalmist recounts the sad story of Israel's 40-year sojourn in the wilderness. Under Moses they had been brought out of Egypt and seen the Egyptian army destroyed by God's mighty hand. But then the complaints began. No food. God provided manna. No water. God directed Moses to strike a rock and water gushed forth at Massah and Meribah (Exodus 17:7).

The crucial test, however, took place on the brink of entering the Promised Land (Numbers 13-14). Twelve spies had been sent north from the Israelite camp at Kadesh-barnea to spy out the land of Canaan prior to the conquest. When they returned, ten reported that they would not be able to defeat the walled cities and giants in the land. Only two – Caleb and Joshua – reported that through trust in God: "We should go up and take possession of the land, for we can certainly do it." (Numbers 13:30).

At that point the people of Israel rebelled. They were filled with fear from the negative report of the ten spies. There was talk of selecting another leader to take them back to Egypt. This wasn't just resistance against the authority of Moses, whom God had appointed, but unbelief of God himself. It was ugly! It constituted treason against both Moses and God.

God's response was anger at the unbelief of the entire generation. His oath in this passage begins "as surely as...." He responded:

"As surely as I live and as surely as the glory of the LORD fills the whole earth, not one of the men who saw my glory and the miraculous signs I performed in Egypt and in the desert but who disobeyed me and tested me ten times – not one of them will ever see the land I promised on oath to their forefathers. No one who has treated me with contempt will ever see it." (Numbers 14:21-23)

None of the men and women 20 years old and older would enter the Promised Land and rest from their sojourn. They would die in the desert; only their children would enter the land. The writer of Hebrews discusses this passage extensively in Hebrews 3 and 4 as a warning against unbelief and apostasy.

Why did the psalmist insert this warning right after high praise and prostrate submission in Psalm 95? The topic of the psalm is worship. His point is that worship not only consists of praise, thanksgiving, and outward submission, but also submissive hearts before the Lord. This is not an outward worship, but inward. Too often our worship is empty words, rather than a submissive spirit full of faith in God and a readiness to obey him. The Apostle Paul reminds us:

"I appeal to you therefore, brothers and sisters, by the mercies of God, to present your bodies as a living sacrifice, holy and acceptable to God, which is your spiritual worship." (Romans 12:1)

The way we live our lives comprises our worship of God, not just what we say with our mouths on "worship days."

Q2. (Psalm 95) In Psalm 95 we are commanded to worship the Lord. What are the reasons *why* we should worship contained in this psalm? Why do you think the warning in verses 8-11 is included in this psalm? How does this fit with the earlier elements of the psalm?

http://www.joyfulheart.com/forums/index.php?showtopic=664

Psalm 98 – Sing to the Lord a New Song

Psalm 98 is typical of many of the praise psalms. The unidentified writer has no complaint to bring before the Lord. Rather he pens a love-song to God meant to be sung and accompanied by instruments, termed "a psalm" (*mizmôr*), from *zāmar*, "to sing, play an instrument."[17]

The structure of the psalm is fairly free flowing:

1. Command: A call to sing a new song (98:1a)
2. Reason: (1b-3) Because of the Lord's record of salvation, righteousness, and faithful love.
3. Command: A call to shout to the Lord and make music (98:4-6)
4. Command: A call to nature to join in the praise (98:7-9a)
5. Reason: Because he is coming with righteous judgment (98:9b).

Sing a New Song (98:1-3)

"Sing to the LORD a new song...." (98:1a)

The psalm begins with a command to sing. Kidner comments, "The 'new song' is not simply a piece newly composed, though it naturally includes such, but a response that will match the freshness of His mercies, which are 'new every morning.'"[18]

Yahweh's Salvation for Israel (98:1b-3)

Now the psalmist gives the reasons that Yahweh is worthy of this song of praise. The words "salvation" (*yeshû'â*) and "save, deliver" (*yāsha'*) occur three times in this section. In the New Testament, the idea of salvation focuses primarily on the forgiveness of sins, deliverance from its power, and the defeat of Satan. But in the Old Testament, salvation is usually in terms of how the Lord has delivered Israel from tangible enemies.[19] As I read verses 1b-3 I think especially of God's deliverance of Israel from Egypt and carving out for them a new homeland in Canaan.

"¹Sing to the LORD a new song,
for he has done marvelous things;
his right hand and his holy arm
have worked **salvation** for him.
²The LORD has made his **salvation** known
and revealed his righteousness to the nations.
³He has remembered his love
and his faithfulness[20] to the house of Israel;

---

[17] Herbert Wolf, *zāmar*, TWOT #558c.
[18] Kidner, *Psalms 73-150*, p. 347
[19] John E. Hartley, *yāsha'*, TWOT #929b.
[20] "Faithfulness" (NIV), "truth" is *ĕmûnâ*, "firmness, fidelity, steadiness" (Jack B. Scott, *'āman*, TWOT #116e).

all the ends of the earth have seen
the **salvation** of our God." (98:1b-3)

The imagery here is of Yahweh as a warrior who wields a sword with his right hand and "holy arm" on behalf of Israel. Yahweh the Warrior is a common image in the Psalms. Notice how through his salvation of Israel from captivity to their home in the Promised Land that God "made his salvation known" and revealed his righteousness to the unbelieving nations around. Because they told the story of what God had done, God's reputation for helping Israel was well known. People learn about God's salvation in our lives by what we share. Part of our praise towards God is furthering his reputation by our testimony of how he has saved and delivered us.

Instrumental Worship (98:4-6)

As we saw in Psalm 150, all the voices and instruments join in worship:

"4Shout for joy[21] to the LORD, all the earth
burst into jubilant song[22] with music;
5make music to the LORD with the harp,
with the harp and the sound of singing,
6with trumpets and the blast of the ram's horn –
shout for joy before the LORD, the King." (98:4-6)

All Nature Praises Yahweh (98:7-9a)

Now the psalmist commands all creation to praise the Lord:

"7Let the sea resound, and everything in it,
the world, and all who live in it.
8Let the rivers clap their hands,
let the mountains sing together for joy;
9let them sing before the LORD...." (98:7-9a)

The psalmist calls upon the sea and the earth and all their inhabitants to praise. Let the sea "roar." The word literally means "to thunder." If you've visited the coast, you know the roar of the breakers and the wind.[23] The rivers are to "clap[24] their hands," the mountains are to "sing."

---

[21] "Shout for joy" (NIV), "make a joyful noise" (KJV) is *rûa'*, "shout, raise a sound, cry out," which we saw above (William White, *rûa'*, TWOT #2135).

[22] "Burst into jubilant song" (NIV), "break forth into joyous song" (KJV), "make a loud noise" (KJV) is *pāsah*, "cause to break or burst forth, break forth with" (BDB 822).

[23] William White, *rā'am*, TWOT #2189.

[24] *Māhā'*, "strike, clap." For more on clapping hands, see the Epilogue, footnote 1.

I once met a Bible school graduate (who should have known better) who claimed that mountains must clap their hands. "If the Bible says they do, then they must do it!" he responded with some passion. This is not a question of inerrancy, but of the poetic use of language. The psalmist is obviously using figurative language. Hebrew poetry – and the Book of Revelation, for that matter – is full of figurative language. We must try to understand the words as the author intended them – in this case figuratively.

When you read this section, you hear the exuberance of praise, the joy of praise, the fullness of praise that we are to bring to God.

The Reason for Praise: The Judge Is Coming with Righteousness (98:9b-d)

> "... For he comes to judge the earth.
> He will judge the world in righteousness.[25]
> and the peoples with equity."[26] (98:9b-d)

You might think that "Here comes the judge!" would be a fearful message, not one that would inspire praise. But if you've been living in a society where the poor are oppressed, where laws are not enforced equally and justly, where the wicked have free rein, you would look at the coming of righteousness and justice with excitement and anticipation.

Righteousness is coming – at last! Hallelujah! For the righteous it is a joy, a hope, an expectation. For the wicked, however, the coming of the Righteous Judge is a fearsome message.

Praise the Lord!
Why? Because he has saved us marvelously!
Praise the Lord with music and instruments.
Let all creation praise the Lord with joy and exuberance!
Why? Because the righteous Judge is coming who will set all injustice aright and bring our final salvation! Hallelujah!

---

[25] "Righteousness" (ṣedeq) is conformance to an ethical or moral standard (Harold G. Stigers, ṣādēq, TWOT 1879a).

[26] "Equity" (mêshār) is "uprightness, straightness" from the verb yāshar, "be level, straight, (up)right, just" (Donald J. Wiseman, yāshar, TWOT #930e).

Q3. (Psalm 98) What are the reasons given for praise in Psalm 98? Why do you think praise is so exuberant in this psalm? How exuberant is praise in your congregation, in your life? Why or why not is it exuberant?
http://www.joyfulheart.com/forums/index.php?showtopic=665

Exercise. For one of the psalms in this lesson – or another psalm with a similar theme – do one of the suggested exercises to help you experience the Psalms in Appendix 1. These include such things as praying a psalm, meditating, reading to a shut-in, paraphrasing, writing your own psalm, singing, preparing a liturgy, and memorizing. Then report to the forum what the exercise meant to you personally or share what you've written with others.
http://www.joyfulheart.com/forums/index.php?showtopic=666

Prayer

Father, what a privilege it is to praise you, to bring joyous happy praises to you with my whole heart. Through praising you, you've filled my life with joy. May my whole life – not just my lips – be a praise to your name. In Jesus' wonderful name, I pray. Amen.

Songs

- **"Break into Songs of Joy"** (in honor of the Lord Most High), words and music by Bill Batstone (© 1986, Maranatha! Music). Psalm 98.
- **"Come Let Us Bow,"** words and music by Andy Park (© 1992, Mercy / Vineyard Publishing). Psalm 95.
- **"Come, Let Us Worship,"** words and music by Chris Tomlin and Jesse Reeves (© 2002, worshiptogether.com songs / sixsteps Music). Psalm 95:6-7
- **"Come, Let Us Worship and Bow Down,"** words and music by Dave Doherty (© 1980, Maranatha Praise, Inc.). Psalm 95:6-7.

- **"Come Worship the Lord,"** words and music by John Michael Talbot (© 1980, Birdwing Music, BMG Songs, Inc.). Psalm 95.
- **"Holy Moment,"** words and music by Matt Redman (© 2000, Thankyou Music). Psalm 95.
- **"Praise Him, Praise Him,"** words: Fanny Crosby (1869), music: Chester G. Allen. Psalm 150.2.
- **"Praise to the Lord, the Almighty, the King of Creation,"** words: Joachim Neander (1680), translated by Catherine Winkworth (1863); music: "Lobe den Herren" (1665), harmony by William S. Bennett (1864). Psalm 150:1-2.
- **"Praise Ye the Lord"** (Psalm 150), words and music by Reta Kelligan (© 1951, 1980, Reta Kelligan). Psalm 150.
- **"Shout to the Lord,"** words and music by Darlene Zschench (© 1993, Hillsong Publishing). Psalm 95:1.
- **"The Battle Song"** (With the High Praises of God in our mouth), words and music by Jimmy Owens (© 1978, Lexicon Music, Inc.). Psalm 149:6.
- **"We Bow Down,"** words and music by Twila Paris (© 1984, New Spring). Psalm 95:6

5. Crying Out for Rescue (Psalms 69, 40, 80)

Many of the psalms are laments that come out of times of great distress and trouble. They are unashamed cries for help, for salvation, for rescue.

These desperate laments may be great Hebrew poetry, but they are not pretty. They speak of times that you and I have faced when all seems lost except for God's intervention. And so at our extremity, we reach out to God and plead for rescue. They have a way of touching the human spirit, of helping us to pray when we are nearly beyond praying.

But most of the laments in our Psalter are not pure laments. Most end on an upswing of hope and praise. Some contain a combination of psalm types, mixing and matching various genre to fit what the poet singer needed to say under the inspiration of the Holy Spirit.

Remember, as you begin to study each of these three psalms of rescue, first read it out loud. Listen to the words, savor them, let them speak to you. After you have done this, then begin to read them carefully to discern specifically what is being said.

Psalm 69 – Deep Waters and Miry Depths

The first psalm we'll examine is attributed to David, a long one, meant to be sung. Even the tune is given, unfortunately now long lost to us:

"For the director of music. To the tune of 'Lilies.' Of David."

David may be referring to trouble and struggle caused by his affair with Bathsheba which ended in her pregnancy and the murder of her husband Uriah as part of the cover-up (2 Samuel 11-12). Some commentators have seen similarities with Jeremiah's prophecy and speculate that Jeremiah was the

The classic symbol of rescue in Christian art is the Good Shepherd rescuing a sheep, very common in the catacombs. "Statue of the Good Shepherd" (third century), 39" high, marble, from the Catacomb of Domitilla, now in Museo Pio Cristino, Vatican.

author of this psalm.[1] There are also some indications that the psalmist may be sick (69:21, 27, 29). We just can't be sure about the details of the psalmist's personal situation.

Going Down for the Third Time (69:1-4)

Whatever the situation, the psalmist is in deep trouble and in that it is easy for us to identify with him. In the first four verses the psalmist describes how he is feeling using the most graphic images:

"[1]Save me, O God,
for the **waters** have come up to my neck.
[2]I sink in the **miry depths**,
where there is no foothold.
I have come into the **deep waters**;
the **floods engulf me**.
[3]I am **worn out** calling for help;
my throat is **parched**.
My **eyes fail**,
looking for my God.
[4]Those who hate me without reason
outnumber the hairs of my head;
many are my enemies without cause,
those who seek to destroy me.
I am forced to restore
what I did not steal." (69:1-4)

David's images are vivid. Water which is over his head, overwhelming him. He describes the mire (*ṭîṭ*) which settles in the bottom of a cistern or perhaps the sinking, grasping mud of a swamp that seems to have no bottom.[2]

One of the refreshing things I see in the Psalms is the writers' ability to just pour out their hearts to God, with all the raw emotions, anger, fear that seem to bubble to the surface. They don't try to "compose themselves" before speaking to God. They tell it like it is, as you might unload on a good friend whom you trust implicitly and who you don't feel will judge you negatively. The Psalms are meant to be an exemplar for us, a guide to prayer. What they teach is that we should be real and honest in our prayers.

---

[1] Kirkpatrick, *Psalms*, p. 397; White, *Psalms*, p. 106.
[2] Ralph H. Alexander, *ṭyṭ*, TWOT #796a. See also Psalm 40:2; Jeremiah 38:6.

You Know My Own Guilt (69:5-12)

> "You know my folly, O God;
> my guilt is not hidden from you." (69:5)

David doesn't pretend here that he is without sin. In fact, his sin and stupidity may have well have contributed to the problems he is facing and enflamed his enemies. If he is referring to the incident with Bathsheba and Uriah in this case, his admission of guilt is quite appropriate.

He realizes also that his sins have brought shame upon other believers, upon God himself, and upon the nation he ruled. When people of faith in prominent places sin publicly, they bring disgrace upon God. When Christians in families sin, they disgrace God before their children and spouse.

> "6May those who hope in you
> not be disgraced because of me,
> O Lord, the LORD Almighty;
> may those who seek you
> not be put to shame because of me,
> O God of Israel.
> 7For I endure scorn for your sake,
> and shame covers my face." (69:6-7)

When we sin, our sin affects others. As John Donne put it, "No man is an island, entire of itself; every man is a piece of the continent, a part of the main."[3]

David isn't merely bearing the just consequences for his sins. God's enemies are having a field day with David's infidelity and have amplified his sin even further. David is now isolated, devastated, the laughing stock of his people:

> "8I am a stranger to my brothers,
> an alien to my own mother's sons;
> 9for zeal for your house consumes me,
> and the insults of those who insult you fall on me.
> 10When I weep and fast,
> I must endure scorn;
> 11when I put on sackcloth,
> people make sport of me.
> 12Those who sit at the gate mock me,
> and I am the song of the drunkards." (69:8-12)

---

[3] John Donne, *Devotions Upon Emergent Occasions* (1624), Meditation 17

David's Appeal to God's Mercy (69:13-18)

David cannot appeal to his own righteousness in this case.[4] Rather he appeals to God's love and mercy as he pleads for deliverance:

> "[13]But I pray to you, O LORD,
> in the time of **your favor**;
> in your **great love**, O God,
> answer me with your **sure salvation**.
> [14]**Rescue** me from the mire,
> do not let me sink;
> deliver me from those who hate me,
> from the deep waters.
> [15]Do not let the floodwaters engulf me
> or the depths swallow me up
> or the pit close its mouth over me.
> [16]Answer me, O LORD, **out of the goodness of your love**;
> in your **great mercy** turn to me.
> [17]Do not hide your face from **your servant**;
> answer me quickly, for I am in trouble.
> [18]Come near and rescue me;
> redeem me because of my foes." (69:13-18)

I look at David's prayer for deliverance. He appeals to God not on the basis of his own worthiness, but on the basis of God's grace. Let's consider some of the words:

- "Time of your favor" (NIV), "in an acceptable time" (NRSV, KJV) is the word *rāsōn*, "pleasure, delight, favor." Here the shade of meaning seems to be "the 'favor' or 'good will' of God."[5] David prays based on God's good will. The New Testament often refers to God's favor as grace.
- "Love" (NIV), "steadfast love" (NRSV), " mercy/lovingkindness" (KJV) in verses 13c and 16a is the word *hesed* that we studied in chapter 2. It carries the ideas of love, including mercy, perhaps "lovingkindness," spells out the meaning more fully.[6]
- "Great mercy" (NIV), "abundant mercy" (NRSV), "tender mercies" (KJV) is *rahămîm*, from a root that refers to deep love, rooted in some natural bond, in this case of us being God's children. Because we are his children, even errant children, his attitude

---

[4] In some cases, David *does* appeal to God based on his own righteousness or the rightness of his cause: Psalms 7:3; 18:20, 24; 26:1-12.
[5] William White, *rāsā*, TWOT #2207a.
[6] R. Laird Harris, *hsd*, TWOT #698a.

towards us is compassion and deep love. A related noun is reḥem, "womb," which suggests the depth of this great mercy.[7]

Our pleas to God are *always* based on his graciousness and never on our own merit. This is one of the basic lessons of faith. And since we can rest on the unchanging character of God's love we are secure in that love.

Calls for Salvation and Rescue

David's call to God is for salvation, rescue, and redemption. We've met these words before, but it won't hurt to examine them again, since they are basic to our understanding of salvation:

- "Salvation" (NIV, KJV) or "faithful help" (NRSV) in verse 13d is *yēsha'*, "salvation, deliverance." The root in a related Arabic word means "to make wide, make sufficient." It carries the idea of moving from distress to safety, that is, rescue.[8] You probably recall that this word is at the root of both the names "Joshua" and "Jesus."
- "Rescue" (NIV, NRSV), "deliver" (KJV) in verse 14a is *nāṣal*, "deliver, rescue, save," with the basic physical sense of drawing out or pulling out.[9]
- "Rescue" (NIV, NRSV), "redeem" (KJV) in verse 18a is *gā'al*, "do the part of a kinsman," in ransoming, buying back, delivering, rescuing one's relative when he is in bondage or danger.[10]
- "Redeem" (NIV, NRSV), "deliver" (KJV) in verse 18b is *pādā*, "ransom, rescue, deliver," with the basic meaning of achieving transfer of ownership from one to another through payment of a price or an equivalent substitute.[11]

Each of these themes is carried over in the New Testament to our salvation from sin through Jesus Christ, the Lamb of God, whose death on the cross paid our ransom (Mark 10:45).

[7] Leonard J. Coppes, *rāḥam*, TWOT #2146b.
[8] John E. Hartley, *yāsha'*, TWOT #929a.
[9] Milton C. Fisher, *nāṣal*, TWOT #1404.
[10] Milton C. Fisher, *gā'al*, TWOT #1404.
[11] William B. Coker, *pādā*, TWOT #1734

> Q1. (Psalm 69:12-18) How could David dare to ask anything from God after the shameful things he had done with Bathsheba and Uriah? How does God's grace and mercy function in the face of our sins?
> http://www.joyfulheart.com/forums/index.php?showtopic=667

Back to David's Enemies (69:19-28)

Now David's mind turns back to the pain that his enemies are heaping upon him:

"19You know how I am scorned, disgraced and shamed;
all my enemies are before you.
20Scorn has broken my heart
and has left me helpless;
I looked for sympathy, but there was none,
for comforters, but I found none.
21They put gall in my food
and gave me vinegar for my thirst." (69:19-21)

What David meant figuratively in verse 21, was fulfilled literally in Jesus Christ, when his crucifiers offered him wine-vinegar mixed with gall (Matthew 27:34, 48). Unlike Jesus, however, who prayed, "Father, forgive them, for they know not what they do" (Luke 23:34), David prays for justice, for vindication, for retribution upon his enemies, not for mercy:

"22May the table set before them become a snare;
may it become retribution and a trap.
23May their eyes be darkened so they cannot see,
and their backs be bent forever.
24Pour out your wrath on them;
let your fierce anger overtake them.
25May their place be deserted;
let there be no one to dwell in their tents.
26For they persecute those you wound
and talk about the pain of those you hurt.

[27]Charge them with crime upon crime;
do not let them share in your salvation.
[28]May they be blotted out of the book of life
and not be listed with the righteous." (69:22-28)

Sometimes in our pain we lash out in anger and hatred. It is "natural." The progressive revelation of the Bible leads us beyond this typical human instinct to something higher – the love of God that transcends our humanness and lifts us to something divine. That is revealed in good time through Jesus Christ our Lord. "We love because he first loved us" (1 John 4:19). For more on the psalmists cursing their enemies, see Appendix 3 below on The Imprecatory Psalms.

A Final Plea (69:29)

Once more David calls out for help:

"I am in pain and distress;
may your salvation, O God, protect me." (69:29)

An Outpouring of Praise (69:30-33)

Like most laments in the Psalms, this psalm turns from complaint and misery to faith with an upswing at the end. David does not stay in his pit of misery. Now he climbs out through praise, the language of faith.

"[30]I will praise God's name in song
and glorify him with thanksgiving.
[31]This will please the LORD more than an ox,
more than a bull with its horns and hoofs.
[32]The poor will see and be glad –
you who seek God, may your hearts live!" (69:30-32)

David understands that faith – expressed by praise and thanksgiving – is more pleasing to God than going through the outward rituals of atonement and cleansing (also Psalm 51:16; 40:6; 50:8; Hosea 6:6). Ultimately, restoration of a person's relationship with God is not an outward exercise, but an inward assurance by the Holy Spirit. It is the answer to David's prayer in Psalm 51:12 to renew a right spirit within him.

A Prophecy for the Restoration of Israel's Homeland (69:33-36)

This psalm ends with what seems to be a prophetic word for the people of Israel during or at the end of their Exile in Babylon. In 587 BC the Babylonian armies had destroyed Jerusalem and their beloved temple, as well as all the fortified cities in Judah. Now God speaks to them words of hope through this psalm:

> "³³The Lord hears the needy
> and does not despise his captive people.
> ³⁴Let heaven and earth praise him,
> the seas and all that move in them,
> ³⁵for God will save Zion
> and rebuild the cities of Judah.
> Then people will settle there and possess it;
> ³⁶the children of his servants will inherit it,
> and those who love his name will dwell there." (69:33-36)

While it is possible that David penned these verses – he was a prophet, you know – I think it is more likely that David's psalm which was being used in the synagogues of Babylon was appended with these by an unknown prophet of the time.

A Psalm for the Brokenhearted

Psalm 69 is a call from the depths of a broken spirit to God. If you've ever been utterly overwhelmed by your circumstances, this psalm can be your prayer to God – and a model prayer for you in future times of struggle. Pour out your soul to Him. Tell him what you are feeling. Then praise him and give him thanks and you'll find that your spirit will begin to lift, your hope will arise, your faith will come out of hiding. No, this is not a psalm that looks to rituals for healing, but the God who heals the hearts of his people. I hear the psalmist's words ring in my own ears:

> "The poor will see and be glad –
> you who seek God, may your hearts live!" (69:32)

Grant it, Lord Jesus!

Q2. (Psalm 69:30-32) Why does this lament (and nearly all laments in the Psalms) end with an upswing of hope and praise? What does this teach us about our own laments and prayers? Why is praise, the language of faith, so important in our prayers, especially prayers of desperate pleas for help?
http://www.joyfulheart.com/forums/index.php?showtopic=668

Psalm 40 – O My God, Do Not Delay

Our second psalm of rescue seems to be, "Out of the frying pan, into the fire." At the beginning of the psalm, David is recounting his long waiting for the Lord to help him and then his spectacular deliverance. He is pumped up by this and shares his testimony "in the great assembly" so that everyone knows how great God is. But at the end of the psalm his sins have overtaken him once more, "troubles without number surround me" (40:12a) and he calls out for help and deliverance again. With hope, with expectation, but also with an urgency that concludes, "O my God, do not delay" (40:17d).

If you've read David's life in 1 and 2 Samuel, you'll recall his numerous troubles. At one period of his life he is pursued again and again by his jealous father-in-law Saul, intent on taking his life. Victory at one turn is followed by trouble at the next. At a later tragic period his own son Absalom chases him from Jerusalem into exile, from which he returns in the anguish of a father whose traitorous but beloved son lies dead.

If you are a person who has seen ups and downs, times of great deliverance followed quickly by great extremity, then this is a psalm for you.

He Put a New Song in My Mouth (40:1-3)

The title tells us: "For the director of music. Of David. A psalm." This psalm, penned by David, "the sweet psalmist of Israel" (2 Samuel 23:1), was meant to be sung. It begins with a recollection of praise after a long period of waiting for deliverance.

> "¹I waited patiently for the LORD;
> he turned to me and heard my cry.
> ²He lifted me out of the slimy pit,
> out of the mud and mire;
> he set my feet on a rock
> and gave me a firm place to stand.
> ³He put a new song in my mouth,
> a hymn of praise to our God.
> Many will see and fear
> and put their trust in the LORD." (40:1-3)

"I waited patiently for the LORD," describes many of our circumstances. In the Hebrew text the verbs are doubled for emphasis (the infinitive absolute), "Expecting, I expected," indicating not so much patience perhaps, than a prolonged period of waiting. The NASB renders it, "I waited intently for the LORD." You've been there, haven't you?

David describes his time of trouble as a "horrible pit" (KJV), "the slimy pit" (NIV), "the desolate pit" (NRSV), literally the "pit of tumult" (NRSV margin). In contrast to mud and mire where he could find no bottom on which to stand, God set his feet on the stability of a rock, "a firm place to stand."

Now he is full of praise and song. David sees his experience as a public testimony of God's powerful ability to deliver that will cause many to "put their trust in the LORD." In verse 10 he mentions speaking openly "in the great congregation" of this deliverance. When God delivers you, do you offer praise and share your testimony openly of how God has helped you, or do you keep it to yourself?

Blessed Is the Person Who Trusts in This Caring God (40:4-5)

Now David offers a couple of verses of praise towards the God of infinite care, blessing, and deliverance.

> "⁴Blessed is the man
> who makes the LORD his trust,
> who does not look to the proud,
> to those who turn aside to false gods.
> ⁵Many, O LORD my God,
> are the wonders you have done.
> The things you planned for us
> no one can recount to you;
> were I to speak and tell of them,
> they would be too many to declare." (40:4-5)

I am struck by verse 5b: "The things you planned for us no one can recount to you" because of their great number. "Your thoughts toward us" (NRSV). When I meditate on this phrase I am filled with quiet joy, almost tears. I am so insignificant, yet mighty Yahweh thinks about me and my path, about you and your path. We would drown in a sea of data about billions of living humans, but God is not overwhelmed. His love, his caring, is personal, individual, unhurried.

I once asked a neighbor who lived down the street if I could pray for his struggling bicycle business. "No," he said. "I wouldn't want to bother God about something as trivial as my business." How tragic to turn away a God who truly cares for you, whose thoughts are toward us and our needs. Not even a sparrow is forgotten by God, much less you! (Luke 12:6-7).

Q3. (Psalm 40:5b) When you realize that God's thoughts and plans are focused on you in particular, how does that make you respond?
http://www.joyfulheart.com/forums/index.php?showtopic=669

In the Scroll of the Book It Is Written of Me (40:6-8)

The next verses are remarkable – and prophetic:

"⁶Sacrifice and offering you did not desire,
but my ears you have pierced
burnt offerings and sin offerings
you did not require.
⁷Then I said, 'Here I am, I have come –
it is written about me in the scroll.
⁸I desire to do your will, O my God;
your law is within my heart.'" (40:6-8)

First, David affirms what other Old Testament prophets have seen: God isn't excited by a heaping up of animal sacrifices. What he wants instead is "an open ear" (6b, NJB, NRSV, "my ears you have pierced," NIV), a willing, obedient spirit, "I desire to do your will" (8a). We see a similar idea in David's great penitential psalm:

"You do not delight in sacrifice, or I would bring it;
you do not take pleasure in burnt offerings.
The sacrifices of God are a broken spirit;
a broken and contrite heart,
O God, you will not despise." (Psalm 51:16-17)

So often we are content to absolve our guilt through some kind of external ritual that God has provided for our assurance. But we must go beyond the external to the inward, to the heart that is willing, to the heart that is now grieved for its folly, to the heart that is broken of its pride and is contrite in its intent.

But David's words in Psalm 40 speak of someone beyond himself, Jesus, about whom the scriptures speak in many places. These verses are quoted in Hebrews, following the early Septuagint translation at key points, pointing to Christ's own coming:

"Sacrifice and offering you did not desire,
but a body you prepared for me;
with burnt offerings and sin offerings
you were not pleased.
Then I said, 'Here I am – it is written about me in the scroll –
I have come to do your will, O God.'" (Hebrews 10:5-7)

David's Public Testimony (40:9-10)

"⁹I proclaim righteousness in the great assembly;
I do not seal my lips,
as you know, O LORD.
¹⁰I do not hide your righteousness in my heart;
I speak of your faithfulness and salvation.
I do not conceal your love and your truth
from the great assembly." (40:9-10)

Part of our thankfulness and praise is to let others know what God has done for us. We're sometimes afraid of what others might think or that we might not be able to measure up in the future to our high calling, and so we are silent. But we are called to give testimony, both in church and to our friends and neighbors with whom we live. How do we know that a simple and humble word of how Jesus has helped us won't be the very thing that God will use to turn a neighbor's heart towards himself?

Troubles without Number Surround Me (40:11-12)

But David's respite from trouble doesn't seem to last long – and neither does ours:

"¹¹Do not withhold your mercy from me, O LORD;
may your love and your truth always protect me.
¹²For troubles without number surround me;
my sins have overtaken me, and I cannot see.
They are more than the hairs of my head,
and my heart fails within me."

David's phrase, "My sins have overtaken me" (*nāśag*, "overtake, catch up with"[12]), suggests a man pursued by enemies and problems, some of which are of his own making.

---

[12] *Nāśag*, Holladay 247. This verb often occurs as a complement to *rādap* "pursue" (Milton C. Fisher, *nāśag*, TWOT #1422).

Sound familiar? David finds it overwhelming: "I cannot see!" His problems seem innumerable to him and he is suddenly afraid: "My heart fails within me." You've been there, surely!

A Returning Confidence that Expects God's Salvation (40:13-16)

But David recovers quickly from his panic and calls out to the Lord with a confidence borne of experience in trouble and seeing God's deliverance:

> "¹³Be pleased, O LORD, to save me;
> O LORD, come quickly to help me.
> ¹⁴May all who seek to take my life
> be put to shame and confusion;
> may all who desire my ruin
> be turned back in disgrace.
> ¹⁵May those who say to me, "Aha! Aha!"
> be appalled at their own shame.
> ¹⁶But may all who seek you
> rejoice and be glad in you;
> may those who love your salvation always say,
> 'The LORD be exalted!'" (40:13-16)

There are always those who will see our trouble and say "Aha! I told you so! I knew this would happen!" David contrasts the shame that he prays for his enemies with the blessing that he calls down upon the believers, "those who love your salvation." Instead of cringing in fear and doubt when trouble comes, they call out confidently "The LORD be exalted!" – or, the way it sometimes comes out of my mouth, "Praise the Lord anyway!"

O My God, Do Not Delay (40:17)

This psalm concludes with faith coupled with humility.

> "Yet I am poor and needy;
> may the Lord think of me.
> You are my help and my deliverer;
> O my God, do not delay." (40:17)

Sometimes we become bold in ourselves. David is careful to remember his true state, "poor and needy," while at the same time calling with confidence on God in *His* true state – "My Help and my Deliverer!" David concludes with a petition that many of us have felt. Yes, we have waited patiently – waited and waited (verse 1), but our desire is to get this over with now! "O my God, do not delay!" (verse 17d).

Psalm 40 is a wonderfully human psalm, the desperate cry of one who is in deep trouble. But what inspires us is not its humanness, but its faith and its hope in the midst of this trouble and the psalmist's sincere surrender to the God whose thoughts are focused on him, the God who holds the plan for his life. And so he responds:

"Here I am, I have come....
I desire to do your will, O my God." (40:7-8)

Q4. (Psalm 40:17) In this verse David combines both humility and faith in his prayer to God. Why are both humility and faith necessary? What happens when one of these qualities is missing?
http://www.joyfulheart.com/forums/index.php?showtopic=670

Psalm 80 – Restore Us, O God

Our third psalm of rescue is a psalm that seems to come from the period of the exile, when the cities of Israel had been destroyed. It was a traumatic time for the people of God, severely chastened for their sin and idolatry, dragged off to a foreign land. They looked with nostalgia upon their days in their homeland and called out to God for restoration. The title reads:

"For the director of music. To the tune of 'The Lilies of the Covenant.' Of Asaph. A psalm."

This psalm came from the musical family of the descendents of Asaph, a temple singer. Even the tune of this song is specified, though no one knows it today.

Rather than studying it verse by verse, read it as it must have been read with its three refrains. Note the powerful images:

- A shepherd with his flock (80:1a)
- The presence of God enthroned upon the ark in all his glory in the temple (80:1b)
- The bread of tears (80:5)

- The vineyard, once fruitful, now destroyed, whose protective walls or hedges are now broken down (80:8-16)

It is a sorrowful psalm. Instead of being a personal lament like Psalms 69 and 40 which we considered above, this is a national lament, a prayer for national deliverance. Once the nation was young, brought out of slavery in Egypt during the Exodus and planted like a tender vine in the vineyard of Canaan land. But now its hope and promise are but a memory. The nation has sinned and God has punished their persistent idolatry and rebellion with foreign armies that have destroyed its cities and carried its people into exile.

Revive Us Again (80:18-19)

The central petition of this psalm is for rebirth, revival, for restoration of the nation. Look at the final verses:

"Revive us, and we will call on your name.
Restore us, O LORD God Almighty...." (80:18b-19a)

"Revive us" (NIV, NASB), "quicken us" (KJV), "give us life" (NRSV, NJB) is the verb *ḥāyā*, "live, have life, remain alive, sustain life, revive from sickness."[13]

"Restore us" (NIV, NRSV, NASB), "bring us back" (NJB), "turn us again" (KJV) is the common verb *shûb*, "turn, return." It is the word used often for "repent." But here it is a plea for God to turn and return his people from their fallen state in exile to a rebirth of the nation in their homeland. We see a similar sentiment in the exile-era psalm from the Sons of Korah and its plaintive prayer in Psalm 85:

"Restore (*shûb*) us again, O God our Savior,
and put away your displeasure toward us.
Will you be angry with us forever?
Will you prolong your anger through all generations?
Will you not revive (*ḥāyā*) us again,
that your people may rejoice in you?" (Psalm 85:4-6)

When I read these words I think of the final verse of a great hymn of a bygone era:

"Revive us again;
Fill each heart with Thy love;
May each soul be rekindled
With fire from above.

---

[13] Elmer B. Smick, *ḥāyā*, TWOT #644.

> Hallelujah! Thine the glory.
> Hallelujah! Amen.
> Hallelujah! Thine the glory.
> Revive us again."[14]

And I think of churches – individual congregations as well as whole denominations and movements – that need revival in the worst possible way. Unless God quickens us, gives us life again, we are but a shell of the former glory that God shone in our midst. We desperately need revival. We see some younger Christian movements that are vibrant and growing, but too many others that are in decline, that are going through the motions but the "the glory is departed" (1 Samuel 4:21).

God grant revival in our churches. Not that we might pride ourselves as we did in the past, but that you might be seen in our midst as you once were! Revive the Baptists! Revive the Presbyterians! Revive the Congregationalists and Nazarenes and Holiness! Revive the Pentecostals! Revive the Catholics! Revive the Orthodox! We need your revival, your life, your power, your glory. Forgive us for our sins and bickering. We repent of our gradual drift away from your purpose for us. Focus our eyes and desire again on our First Love. And revive your life in us, we pray!

Q5. (Psalm 80) If you were to formulate a personal prayer for revival for your own life or for your congregation, how would you word it? What elements should be present in a prayer for personal or congregational revival? What would this prayer have in common with 2 Chronicles 7:14? How does this kind of prayer pave the way for revival and restoration to take place?
http://www.joyfulheart.com/forums/index.php?showtopic=671

Make Your Face Shine upon Us (80:3, 17, 19)

The refrain of Psalm 80 refocuses the participants in this corporate song and prayer onto God himself:

---

[14] "Revive Us Again," words by William P. Mackay (1863), music by John J. Husband (1815).

"Restore us, O Lord God Almighty;
make your face shine upon us,
that we may be saved." (80:3, 17, 19)

It is a three-fold prayer to Yahweh, the God Almighty, the only one who is powerful enough to turn around the decay of the past into the fresh life that we long for.

1. Restore us
2. Make your face shine upon us
3. Save us

What does it mean to ask God to "make your face shine upon us"? We are familiar with the words from the Aaronic benediction that is repeated in many congregations:

"The Lord bless you, and keep you.
The Lord make his face shine upon you,
and be gracious unto you.
The Lord lift up his countenance upon you,
and give you peace." (Numbers 6:25-26)

In Near Eastern thought, a person's face referred to his presence before you. We looked at this concept in conjunction with Psalm 27 about seeking the face of the Lord. For Yahweh to "make his face shine upon you" and the parallel "lift up his countenance upon you," means to smile when he is with us, to show favor to us because he is pleased with us, "to be gracious toward." To "lift up his countenance upon you" meant to look directly at his people, to give them his full attention resulting in peace.[15]

The psalms of lament have taught us much about prayer with praise, about grace and mercy, about our need for revival and renewal. May the prayers of your servants the psalmists be answered in our own lives! Grant it, Lord God.

Exercise. For one of the psalms in this lesson – or another psalm with a similar theme – do one of the suggested exercises to help you experience the Psalms in Appendix 1. These include such things as praying a psalm, meditating, reading to a shut-in, paraphrasing, writing your own psalm, singing, preparing a liturgy, and memorizing. Then report to the forum what the exercise meant to you personally or share what you've written with others.
http://www.joyfulheart.com/forums/index.php?showtopic=672

---

[15] R.K. Harrison, *Numbers: An Exegetical Commentary* (Baker Book House, 1992), p. 133.

Prayer

Lord, you know us. You know our sorrows and our personal laments. Teach us – teach me – to turn my laments into a prayer of faith that you can answer. Heal the broken elements of my life that I might be whole. Bring me and my congregation the grace of a God-sent restoration and revival. Restore us again, O God our Savior, to our first love – Jesus. In His name, we pray. Amen.

Songs

- **"Eternal Father, Strong to Save"** (Navy Hymn), words by William Whiting (1860), music by John B. Dykes (1861).
- **"He Brought Me Out of the Miry Clay,"** words Henry J. Zelley (1898), refrain and music by Henry L. Gilmour
- **"He Took My Feet from the Miry Clay,"** traditional African American spiritual.
- **"I Waited for the Lord"** (Psalm 40:1-6), words and music by Bill Bastone (© 1982 Maranatha! Music)
- **"Psalm 5"** (Give ear to my words, O Lord), words and music by Bill Sprouse, Jr. (© 1975,Marnatha! Music). Psalm 5.
- **"Revive Us Again,"** words by William P. Mackay (1863), music by John J. Husband (1815)
- **"Save Me, O God, the Swelling Floods,"** words: Isaac Watts (1719), Music: Cheshire (1579)
- **"Wait on the Lord,"** words and music by Bob Cull (© 1978, Maranatha! Music)
- **"Unto Thee, O Lord,"** words and music by Charles Monroe (© 1971, 1973, Maranatha! Music)

6. Trusting in God's Protection (Psalms 61, 91, 121)

When trouble is all around we can either panic or find strength in faith. In these psalms the writer sees God as his ultimate Protector. In this lesson we'll be focusing on the portions of several psalms that describe a person seeking the protection of God. These are generally categorized in the genre of psalms of confidence.

Wartburg Castle (founded 1067 AD) is the site where Martin Luther was protected 1521-22 and where he translated the New Testament into German. It may have been the inspiration for his song, *"Ein' Feste Berg"* or "A Mighty Fortress Is Our God.".

Psalm 61 – Lead Me to the Rock that Is Higher than I

Our first psalm of protection endears itself to us because we can so easily identify with the sense of vulnerability of the author in the first couple of verses. Psalm 61 is meant to be sung and accompanied:

"For the director of music. With stringed instruments. Of David."

Since the psalm is attributed to David, the first four verses would seem to come from his hand. Verses 5-8 speak of the king in the third person, so they may have been added in subsequent generations as a prayer for the king. We're not sure.

Hear My Faint Cry, O God (61:1-2b)

I love this brief psalm, that begins:

"¹Hear my cry, O God;
listen to my prayer.
²From the ends of the earth I call to you,
I call as my heart grows faint." (61:1-2b)

The first couplet (or pair of parallel lines) has the psalmist asking God to listen to him.[1] The second couplet seem to emphasize the distance he feels from God at the moment – "from the ends of the earth." He is at an extremity: "I call as my heart grows faint" (NIV) or is "overwhelmed" (KJV). The verb is *'āṭap*, "be feeble, faint, grow weak." The word can pertain to physical exhaustion or the languishing of a man's innermost being.[2] Even though he has almost given up, he calls.

The Rock that is Higher than I (61:2c)

His prayer inspires me every time I read it:

"Lead me to the rock that is higher than I." (61:2c)

The image is of a man seeking refuge from his enemy by hiding in the towering rocks of a mountain. He has found a place of concealment but realizes the vulnerability of his position. And so he asks a person to lead him to a rocky prominence that is yet higher up and more difficult to attack than his current position. And so the person leads him up the hidden trail to the higher rock.

But the Rock in this psalm is God himself, who is often referred to as "the Rock" in the Bible. The word here is *ṣûr*, "massive rock," used for boulders or formations of stone, and for the material which composes mountains. The caves of the rocks are places where David and his men sought safety when they were being hunted by King Saul and his armies.[3]

My Refuge and Strong Tower Against the Foe (61:3)

The next images are military in nature:

"[3]For you have been my **refuge**,
a **strong tower** against the foe." (61:3)

Two words in this couplet describe the defensive protection that God offers:

"Refuge" (NIV, NRSV), "shelter" (KJV) is *maḥseh*, "place of refuge, shelter," from the verb *ḥāsā*, "to seek refuge, flee for protection."[4]

"Strong tower," is a tall building on the city wall or in a walled city that could be defended against even a determined enemy, due to its height and strength of construction.[5]

---

[1] "Listen" (NIV, NRSV), "attend" (KJV) is *qāshab*, "hear, be attentive, heed." It is not a command to God, but a request,

[2] Carl Schultz, *'āṭap*, TWOT #1607.

[3] John E. Hartley, *ṣwr*, TWOT 1901a.

[4] Donald J. Wiseman, *ḥāsā*, TWOT #700b.

[5] Two words are used: *'ōz*, "strength, power," used primarily of God (Carl Schultz, *'āzaz*, TWOT #1596b) and *migdāl*, "tower," from the root *gādal*, "to grow up, become great," deriving from early times when the tower was the largest (greatest) structure in a town (Elmer B. Smick, *gādal*, TWOT #315f)

This image of God as a place of refuge is common, especially in the Psalms. He is a safe place, a place to which one can retreat when all hell is breaking loose. He is a sure bastion against any foe. God is our source of protection.

The Shelter of Your Wings (61:4)

The final images in this psalm of protection are more gentle, more intimate places of solace:

"I long to dwell in your tent forever
and take refuge in the shelter of your wings." (61:4)

"Your tent" refers to God's dwelling place. Initially it referred to the "tent of meeting" or the "tabernacle" in the wilderness, later the temple in Jerusalem. In the Psalms to "dwell in the house of the Lord" is an idiom that describes a closeness to and intimacy with God (Psalm 15:1; 23:6; 27:4; 90:1; 92:13).

"The shelter of your wings" calls on the image of a mother bird sheltering and protecting her young with her wings (Psalm 17:8; 57:1; 63:7; 91:4; Ruth 2:12). Jesus used this image as he prophesied the destruction of Jerusalem:

"O Jerusalem, Jerusalem ... how often I have longed to gather your children together, as
a hen gathers her chicks under her wings, but you were not willing." (Matthew 23:37)

In chapter 2 of our study we already looked at Psalm 63, where we find this poignant verse:

"Because you are my help,
I sing in the shadow of your wings." (Psalm 63:7)

We'll see yet another reference to the protection of God's wings in Psalm 91 below. Does God have literal wings? Of course not. God the Father is a spirit without a physical body (John 4:24). But the imagery of his wings helps us to understand the intimacy of his protection.

After "Selah" (which may signify some kind of pause), the psalm turns from God as a refuge and concludes with a prayer for the king:

"⁵For you have heard my vows, O God;
you have given me the heritage of those who fear your name.
⁶Increase the days of the king's life,
his years for many generations.
⁷May he be enthroned in God's presence forever;
appoint your love and faithfulness to protect him.
⁸Then will I ever sing praise to your name
and fulfill my vows day after day." (61:5-8)

Q1. (Psalm 61:1-4) What images does the psalmist evoke to communicate his trust in God's protection? How do the first four verses of this psalm make you feel?
http://www.joyfulheart.com/forums/index.php?showtopic=673

Psalm 91 – Dwelling in the Shelter of the Most High

Psalm 91 is a wonderful psalm that has been a comfort and source of faith to many who have faced physical danger. It has the distinction of being misquoted by Satan to tempt Jesus (Matthew 4:6; Luke 4:10-11) and referred to by Jesus to strengthen his disciples in spiritual warfare (Luke 10:19).

The Mighty Names of God (91:1-2)

Notice how this psalm begins: by invoking four of the most common strong names of God:

- The Most High (*'elyôn*), the name by which he was known by Abraham and the patriarchs. The Exalted God, the God higher than every false god.
- The Almighty (*shadday*), the God of Might, the ruler of all.
- The LORD or Yahweh, is the name by which God revealed himself to Moses, the great I Am, the eternally existent God.
- My God (*'ĕlōhīm*), the Strong One, using the plural of majesty.[6]

We must never forget Who is with us: God in all his might and power!

Metaphors of Protection

Observe how the psalm uses a number of protection metaphors for God, some of which we've explored above:

---

[6] For more on this, see my *Names and Titles of God* (JesusWalk Publications, 2010).

"¹He who dwells in the shelter of the Most High
will rest in the shadow of the Almighty.
²I will say of the LORD, 'He is my refuge and my fortress,
my God, in whom I trust.'" (91:1-2)

"He will cover you with his feathers,
and under his wings you will find refuge;
his faithfulness will be your shield and rampart." (91:4)

"If you make the Most High your dwelling –
even the LORD, who is my refuge...." (91:9)

Consider the words and what they convey:[7]

- **"Shelter, secret place"** (1a, *sēter*) is a "hiding place," from *sātar*, "hide, conceal," which includes the thought of protection.[8] Most notably, the noun is used in Psalm 32:7 of God, "You are my hiding place."
- **"Shadow"** (1b, *(ṣel)* refers to "shadow," which, in an arid, sun-baked land, conveys the positive ideas of shade, protection, and defense.[9] Elsewhere we see references to "the shadow of his wings" (Psalm 17:8; 36:7).
- **"Refuge"** (2a, *maḥseh*) denotes "refuge, shelter,"[10] which we saw above in 61:3.
- **"Fortress"** (2b, *meṣûdâ*) refers to a "fastness, stronghold," related to the word for Masada, the fortress-palace plateau of Herod near the Dead Sea.[11]
- **"Feathers"** and **"wings"** (4a,b), of course carry on the protection analogy of the mother bird, which we explored above in 61:4.
- **"Shield"** (4c, *ṣinnâ*) refers here to a "large shield (covering the whole body)."[12] A shield is used as a metaphor of God's protection a number of times in Scripture (for example, Genesis 15:1; Deuteronomy 33:29; Psalm 3:3; 115:9-11).
- **"Buckler"** or "rampart" (4c, *sōḥērâ*) is difficult to translate with certainty. It could mean some kind of surrounding wall, but because of the parallelism in this verse is

---

[7] For more on God's names of protection, see my *Names and Titles of God* (JesusWalk Publications, 2010), chapter 7.

[8] R. D. Patterson, *sātar*, TWOT #1551a.

[9] John E. Harley, *ṣālal* , TWOT #1921a.

[10] Donald J. Wiseman, *ḥāsā*, TWOT #700b.

[11] *Meṣûdâ* is related to *meṣād*, which means "mountain-height" or "summit"; then "fortress, castle" (Arabic *maṣādun*) (John E. Harley, *ṣûd*, TWOT #1885i).

[12] *Ṣinnâ*, BDB 857.

usually understood as the small shield used in closest combat or some type of armor ... and is clearly related to the verbal root, *sāḥar*, 'go around, turn about/away.'"[13]

- **"Refuge"** (9a, *maḥseh*) is a "place of refuge, shelter," which we saw in Psalm 61:3 above.[14]
- **"Dwelling place, habitation"** (9b, *mā'ōn*) refers to a "place of habitation, dwelling," from *'ûn*, "to dwell."[15]

What a wonderful picture of God is fleshed out by the imagery in this psalm!

The Fowler's Snare (91:3)

In Psalm 91 the author enumerates the various dangers that one can experience and assures the reader that God is able to save from all of these:

> "Surely he will save you from the fowler's snare
> and from the deadly pestilence." (91:3)

A fowler, of course, was a person who hunted fowl, birds, either for amusement or to supply birds for food, pets, or sacrifice. Birds were caught by many means – net, trap, decoy birds, bird lime – a sticky substance that would stop birds from flying away, throw stick, and the bow and sling. Here the psalmist refers to a bird trap (*pah*) that would catch the bird unawares. It is used figuratively for the plots of the wicked to try to entrap and bring down their enemies.

"Noisome" (KJV) has nothing to do with noise, but is an archaic word meaning "noxious, harmful," or as the NIV and NRSV render it, "deadly." "Pestilence" is *deber*, "pestilence, murrain, and plague," perhaps bubonic plague, any kind of pestilence which results in death.[16]

The promise here is that God's protection can extend both to the plots of evil men and the diseases that ravage mankind.

---

[13] R. D. Patterson, *sāḥar*, TWOT #1486c. NIV translates it "rampart" in Psalm 91:4b. Holladay translates it as "wall." (Holladay 255a). The New English Bible and NIV translations as "rampart" follows a Syriac root with the idea of "walled enclosure, bulwark" (Marvin E. Tate, *Psalms 51-100* (Word Biblical Commentary 20; Word: 1990), p. 448). The Targum saw it as a small round shield. "Technically the buckler is a small rounded shield usually worn on the forearm rather than carried in the hand." The large shield may be a better interpretation of *sinnâ* (James K. Hoffmeier, "Weapons of War," ISBE 4:1040-1041).

[14] Donald J. Wiseman, *ḥāsā*, TWOT #700b.

[15] *'Ûn*, TWOT #1581a.

[16] Earl S. Kalland, *dābar*, TWOT #399b; Holladay, 68a.

The Terror of Night (91:5-6)

Now the psalmist continues to spell out the kinds of places where God's protection can extend:

"[5]You will not fear the terror of night,
nor the arrow that flies by day,
[6]nor the pestilence (*deber*) that stalks in the darkness,
nor the plague that destroys at midday." (91:5-6)

"Plague" (NIV) or "destruction" (KJV, NRSV) is *qeṭeb*, "destruction"[17] or perhaps "sting," as the name of a disease, perhaps measles.[18] God can protect us from the terrors of both night and day, while we sleep and when we are awake.

It Will Not Come Near You (91:7-8)

And now an astounding promise that God will protect us, even though others around us are stricken:

"[7]A thousand may fall at your side,
ten thousand at your right hand,
but it will not come near you.
[8]You will only observe with your eyes
and see the punishment of the wicked." (91:7-8)

Dwelling with the Most High (91:9-10)

"[9]If you make the Most High your dwelling –
even the LORD, who is my refuge –
[10]then no harm[19] will befall you,
no disaster[20] will come near your tent." (91:9-10)

What does it mean to "make the Most High your dwelling"? It means to consciously adhere to him in faith continually. Many people speak God's name in times of danger. But the psalmist here is speaking of those who "abide" with God, who trust him continually, who constantly look to him.

---

[17] *Qeṭeb*, BDB 881.

[18] *Qeṭeb*, Holladay 317a.

[19] *Ra'* is "evil, distress, the opposite of what is good, and can refer to misfortune, calamity, and wickedness (G. Herbert Livingston, *rā'a'*, TWOT #2191a).

[20] *Nega'* is "stroke, plague, disease," with the basic idea of "to touch" or "to strike."(Leonard J. Coppes, *nāga'*, TWOT #1293a).

Angels Protecting Us (91:11-12)

Now the psalmist speaks of the agents of this protection – angels, messengers:

"¹¹For he will command his angels concerning you
to guard you in all your ways;
¹²they will lift you up in their hands,
so that you will not strike your foot against a stone." (91:11-12)

Though Satan used this verse to try to tempt Jesus to do a spectacular miracle outside of God's will (Matthew 4:6; Luke 4:10, 11), that doesn't detract from the truth in Scripture that angels are sent to protect and care for us humans (Genesis 19; Matthew 18:10; 26:53; Hebrews 1:14; etc.). You have probably experienced miraculous protection from accidents that could have killed you. I have no doubt that angels are often at work to protect us.

Power Over Evil Forces (91:13)

Now the psalm down-shifts to a new level of power. Previously, the psalmist spoke of God's protection for his people – defensive. Now he speaks of his people's power and ability to destroy the forces arrayed against them – offensive. Verse 13 promises God's protection over deadly creatures – the large, powerful lion and the small but venomous serpent.

"You will tread upon the lion and the cobra;
you will trample the great lion and the serpent."
(91:13)

"Cobra" (NIV) or "adder" (NRSV, KJV) is *peten*, which designates a venomous serpent, perhaps a hooded Egyptian Cobra or asp (*Naja haje*) or horned viper (*Cerastes cerastes*).[21] "Serpent" (NIV, NRSV) or "dragon" (KJV) is *tannîn*, "dragon, sea monster, serpent, whale," here used in the generic sense of "any large

Above: Egyptian Cobra (Naja haje). Below: Saharan Horned Viper (Cerastes cerastes).

---

[21] *Peten*, Holladay 301b.

reptile."[22] The Egyptian Cobra's venom is extremely toxic and can induce quick and painless death, probably used by Cleopatra to commit suicide. The horned viper's venom is much less toxic.

Serpents, of course, have been identified as symbolic of Satan from the Garden of Eden (Genesis 3:1) to the Book of Revelation (Revelation 12:9). Jesus refers to this passage when he seeks to clarify the disciples' power when they come back exuberant from a mission having cast out demons:

> "I have given you authority to trample on snakes and scorpions and to overcome all the power of the enemy; nothing will harm you." (Luke 10:19)

In Jesus' name we have power greater than that of our powerful enemy. In Jesus we have the power to push him back, to resist him, to wage war against him. Hallelujah! The last phrase, rendered by the NIV as "Nothing will harm you," is a double negative in Greek, emphasizing and reinforcing its truth.

Because He Loves Me I Will Rescue Him (91:14-16)

In verses 14 to 16 the psalmist speaks as God's spokesman about the reasons for his protection and the qualities of the person he protects:

> "14'Because he loves me,' says the LORD, 'I will rescue him;
> I will protect him, for he acknowledges my name.
> 15He will call upon me, and I will answer him;
> I will be with him in trouble,
> I will deliver him and honor him.
> 16With long life will I satisfy him
> and show him my salvation.'" (91:14-16)

First, the qualities of the person the Lord watches out for:

- **Loves God** (*ḥāshaq*), "to be attached to, to love, to cling to." The root emphasizes that which attaches to something or someone. In the case of emotions it is that love which is already bound to its object.[23]
- **Knows God's name**. *Yāda'*, "to know," refers here to intimate knowledge, personal relationship. "Name" *(shēm)* means more than merely a way to designate a person. In Hebrew thought the name often included ideas of existence, character and reputa-

---

[22] Ronald F. Youngblood, *tnn*, TWOT #2528b.
[23] Leonard J. Coppes, *ḥāshaq*, TWOT #773. Tate, *Psalms*, p. 450.

tion.[24] It embraces the idea of how God reveals himself. Thus the idiom "to know the name" means to know God, to have a close relationship with him.[25]

• **Calls upon God**. "He will call upon me," expresses the bond between the Helper and the helped, rooted in a trust in God's infinite grace, God's unmerited favor. This quality is of one reliance, of trust, of faith.[26]

These verses also spell out God's eight forthright promises to his people:

1. I will rescue him (14a)
2. I will protect him (14b)
3. I will answer him (15a)
4. I will be with him in trouble (15b)
5. I will deliver him (15c)
6. I will honor him (15c)
7. I satisfy him with long life (16a)
8. I will show him my salvation (16b)

Meditate on *that*, dear friends, when you are overtaken by fear!

Q2. (Psalm 91) What does this psalm teach us about God's protection when in danger? What does it teach about our authority to vanquish our enemies? What promises does Psalm 91 contain? How does this psalm make you feel?
http://www.joyfulheart.com/forums/index.php?showtopic=674

---

[24] Walter C. Kaiser, *shēm*, TWOT #2405.
[25] Tate, *Psalms*, p. 457.
[26] Kidner, *Psalms 73-150*, p. 334.

Psalms 56 and 57

There are many, many psalms that talk about protection that we must skip over because of time, such as:

> "When I am afraid,
> I will trust in you.
> In God, whose word I praise,
> in God I trust; I will not be afraid.
> What can mortal man do to me?" (Psalm 56:3-4)

and

> "Have mercy on me, O God, have mercy on me,
> for in you my soul takes refuge.
> I will take refuge in the shadow of your wings
> until the disaster has passed." (Psalm 57:1)

... and a dozen more.

Psalm 121 – I Will Lift Up My Eyes to the Hills

Our final psalm of protection is a brief one, but beloved because it expresses the faith of the believer. It is titled as "a song of ascents," a psalm that was sung as pilgrims approached Jerusalem on the high feast days of Passover, Pentecost, and others. The author is not disclosed to us.

I Lift Up My Eyes to the Hills (121:1-2)

The psalm begins with a mention of hills and mountains. For most Israelites on a pilgrimage to the Holy City, their journey concluded with climbing up the rugged hills where Jerusalem sits at 2,460 feet above sea level. For those passing through Jericho it was an ascent of 3,300 feet, since Jericho in the plain of the Jordan is at 850 feet *below* sea level in the Great Rift Valley. Jerusalem's location is celebrated in Psalm 48:2 as "beautiful for situation" (KJV), "beautiful in elevation" (NRSV), "beautiful in its loftiness" (NIV), "towering in beauty" (NJB).

But the journey could be fraught with danger from bandits such as those who attacked the man in Jesus' parable of the Good Samaritan (Luke 10:30-37). These brigands would hide in the Judean hills and, when they found a person or small group traveling, would swoop down and rob them of everything they had. Thus pilgrims usually traveled to Jerusalem together in large groups for protection.

> "¹I lift up my eyes to the hills –
> where does my help come from?
> ²My help comes from the LORD,
> the Maker of heaven and earth." (121:1-2)

Scholars have argued about the meaning of the hills. They could refer to:

1. A source of danger from highwaymen (as outlined in the paragraph above, which makes most sense to me),
2. A place to take refuge, like David did from Saul (Psalm 11:1),
3. Suggestive of high places where false gods were worshipped (Jeremiah 3:23), or
4. A reminder to pilgrims of Yahweh who was their mighty Rock.[27]

Whatever the meaning of the hills in verse 1, the psalmist very clearly sees the source of his help:

> "My help comes from the LORD,
> the Maker of heaven and earth." (121:2)

"Help" is 'ēzer, "help, support, helper," from the verb 'āzar, "help, support." Many times it refers to military assistance. In the Psalms it usually refers to divine aid, both material and spiritual.[28] In a number of places Helper is used as a title or descriptor of God (Psalm 10:14; 22:19; 40:17; 54:4; 118:6-7 quoted in Hebrews 13:6).[29] In contrast to the towering hills where one can feel very small, the pilgrim proclaims that his Helper is the one who created these very mountains, "the Maker ('āśā) of heaven and earth," invoking another title of God (also Psalm 115:15; 134:3; 146:6; 149:2; Isaiah 27:11, 54:5, etc.).[30]

The Lord Who Watches Over You (121:3-8)

Now the psalmist begins to expand on the ways the Lord protects his people. Notice how the keywords "watch," "keep," "preserve," continue to pop up through the rest of the psalm:

> "³He will not let your foot slip –
> he who **watches over** you will not slumber;

---

[27] For a summary of various explanations see Allen, *Psalms*, p. 151; Allen follows T. H. Weir in seeing verse 1b as an indirect question. See also Kidner, *Psalms 73-150*, p. 431.

[28] Carl Schultz, *'āzar*, TWOT #1598.

[29] "Helper" in most of the titles of God is a participle form of the verb *'āzar*. More on this in my *Names and Titles of God*.

[30] *'Āśā*, "do, make," with emphasis on fashioning the object (TWOT #1708).

⁴indeed, he who **watches over** Israel
will neither slumber nor sleep.

⁵The LORD **watches** over you –
the LORD is your shade at your right hand;
⁶the sun will not harm you by day,
nor the moon by night.

⁷The LORD will **keep** you from all harm –
he will **watch over** your life;
⁸the LORD will **watch over** your coming and going
both now and forevermore." (Psalm 121:1-8)

The word variously translated "watch," "keep," or "preserve" is *shāmar*, "keep, guard, observe, give heed." The basic root means "to exercise great care over," with the connotation of carefulness, faithfulness, diligence. The word can be used in tending a garden, a flock, or a house, guarding against intruders, of gatekeepers or watchmen. We'll see it again when we discuss psalms that talk about God as our Shepherd. Here the word carries the idea of "to guard, take care of."[31]

God's protection involves his own careful guarding of us from danger. God is like a watchful Mom always keeping tabs on her toddler to keep him from any kind of danger that might approach. Mom is there to defend her pup against any alarm, rescue him from any tumble, and stand in the way of any possible threat to her child.

We could be tempted to rebel at God acting like a "mother hen." Or we could relax and realize that it is out of love that he is caring for us.

Notice the details of his protection:

1. Protection from falling. "He will not let your foot slip" (verse 3a)
2. Protection 24/7. "He who watches over you will not slumber" (verses 3b-4)
3. Protection from the sun and moon. "The LORD is your shade at your right hand" (verses 5-6)
4. Protection of an all-hazard policy. "The LORD will keep you from all harm" (verse 7)

The psalm concludes with an all-inclusive statement of God's watch-care over you.

- All harm
- Your life
- Your coming and going
- Now and forever.

---

[31] *Shāmar*, TWOT #2414.

His watchfulness is rooted in his great love that encompasses us. Elisha Hoffman and Anthony Showalter summed it up well in this memorable chorus:

"Leaning, leaning
Safe and secure from all alarms.
Leaning, leaning,
Leaning on the Everlasting Arms." [32]

Q3. (Psalm 121). What reassurance is it to you that God keeps you and watches over you? How does Psalm 121 make you feel?
http://www.joyfulheart.com/forums/index.php?showtopic=675

Will God *Really* Protect Us?

How can this be? we wonder. Surely, godly believers have died in dangerous situations. Does God *really* protect us? This very question, of course, probably results from sad negative experiences mixed with unbelief. The promises in these protection psalms are for people who will actually put their trust in God and his word. The promises are activated by faith. Let me remind you of two passages from Hebrews:

"We do not want you to become lazy, but to imitate those who **through faith and patience** inherit what has been promised." (Hebrews 6:12)

"I do not have time to tell about Gideon, Barak, Samson, Jephthah, David, Samuel and the prophets, who **through faith** conquered kingdoms, administered justice, and **gained what was promised**; who shut the mouths of lions, quenched the fury of the flames, and escaped the edge of the sword; whose weakness was turned to strength; and who became powerful in battle and routed foreign armies." (Hebrews 11:32b-34)

The Bible is full of people who by faith experienced God's supernatural protection. Today's world, as well, is full of believers who have seen the fulfillment of these promises

---

[32] "Leaning on the Everlasting Arms," words by Elisha A. Hoffman (1887), music and refrain by Anthony J. Showalter.

first hand. God is not impotent, but our unbelief can make us impotent, preventing us from seeing these things (Matthew 13:58; Mark 6:5).

But consider: Christians don't seem to be immune to death in accidents, war, persecution, etc. How do we understand this in light of Psalm 91? Did all those who succumb to enemies just lack enough faith? Some did, of course, but surely not all. Two passages of Scripture may shed some light on this. The first is from the Apostle Paul:

> "And we know that in all things God works for the good of those who love him, who have been called according to his purpose." (Romans 8:28)

But this truth does not exclude verse 35:

> "Who shall separate us from the love of Christ? Shall trouble or hardship or persecution or famine or nakedness or danger or sword?" (Romans 8:35)

The second passage is Jesus' teaching about the end times:

> "You will be betrayed even by parents, brothers, relatives and friends, and they will put some of you to death. All men will hate you because of me. **But not a hair of your head will perish**. By standing firm you will gain life." (Luke 21:16-19)

People without faith look only at what happens in *this* life. And God is quite able to protect us in this life! But people of faith look beyond this life to the *next*. In the ultimate sense – and that is what is important to us Christians – our enemies cannot harm even one hair on our head. They can kill the body, but they cannot kill the soul (Matthew 10:28). And God will have the very last word on Judgment Day. In Revelation, the martyrs in heaven cry out:

> "How long, Sovereign Lord, holy and true, until you judge the inhabitants of the earth and avenge our blood?" (Revelation 6:10)

The answer is not quite yet, but soon. When Jesus comes in his kingdom there will be singing and shouting and the fulfillment of all the promises of the Bible on that Day. Come, Lord Jesus!

So if you are in danger, by all means come to Psalm 91 for strength and encouragement. God is our Great Protector and we have been given mighty power to overcome our enemies. May you be one of those saints who through faith, "shut the mouths of lions, quench the fury of the flames, and escape the edge of the sword" (Hebrews 13:34). Just realize that the final chapter of your life and mine is not written in the here and now, but on that Day it will all be revealed in victory and glory. God has us all in his hands.

Q4. Since Christians don't seem immune to accident, persecution, and death, how are we to understand these psalms of protection? Why don't some believers seem to be protected? Does God *really* protect us? How?
http://www.joyfulheart.com/forums/index.php?showtopic=676

Exercise. For one of the psalms in this lesson – or another psalm with a similar theme – do one of the suggested exercises to help you experience the Psalms in Appendix 1. These include such things as praying a psalm, meditating, reading to a shut-in, paraphrasing, writing your own psalm, singing, preparing a liturgy, and memorizing. Then report to the forum what the exercise meant to you personally or share what you've written with others.
http://www.joyfulheart.com/forums/index.php?showtopic=677

Prayer

Father, thank you for the knowledge of your intimate watch-care over us. Strengthen our faith, we pray. When we are afraid, help us to trust in you. Protect us from our human enemies and the enemy of our souls. And bring us intact, we pray, into your eternal Kingdom. In Jesus' mighty name, we pray. Amen.

Songs

- **"A Mighty Fortress Is Our God,"** words and music, Martin Luther (1529). Verse 1: Our Helper He, amid the flood of mortal ills prevailing...."
- **"A Shelter in the Time of Storm,"** words: Vernon J. Charlesworth (1880), music by Ira D. Sankey (1885)
- **"Dwelling Place,"** words and music by Walt Harrah (© 1986, Maranatha! Music). Psalm 91:1.
- **"He Hideth My Soul in the Cleft of the Rock,"** words by Fanny Crosby (1890), music by William J. Kirkpatrick

- **"Hear My Cry, O Lord, Listen to My Prayer,"** Psalm 61, unknown composer.
- **"I Lift My Eyes Up,"** words and music by Brian Doerksen (© 1990 Vineyard Songs Canada, Admin. by Music Services). Psalm 121.
- **"I Will Lift Up My Eyes,"** words and music by Dale Garratt (© 1970, Scripture in Song). Psalm 121.
- **"In the Secret of His Presence,"** words: Ellen L. Goreh (1883), music: George C. Stebbins (1883)
- **"Lead Me to the Rock,"** words and music by Lynn DeShazo (© 1989, Integrity's Hosanna! Music). Psalm 61:2
- **"Leaning on the Everlasting Arms,"** words (1887) by Elisha A. Hoffman, music and refrain by Anthony J. Showalter (1858-1924).
- **"On Eagle's Wings,"** words and music by Michael Joncas (© 1979, 1991, New Dawn Music), in the Chalice Hymnal (1995), #77.
- **"Praise the Name of Jesus,"** ("He's my Rock, He's my Fortress...."), words and music by Roy Hicks, Jr. (©1976 Latter Rain Music, Admin. by EMI Christian Music Publishing)
- **"Rock of Ages, Cleft for Me,"** words by Augustus Toplady (1776), music by Thomas Hastings (1830)
- **"The Rock that Is Higher than I,"** words by Erastus Johnson (1871), music by William G. Fischer (1871). Psalm 61:2.
- **"You Are My Hiding Place,"** words and music by Michael Ledner (© 1981 Maranatha! Music, Admin. by The Copyright Company). Psalm 32:7

7. Resting in God's Care (Psalms 131, 23, 16, 3, 31, 46)

The Psalms are about trust. They have been penned in all sorts of circumstances, many of them crisis times when nerves are on edge and fear is nibbling at the heart. The theme of some of our most beloved psalms is peace in the midst of the storm. In this lesson we'll examine several psalms that speak about resting in God, no matter what is going on outside.

Psalm 131 – I Have Stilled and Quieted My Soul

The first "resting psalm" we'll consider is a short little gem, Psalm 131. It contains only three verses. It is attributed to David and was included by the editor of Psalms as one of the psalms termed "a song of ascents," traditionally sung by pilgrims going up to Jerusalem for a feast.

Detail of "The Good Shepherd," Tiffany stained glass memorial window (designed in 1898, created and installed later), Arlington Street Church, Boston. Photo ©2002, cambridge2000.com. Used by permission.

Humility and Trust (131:1)

It begins with an attitude of humility. We can't rest when we feel we have to be in control. We can't relax when we have to feel like we're in charge.

> "My heart is not proud, O LORD,
> my eyes are not haughty;[1]
> I do not concern myself with great matters
> or things too wonderful[2] for me." (131:1)

---

[1] Proud" (NIV, NASB), "haughty" (KJV), "lifted up" (NRSV) is *gābah*, "be high, exalted," from a root that means "to be high or lofty" (Victor P. Hamilton, *gābah*, TWOT #305). The second line has the synonym, *rûm*, "be high, lofty, rise up," here representing pride and presumption (AB, *rûm*, TWOT #2133).

[2] "Wonderful" (NIV), "marvelous" (NRSV), "high" (KJV) is *pālā'*, "be marvelous, wonderful," things that are unusual, beyond human capacities (Victor P. Hamilton, *pālā'*, TWOT #1768).

Resting in God begins with humility – and perspective. He's not talking about squelching normal curiosity and inquiry. But there comes a point of obsession where we *must* understand. That attitude is part of the urge to control everything. There are some things beyond my knowledge. Therefore, those things that I can't fathom, that I can't understand why, I must be willing to let them go in order to rest in God.

I Have Stilled and Quieted My Soul (131:2)

The second verse describes the psalmist's participation in settling down in trust and rest.

"But I have stilled[3] and quieted[4] my soul;[5]
like a weaned[6] child with its mother,
like a weaned child is my soul within me." (131:2)

You'd think that there's nothing more peaceful than a little babe nursing. But that's not the imagery here. It's a weaned child that is our image. If you've observed breast-feeding, you've know that the tiny little baby can become a tyrant when he's hungry. He'll start fussing, reaching for his mother, and won't quit until he gets the milk he needs. But the demanding baby isn't forever. Children were probably weaned by age three in most cases, perhaps sooner.

As much as the mother may enjoy the intimacy of breast-feeding, a weaned child moves one more step toward maturity. He is no longer so demanding of his mother. He doesn't have to satisfy his own needs instantly – at least *quite* as fast! That's what David means here. When we are at rest with God, we are like a weaned child with his mother, in contrast to a still-nursing child.

If we are like weaned children with God, we're beginning to move beyond the place of acting out of "selfish ambition or vain conceit" (Philippians 2:3-4). Rather, with the Apostle Paul we can say, " I have learned to be content whatever the circumstances" (Philippians 4:12). We have moved to a place of trust.

Hoping, Trusting in the Lord (131:3)

This short psalm concludes with a note of hope:

---

[3] "Stilled" (NIV), "calmed" (NRSV), "behaved" (KJV) is *shāwā*, "agree with, be(come) like, level." It is to be distinguished from another similar word, "to set, place" (Victor P. Hamilton, *shāwā*, TWOT #2342). In the Piel stem it means to "make (ground) level," and thus in our verse "to sooth" (*shāwā*, Holladay 364a).

[4] "Quieted" is *dāmam*, "be silent, still; wait." Several times the word is used in the Psalms of being still before the Lord in quiet meditation (Psalm 4:4; 30:12; 37:7) (*Dāmam*, TWOT #439).

[5] "Myself" (KJV) or "my soul" (NIV, NRSV) is *nepesh*, "life, soul, creature, person, appetite, mind" (Bruce K. Waltke, *nāpash*, TWOT #1395a).

[6] "Weaned" is *gāmal*, "to wean a child." (1 Samuel 1:23-24; Hosea 1:8) (Jack P. Lewis, *gāmal*, TWOT #360).

"O Israel, put your hope in the LORD
both now and forevermore." (131:3)

To hope (*yāḥal*) carries the ideas of "tarrying" and "confident expectation, trust."[7] When we are expectant of God to act on our behalf, then we can rest in that confidence. Our attitude is not one of insistence, but one of trust.

This little psalm carries a big message.

Q1. According to Psalm 131, just *how* does David quiet his inner person before the Lord? What are the elements mentioned in this psalm?
http://www.joyfulheart.com/forums/index.php?showtopic=678

Psalm 23 – The Lord Is My Shepherd

Our next psalm of resting and trust is the 23rd Psalm, probably the most popular and beloved psalm in the entire Psalter. As I've asked people why they like it, they tell me that it is comforting, peaceful. In short, it speaks of a rest and confidence in God that the sheep experiences with a good shepherd.

The psalm is attributed to David, probably a reflection that drew on his years as a shepherd for his father's flock. The imagery is strong and compelling.[8]

The shepherd was often a younger family member, though sometimes individuals were employed to shepherd an owner's flock. A shepherd was expected to:

1. **Lead the sheep** to watering holes and fresh green pasture when they had eaten off the grass in one place.
2. **Protect the sheep** from dangers such as wolves, lions, and bears.
3. **Heal the sheep** when they were injured and help during birthing.

---

[7] Paul R. Gilchrist, *yāḥal*, TWOT #859.

[8] For more detail on Psalm 23, see my exposition of the Psalm in *Names and Titles of God* (JesusWalk Publications, 2010), chapter 8.

4. **Rescue the lost sheep.** If a sheep wandered off, the shepherd would look for it until he found it.

The Lord our Shepherd (23:1)

Psalm 23:1 identifies Yahweh as "my shepherd," from the verb *rā'ā*, "to pasture, herd, tend."[9] Look at this psalm with me as one which invites us to rest in God.

"The LORD is my shepherd,
I shall not be in want." (23:1)

The basic premise is that since Yahweh is my shepherd, then I shall never be in need for anything. "Be in want" is *ḥāsēr*, "lack, have a need, be lacking."[10]

The Shepherd Provides Food (23:2)

The Shepherd helps the sheep find rest, pasture, and water to meet their physical needs.

"He makes me lie down in green pastures,
he leads me beside quiet waters." (Psalm 23:2)

"Leads" is *nāhal*, "lead with care, guide to a watering-place or station, and cause to rest there, lead, guide, refresh."[11] Lying in green pastures is the image of sheep that are content in the abundance found for them by their shepherd. The quiet waters refer to the part of the stream where the water isn't rushing and dangerous, but easy and safe to drink from and be refreshed.

The Shepherd Provides Restoration and Refreshing (23:3a)

Verse 3a continues the parallelism begun in verse 2 of the shepherd's ministry of caring for the sheep:

"He restores my soul[12]" (23:3a).

"Restore" is *shûb*, which we saw in Psalm 80:19 above. Here it means figuratively, "refresh, restore," literally, "repair."[13] For a sheep, this might include rescue from danger and then getting the animal back into good health through rest and recuperation. For a person, it might include rescue from a messed up life, and the gradual restoration to wholeness through loving care. God is in the restoration and wholeness business. He wants you to be refreshed and renewed as you rest in him.

---

[9] William White, *rā'ā*, TWOT #2185.
[10] Jack B. Scott, *ḥāsēr*, TWOT #705.
[11] *Nāhal*, BDB 625.
[12] "Soul" is *nephesh*, which we saw in 131:2, footnote 5 above.
[13] *Shûb* comes from a root meaning of "turn, return," and is often used with reference to repentance (BDB 1000, Po'l stem, 2a.

The Shepherd Guides in Righteous Ways (23:3b)

Now the psalm takes a moral turn.

"He guides me in paths of righteousness
for his name's sake" (23:3b).

"Guide" (NIV) and "lead" (KJV, NRSV) here is *nāḥâ*, "lead, guide," with the idea of conducting one along the right path.[14] Notice the reason that he leads us in these particular paths – "for his name's sake," that is, because the Lord's reputation and character require that he lead in righteous ways. We are tempted to get off the trail by taking moral short-cuts, but our Shepherd leads us in paths of righteousness.

Protection and Assurance in Fear (23:4)

When we are afraid, it is difficult to relax and rest. But the shepherd calms the sheep in times of danger, too.

"Even though I walk
through the valley of the shadow of death,
I will fear no evil,
for you are with me;
your rod and your staff,
they comfort me." (Psalm 23:4)

The shepherd will sometimes need to lead the flock through uncomfortable places to get them to the next pasture. John Muir, founder of the Sierra Club and father of the American national park movement, was a shepherd when he was young. Early in the summer he would be given a flock and take it higher and higher into the Sierra to bring it to fresh, green pasture. Sometimes the trail between pasture in Yosemite Valley and Tuolumne Meadows might be terrifying to the sheep. They wouldn't know where he was going. If they had been people they would have second-guessed their shepherd: "Do you know where in the world you are going?" they might ask – as we sometimes ask of God.

The "valley of the shadow of death" could be rendered "darkest valley" (NRSV, NIV margin). *Salmāwet*, means "deep darkness," sometimes translated "thick darkness," "thick gloom," from *sālal*, "to be dark."[15]

What encourages and comforts the sheep in the fearful darkness of this mountain canyon is the sight of the shepherd's rod and staff. They are the elements of protection that will ward off the wolf. The sheep see the rod and they know that the shepherd will use it to protect them, even to the extent of putting his life at risk – and they are comforted. Your

---

[14] Hiphil, *nāḥâ*, TWOT #1341. BDB 635.

[15] The word for shadow (*sel*) comes from this root also (John E. Hartley, *sālal*, TWOT #1921b).

Shepherd is committed to delivering you from your enemies and has indeed laid down his life for you in the battle for your soul.

The Gracious Host (23:5)

Now David strays from the sheep analogy, but Yahweh is still the subject of his thoughts:

"You prepare a table before me
in the presence of my enemies.
You anoint my head with oil;
my cup overflows." (Psalm 23:5)

The word for "table" (*shūlḥān*) means properly "skin or leather mat" spread on the ground.[16] I imagine a sumptuous picnic set by a gracious host. Enemies are hiding in rocks around about, spying on the feast set for the guest by the host. But their malevolence doesn't ruin the party because of the host's loving attention. The psalm is about rest, about the host putting the guest at ease.

When guests were welcomed in a Near Eastern home it was polite to provide a basin for them to wash their feet, they would receive a kiss, and the host would pour fragrant olive oil on their hair (Luke 7:44-46).

"My cup overflows," is a metaphor of abundance. The host doesn't just pour it almost full, but overfull – it is figurative, of course, not literal. God's love for us and provision for us is not meager or stingy, but liberal and abundant. We can trust him. We can rest in his presence.

Eternal Life (23:6)

"Surely goodness and mercy shall follow me
all the days of my life,
and I will dwell in the house of the LORD
forever" (Psalm 23:6).

"Surely goodness and mercy shall follow me," is David's firm assurance of his future, since Yahweh is his Shepherd and Host. "Follow" is *rādap*, "be behind, follow after, pursue, persecute."[17] In this context, enemies will not chase after him, but he will be pursued by goodness and mercy. What a positive, hopeful, wonderful promise. The psalmist is not a bitter pessimist, but a faith-filled, in-awe-of-God optimist.

"Forever" (NIV, KJV, NASB), "my whole life long" (NRSV), "for all time to come" (New Jerusalem Bible) translate two words: *'ōrek*, "length" (from *'ārak*, "to be long") and *yôm*, "day,

---

[16] *Shūlḥān*, BDB 1020.
[17] William White, *rādap*, TWOT #2124.

time, year." Hebrew really has no synonym for "eternity" and "forever." But the phrase "to the length of days" found here can be used to express "a protracted period of time" and "in some contexts signify the everlasting afterlife."[18]

Verse 6a and b show the synonymous parallelism characteristic of Hebrew poetry. As is common, the second line of the couplet carries the thought a bit further than the first. The first line speaks confidently of this life, the second speaks of the life beyond this earthly life.

We are comforted by Psalm 23. With dangers and perils all around us, only in the presence of one who we believe really cares for us can we afford to rest. In a sense, our ability to rest is directly dependent upon the degree of our faith in the care of the Shepherd.

Rest, O sheep. Your Shepherd does indeed care for you and interposed his own life for the sheep (John 10:11) to give them eternal life.

> Q2. According to Psalm 23, how does the Lord our Shepherd quiet his sheep and give them confidence? How many ways can you find in this psalm?
> http://www.joyfulheart.com/forums/index.php?showtopic=679

Psalm 16 – You Will Not Abandon Me to the Grave

Let's look at portions of a few more psalms of rest. David's "miktam" in Psalm 16 also considers the rest we look forward to, even in death. The psalm begins with a general plea for safety:

"Keep of me safe, O God,
for in you I take refuge." (16:1)

But the psalm concludes with a remarkable insight for David, one of life after the grave:

"[9]Therefore my heart is glad and my tongue rejoices;
my body also will rest secure,
[10]because you will not abandon me to the grave,

---

[18] Victor B. Hamilton, 'ārak, TWOT #162a.

nor will you let your Holy One see decay.
[11]You have made known to me the path of life;
you will fill me with joy in your presence,
with eternal pleasures at your right hand." (16:9-11)

Notice that David is able to "rest secure" physically in verse 9 because of his confidence in the bodily resurrection, that the termination death brings is not the end.

Verse 10 is quoted as a prophecy of the Messiah ("your Holy One") in Peter's sermon on the Day of Pentecost (Acts 2:24-28) and Paul's sermon in the synagogue at Pisidian Antioch (Acts 13:35).

How do you rest in the Lord at *your* deathbed or the bedside of one you love? With this confidence that death is not the end – resurrection is! Look at his expectation of eternal life in verse 11:

- Joy in Yahweh's presence and
- Eternal pleasures at his right hand!

Psalm 3 – I Lie Down and Sleep

Psalm 3 is another psalm of David, penned "when he fled from his son Absalom" (2 Samuel 15-18). Even in flight for his life he senses the protection of God and is able to rest.

"[3]But you are a shield around me, O LORD;
you bestow glory on me and lift up my head.
[4]To the LORD I cry aloud,
and he answers me from his holy hill. *Selah*
[5]I lie down and sleep;
I wake again, because the LORD sustains me.
[6]I will not fear the tens of thousands
drawn up against me on every side." (Psalm 3:3-6)

I think of that hymn, written by Cleland B. McAfee after two of his nieces died of diphtheria:

"There is a place of quiet rest,
Near to the heart of God,
A place where sin cannot molest,
Near to the heart of God."[19]

---

[19] "Near to the Heart of God," by Cleland B. McAfee (1903).

We Christians have a great hope – in this life and beyond the grave! Since we have that confidence, we can rest in God. We can relax in his care.

Psalm 31 – Into Your Hands I Commit My Spirit

Psalm 31 is another psalm attributed to David, a musical psalm no doubt sung later in the temple: "for the director of music." Look at the place of rest that David finds amidst the machinations of his foes:

> "³Since you are my rock and my fortress,
> for the sake of your name lead and guide me.
> ⁴Free me from the trap that is set for me,
> for you are my refuge.
> ⁵Into your hands I commit my spirit;
> redeem me, O LORD, the God of truth." (31:3-5)

Verse 5a was on Jesus' lips at his death:

> "Then Jesus, crying with a loud voice, said, 'Father, into your hands I commend my spirit.' Having said this, he breathed his last." (Luke 23:46)

How can a Christian be composed at his own death? By resting in faith in the promises of God. In this Jesus was the Pioneer and Perfecter of our faith (Hebrews 12:2, NRSV).

Psalm 31 also contains another passage expressive of resting in the Lord:

> "¹⁴But I trust in you, O LORD;
> I say, 'You are my God.'
> ¹⁵My times are in your hands;
> deliver me from my enemies
> and from those who pursue me.
> ¹⁶Let your face shine on your servant;
> save me in your unfailing love." (31:14-16)

The insight, "My times are in your hands," can help us with *our* trust issues, too. Times ('ēt) is found in the plural and refers here to the specific "appointed times" in our lives that are ordained by God for us. "The basic meaning of the word relates to time conceived as an opportunity or season."[20]

We're often in a hurry. Or the opposite: dreading the future and trying to repel it with every ounce of strength we have. Verse 15 does not express the fatalism of the song, *"Que*

<hr />

[20] Leonard J. Coppes, *'ōnā,* TWOT #1650b.

sera, sera, whatever will be will be....."[21] Rather it demonstrates an active trust in the Living God who loves us and will order our lives in love according to his plan for us.

Q3. (Psalm 31) What does it mean to say to the Lord, "Into your hands I commit my spirit" (31:5)? How does that statement bring peace to a person? How does the statement, "My times are in your hands" (31:15), bring peace to the troubled soul? http://www.joyfulheart.com/forums/index.php?showtopic=680

Psalm 46 – Our Ever-Present Help in Trouble

The final psalm I want to consider under psalms of rest is Psalm 46, attributed to "the Sons of Korah," a school of temple singers. "According to *alamoth*" may refer to a song in the treble range, though we're not sure. See how the psalmist rests his soul in God in the midst of the commotion he describes:

"¹God is our refuge and strength,
an ever-present help in trouble.
²Therefore we will not fear, though the earth give way
and the mountains fall into the heart of the sea,
³though its waters roar and foam
and the mountains quake with their surging. *Selah.*" (46:1-3)

In verse 1 he sees God, "an ever-present help in trouble." In verses 2 and 3 he pictures the trouble as a great earthquakes and cataclysms of mountains and ocean. The imagery expresses vividly the turmoil, agitation, confusion, chaos that we feel sometimes, where life seems to be spinning out of control around us. "Selah" probably directs there to be pause in the music at this point.

---

[21] "*Que Sera, Sera* (Whatever Will Be, Will Be)," words by Ray Evans, music by Jay Livingston (1956). In 1956 it won an Academy Award for Best Original Song.

But in the middle of the turmoil, the scene shifts to a river, a stream that flows in the midst of the "city of God."

"There is a river whose streams make glad the city of God,
the holy place where the Most High dwells." (46:4)

It brings the same feeling as the "still waters" of Psalm 23:2. It is an image of refreshment, of life, of peace. We see this same fabled river pictured in Ezekiel 47 flowing out from under the threshold of the temple and flowing down to bring life to whatever it touches. In Revelation 22 it flows in the Heavenly City:

"Then the angel showed me the river of the water of life, as clear as crystal, flowing from the throne of God and of the Lamb down the middle of the great street of the city. On each side of the river stood the tree of life, bearing twelve crops of fruit, yielding its fruit every month. And the leaves of the tree are for the healing of the nations." (Revelation 22:1-2)

The water of life is to refresh *you*, to sustain *you* in trouble. It is God's provision for you, though outside of the City of God there is clamor:

"⁵God is within her, she will not fall;
God will help her at break of day.
⁶Nations are in uproar, kingdoms fall;
he lifts his voice, the earth melts.
⁷The LORD Almighty is with us;
the God of Jacob is our fortress. *Selah*" (46:5-7)

The psalm concludes recounting what God has done to bring peace.

"⁸Come and see the works of the LORD,
the desolations he has brought on the earth.
⁹He makes wars cease to the ends of the earth;
he breaks the bow and shatters the spear,
he burns the shields with fire." (46:8-9)

Then the psalmist speaks prophetically for God:

"Be still, and know that I am God;
I will be exalted among the nations,
I will be exalted in the earth."
The LORD Almighty is with us;
the God of Jacob is our fortress. *Selah*" (46:10-11)

We are to still ourselves before God, he tells us. Why should we be still? What should we know? That in spite of all the chaos round about, the One who is with us is God himself. He is the Authority. He is the Power. He is the Might. Nothing can withstand Him!

Because He is with us we must still our fears and worries about our circumstances. He is enough! Because He is in the "City," the city is impregnable. Because God is with us, no one can stand against us. Because God is with us – and more importantly, we are with God – we cannot fail!

The ultimate source of peace in this troubled world is a clear vision of who God is and faith that He is completely in charge. Outside life may be full of confusion, but in God's presence – in the City of God, in his Hiding Place, in the Shelter of the Most High – there is peace. There is rest – for you!

Q4. (Psalm 46) How does the imagery of the river and streams in verse 4 function in Psalm 46 to speak peace to the harassed and harried person? Verse 10 tells us: "Be still and know that I am God." How does knowledge of who He is affect our peace? How should it affect our words? Why does He command us to "be still" as a result of this knowledge?
http://www.joyfulheart.com/forums/index.php?showtopic=681

Q5. After you've studied the psalms in this chapter, what do you think it means to "rest" in God? How do you seek God's peace when you have a dozen things coming against you?
http://www.joyfulheart.com/forums/index.php?showtopic=682

Exercise. For one of the psalms in this lesson – or another psalm with a similar theme – do one of the suggested exercises to help you experience the Psalms in Appendix 1. These include such things as praying a psalm, meditating, reading to a shut-in, paraphrasing, writing your own psalm, singing, preparing a liturgy, and memorizing. Then report to the forum what the exercise meant to you personally or share what you've written with others.
http://www.joyfulheart.com/forums/index.php?showtopic=683

Prayer

Lord, we worry so much, "cumbered with a load of care." I pray that you would teach me more deeply in my heart to rest in you in faith and confidence. Help me to unload my fears at your feet. Help me to put my petty frets down before you and rest the weight of my life upon You. In Jesus' name, I pray. Amen.

Songs

- **"A Shield About Me,"** words by Donn Thomas, music by Donn Thomas and Charles Williams (© 1980, 1982, Spoone Music Corp and Word Music). Psalm 3:3.
- **"Be Still,"** words and music by David J. Evans (© 1986, Thankyou Music). Psalm 46:10.
- **"Be Still and Know,"** composer unknown. Psalm 46:10.
- **"Be Still, My Soul,"** words: Katharina A. von Schlegel (1752), translated to English by Jane L. Borthwick (1855), music: Finlandia, Jean Sibelius (1899). Psalm 131.
- **"Cause Me to Come to Thy River, O Lord."** words and music by R. Edward Miller (© 1974, Maranatha! Music). Psalm 46:4.
- **"Gentle Shepherd,"** by Gloria and Bill Gaither (©1974 William J. Gaither, Inc., Gaither Copyright Management). Psalm 23.
- **"God Is My Shepherd,"** words: Scottish Psalter (1650), music: J.L. Macbeth Bain (1915), Chalice Hymnal #79. Psalm 23.
- **"God Will Take Care of You,"** words by Civilla D. Martin (1905), music by W. Stillman Martin (1905)
- **"He Leadeth Me! O Blessed Thought,"** words by Joseph H. Gilmore (1862), music by William B. Bradbury (1864). Psalm 23.
- **"His Sheep Am I"** ("in God's green pastures feeding..."), words and music by Orien Johnson (©1984, Word Music, LLC, a div. of Word Music Group, Inc.). Psalm 23.

- **"My Glory and the Lifter of My Head,"** words and music by Mae McAlister (© 1967, A Christian Church on a Hill, Thornhill, Ontario, CA). Psalm 3:3.
- **"My Shepherd, You Supply My Need,"** words: from Isaac Watts (1719), music: "Resignation," *Southern Harmony* (1835). Psalm 23.
- **"My Times Are in Thy Hand,"** words by William F. Lloyd (1835), music: Virgil (Albans), arranged from Giovanni Paisiello (1875)
- **"Quiet, Lord, My Froward Heart,"** words by John Newton (1779), music: Jesu, Jesu, du Mein Hirt, Paul Heinlein (1676). Psalm 131.
- **"Savior, Like a Shepherd Lead Us,"** words: attributed to Dorothy A. Thrupp (1836), music by William B. Bradbury (1859). Psalm 23.
- **"Shepherd of My Soul,"** words and music by Martin Nystrom (©1986, Maranatha Praise, Admin. by Music Services). Psalm 23.
- **"Still"** ("Hide me now..."), words and music by Reuben Morgan (© 2002, Hillsong Publishing)
- **"Stilled and Quieted My Soul,"** words and music by Tom Howard (© 1982 Maranatha! Music). Psalm 131.
- **"Surely Goodness and Mercy,"** by John Peterson & Alfred B. Smith (©1958, Singspiration). Psalm 23.
- **"The King of Love My Shepherd Is,"** words by Henry W. Baker (1868), music ancient Irish melody. Psalm 23.
- **"The Lord's My Shepherd,"** words: Scottish Psalter (1650), music: "Crimond," by Jessie Seymour Irvine (1871), descant by W. Baird Ross (20th century). Chalice Hymnal #78.
- **"There Is a River"** (that flows from deep within), words and music by David and Max Sapp (© 1969, David Sapp Ministries). John 4; Psalm 46:4.

8. Exulting in God (Psalms 57, 96, 126, and 24)

The first question of the Westminster Shorter Catechism reads: "What is the chief end of man?" The answer is: "Man's chief end is to glorify God and to enjoy him forever." These psalms teach us to express that joy – and as we express joy we are caught up in that joy ourselves. One gift to us from the Psalter is to learn how to praise our God and *enjoy* Him in that praise.

There comes a time to exult in the Lord, to enjoy him, to delight in him, to proclaim his greatness out of sheer joy. The psalms in this chapter are similar to those we saw in chapter 4; they belong to the genre of hymns. As you read each of these psalms out loud, try to enter in to the psalmist's joy. God has given us these psalms to instruct us in how to praise. Open your heart to learn.

Gerrit van Honthorst (1590-1656), King David Playing the Harp (1611), 82x65cm, Centraal Museum, Utrecht, Holland.

Psalm 57 – I Will Awake the Dawn!

Psalm 57 is attributed to David, "when he had fled from Saul into the cave." You can read about that incident in 1 Samuel 24. As a teenager David had been anointed king, though Saul was still reigning. His victory over Goliath made him a national hero overnight. King Saul gave him his daughter Michal in marriage. But as David's acclaim increased, Saul's fear of David's popularity turned to paranoia. Now he sought for David's very life, while David resorted to hiding in a cave. Even so, God shows him there that Saul is in his power.

David's Lament (57:1-6)

Psalm 57 isn't a pure hymn genre. It begins as a lament reflecting David's fear that his presence in the cave would be discovered, but then turns into a full-blown hymn near the end as he realizes that the Lord has wonderfully protected him.

The first part is the lament:

"[1]Have mercy on me, O God, have mercy on me,
for in you my soul takes refuge.
I will take refuge in the shadow of your wings
until the disaster has passed.

[2]I cry out to God Most High,
to God, who fulfills [his purpose] for me.
3 He sends from heaven and saves me,
rebuking those who hotly pursue me. *Selah*

[4]I am in the midst of lions;
I lie among ravenous beasts –
men whose teeth are spears and arrows,
whose tongues are sharp swords." (57:1-4)

Be Exalted, O God (57:5, 11)

Now we hear a glimmer of praise as David begins to see God's deliverance.

"Be exalted, O God, above the heavens;
let your glory be over all the earth." (57:5, 11)

These words of praise appear both at the midpoint of the psalm and at the end, perhaps as a musical refrain that concludes each section of the psalm. "Exalted" is *rûm*, "be high, lofty." Here height is symbolic of positive notions such as glory and exaltation.[1] When we speak highly of God, when he becomes the focus of our hearts and minds, it is difficult to lift up ourselves, to be proud. Christian songwriter Brian Doerksen characterizes this kind of worship as, "Notice God, don't notice me."[2] Worship is not about us. It is all about God. John the Baptist understood: "He must increase, but I must decrease" (John 3:30).

The prayer, "Be exalted above the heavens," is to pray that God's glory may be seen for what it is, in the same way that we pray, "Thy kingdom come, thy will be done...." Our praying will not make it happen any sooner, but it is a prayer that puts us in the proper attitude towards the Father, giving us proper perspective of who God really is!

[1] Andrew Bowling, *rûm*, TWOT #2133.
[2] Brian Doerksen quoted by Andree Farias, "Pioneer Doerksen on What's Wrong with Worship Music," *Christianity Today*, July 2007.

They Have Been Caught in Their Own Trap (57:6)

Verse 6 comes back to the traps that men set – nets to ensnare birds, covered pits to catch larger animals. David's enemies are tricky:

"They spread a net for my feet –
I was bowed down in distress.
They dug a pit in my path –
but they have fallen into it themselves. *Selah*" (57:6)

Saul's army has surged up into the Judean mountains in search of David. But when Saul comes (in order to "relieve himself") into the very cave where David is hiding with his men, God shows David that his enemy is in his power. Instead of killing Saul – "the Lord's anointed" king – when he has a chance, David instead proclaims his honor and loyalty publicly. God is glorified and his enemy shamed.

David's Exultation (57:7-11)

Now David breaks into full-blown exultation.

"My heart is steadfast, O God,
my heart is steadfast;
I will sing and make music." (57:7)

David's steadfast heart is much different than being "bowed down" just a verse before (verse 6b). In my own personal experience, when my heart is "bowed down," I just don't feel like praising. When I determine to praise God anyway, eventually my emotions come along and I can find myself full of heart-felt praise to God.

"Steadfast" (NIV, NRSV), "ready" (NJB), "fixed" (KJV) is *kûn*, "established, prepared, made ready, fixed." The root meaning is to bring something into being with the consequence that its existence is a certainty.[3] David's heart is now steady, focused, fixed on praise.

"Awake, my soul!
Awake, harp and lyre!
I will awaken the dawn." (57:8)

Now he calls to himself, "Wake up!" He calls to his familiar instruments, the harp and lyre, "Wake up! Get ready to play!" The "dawn" (NIV, NRSV) or "early" (KJV) is *shaḥar*, "dawn," the breaking of the day, that time just prior to sunrise.[4] Before light he will begin to

---

[3] John N. Oswalt, *kûn*, TWOT #964. This is the Niphal stem. Holladay references this verse for the meaning, "2. be stable, secure, b. steady spirit" (Holladay 153a).
[4] Victor B. Hamilton, *shaḥar*, TWOT #2369.

praise and sing at full volume so that even the dawn will be aroused from sleep by his melodies.

David will not be quiet. Even among the gentiles with whom he sometimes sojourns in his self-imposed exile from Saul's kingdom, he is not quiet.

> "[9]I will praise you, O Lord, among the nations;
> I will sing of you among the peoples.
> [10]For great is your love, reaching to the heavens;
> your faithfulness reaches to the skies.
> [11]Be exalted, O God, above the heavens;
> let your glory be over all the earth." (57:9-11)

In verse 10 he praises God's wonderful love (*ḥesed*). It is so great (*gādōl*) that it fills all creation, full up to the brim of heaven. The parallel line boasts that his "faithfulness" (NIV, NRSV), "constancy" (NJB), "truth" (KJV, *'ĕmet*) fills up to the "skies" (NIV) or to the "clouds" (NRSV, KJV).

The lines in verse 10 employ the preposition *'ad*, "movement up to, until, as far as."[5] But God's person in verse 11 is *above* the heavens, above the earth, employing the preposition, *'al*, "higher than, on over."[6]

Our God is worthy of our praise, no matter what situation we find ourselves in. He transcends our universe and our categories of what is possible. He is above it all, and thus nothing is impossible for him! Be exalted, O God, in my heart and attitudes and priorities. You are so far higher than I can imagine, yet you bend down to hear my prayers, like a father with a tiny child. Yes! Be exalted, O God, in your greatness!

Q1. (Psalm 57) Why is praise difficult in the midst of trying circumstances? How does praise affect our faith? Our attitude? Our motivation?
http://www.joyfulheart.com/forums/index.php?showtopic=684

---

[5] *'Ad*, Holladay 264b-206c, II.
[6] *'Al*, Holladay 272b-273a.

Psalm 96 – Ascribe to the Lord the Glory Due His Name

This song of praise commands the hearers to worship and bless Yahweh:

"¹Sing to the LORD a new song;
sing to the LORD, all the earth.
²Sing to the LORD, praise (*bārak*) his name;
proclaim his salvation day after day." (96:1-2)

The praise is to be joyful, characterized by singing (*shîr*). Singing worship is to be both universal ("all the earth") and constant ("day after day").

Blessing Yahweh (96:2)

We are called upon to "praise" (NIV) or "bless" (KJV, NRSV, NJB) his name, that is his person. The verb is *bārak*, "bless, praise, salute." When one greater blesses a person of lower status it means "to endue with power for success, prosperity, fecundity, longevity, etc."[7] When the lesser blesses the greater, that is, God, the word means "to declare God the origin of power for success, prosperity, fertility," that is, to "praise God."[8] In this sense it appears often in the Psalms:

"I will bless the LORD at all times;
his praise shall continually be in my mouth." (Psalm 34:1; NRSV)

"So I will bless you as long as I live;
I will lift up my hands and call on your name." (Psalm 63:4; NRSV)

Declaring His Glory to the Nations (96:3-6)

Israel is not to keep God to themselves. As God spoke through the prophet Isaiah, Israel is to be a "light to the nations" (Isaiah 42:6; 49:6; 51:4; 60:3). The so-called gods of other religions are bogus. Their followers are sadly deluded. Our God is the true God. Here is the germ of the missionary call:

"³Declare his glory among the nations,
his marvelous deeds among all peoples.
⁴For great is the LORD and most worthy of praise;
he is to be feared above all gods.
⁵For all the gods of the nations are idols,
but the LORD made the heavens.
⁶Splendor and majesty are before him;
strength and glory are in his sanctuary." (96:3-6)

---

[7] John N. Oswalt, *bārak*, TWOT #285.
[8] *Bārak*, Holladay 49-50.

Great Is the Lord and Greatly to Be Praised (96:4a)

Verse 4a gives two more reasons *why* we should praise the Lord that are echoed in Psalms 48:1 and 145:3:

- **"Great is the LORD."** We should praise God because of his immense greatness, before which we are but grasshoppers (Isaiah 40:22). To do otherwise is immensely ignorant and unrealistic.
- He is **"most worthy of praise."** "Worthy" (NIV, NJB) or "greatly" (KJV, NRSV) is *me'ōd*, "exceedingly, much, abundance." The word is found in many combinations, all expressing the idea of exceeding.[9] Literally this phrase is "to be praised greatly." Only exceedingly great praise is appropriate before such a great God.

Ascribe to the Lord the Glory Due His Name (96:7-8)

Next we are called upon to ascribe to or credit God with the glory that is his:

"[7]Ascribe to the LORD, O families of nations,
ascribe to the LORD glory and strength.
[8]Ascribe to the LORD the glory due his name;
bring an offering and come into his courts." (96:7-8)

The psalmist, echoing Psalm 29:1-2 calls on the peoples of the earth to "ascribe" glory and strength to Yahweh. "Ascribe" (NIV, NRSV), "give" (KJV, NJB) is *yāhab*, "give, ascribe." Several passages are practically the same: verses 7 and 8 in our passage, Psalm 29:1-2; and 1 Chronicles 16:28-29, with a similar use in Deuteronomy 32:3. Delitzsch explains this use of *yāhab* this way: "to render back to Him cheerfully and joyously in a laudatory recognition, as it were by an echo, His glory and might, which are revealed and to be revealed in the created world."[10]

Why should the nations credit God with glory and strength? Because these qualities conform with his name, his reputation, his very character. The word "due" is clearly implied but not explicitly stated in the Hebrew text. To credit God with glory and strength is appropriate to who he is. Other psalms explain:

---

[9] Walter C. Kaiser, *m'd*, TWOT #1134a.

[10] KD 5:368 on Psalm 22:2. In the Greek Septuagint translation, *yāhab* is translated by *didōmi*, "give," in 1 Chronicles 16:28-29 and by *pherō*, "to bring, present, bear," in the Psalms passages. "'Ascribe' with synonyms 'attribute' or 'credit' would suggest 'inferring of cause, quality, authorship' (Webster). Hence the passages would demand everyone to acknowledge the Lord Yahweh as the great king and offer such ascription of glory and greatness as is commensurate with his majesty" (Paul R. Gilchrist, *yāhab*, TWOT #849).

> "Sing joyfully to the LORD, you righteous;
> it is **fitting** for the upright to praise him." (Psalm 33:1)

> "Praise the LORD.
> How good it is to sing praises to our God,
> how pleasant and **fitting** to praise him!" (Psalm 147:1)

The adjective "fitting" (NIV), "befits" (NRSV), "comely," *nā'weh*, denotes beauty or suitability.[11] It suits upright, honest people to offer praise to God. Is God so ego-centered that he demands our praise? No. But only when we ourselves are hopelessly ego-centric do we deny to God the worship that is befitting who he is. When we praise and worship him we line up with the reality of the universe.

Worship Yahweh in the Splendor of His Holiness (96:9)

> "Worship the LORD in the splendor of his holiness;
> tremble before him, all the earth." (96:9)

"Worship" (*ḥāwā*) means "bow down deeply, do obeisance" in worship.[12] The next phrase (also found in 29:2) has been interpreted several ways:

- "the splendor of his holiness" (NIV, KJV)
- "the beauty of holiness" (KJV)
- "holy splendor" (NRSV)
- "holy array" (RSV)

The word is *hădārâ*, "adornment, glory," is also found in a few verses previously in 96:6a, referring to God. The RSV's "holy array" takes this as the beauty of the priests' holy garments in worship. But it is probably better to see this as descriptive of God as the NIV and NRSV, "holy splendor."[13]

The Lord Reigns! (96:10a)

> "Say among the nations, 'The LORD reigns.'" (96:10a)

---

[11] Leonard J. Coppes, *nā'weh*, TWOT #1271a.

[12] The histafal stem of *ḥāwā*, Holladay, 97a.

[13] So Kidner, *Psalms 1-72*, on Psalm 29:2, p. 125. However, Craigie (*Psalms*, p. 242-243), renders this as "holy attire," rejecting a supposed Ugaritic etymology of a cognate word. "The reference is probably a poetic reflection on the holy (or purified) attire in which human worshipers were dressed for their celebration of the Lord's victory" (p. 247). Tate (*Psalms*, p. 510) translates Psalm 96:9a: "Bow down before Yahweh in (his) holy splendor." In footnote he gives different uses of the word.

Part of our worship of God is proclamation to unbelievers. Evangelism is not an option, it is a command connected with the startling reality of who God really is. We cannot be silent about our faith and worship God adequately.

Let Heavens, Earth, Sea, Fields, and Trees Worship Yahweh (96:10-13)

The final verses of this psalm build up a glorious momentum of praise. The whole creation is to be caught up in praise. You can only catch the real power of it by reading it out loud with emphasis:

> "[10]Say among the nations, 'The LORD reigns.'
> The world is firmly established, it cannot be moved;
> he will judge the peoples with equity.
> [11]Let the heavens rejoice, let the earth be glad;
> let the sea resound, and all that is in it;
> [12]let the fields be jubilant, and everything in them.
> Then all the trees of the forest will sing for joy;
> [13]they will sing before the LORD, for he comes,
> he comes to judge the earth.
> He will judge the world in righteousness
> and the peoples in his truth." (96:10-13)

Why praise? Because the Lord reigns. The Hebrew verb *mālak*, "to reign, that is, to be and exercise the functions of a monarch."[14] Yahweh is coming to judge (*shāpat*) the earth, in the sense of "to govern, rule, exercise of government."[15] When both John the Baptist and Jesus declared that "The Kingdom of God is at hand" (Mark 1:15; Matthew 3:2; 4:17; 10:7), they were declaring that the reign of God had come in the Messiah himself. In Jesus the Messiah "our God reigns!" (Revelation 19:6; Isaiah 52:7). The King has come to his Kingdom. This will reach its complete fulfillment at the Second Coming of Christ at the end of the ages.

This psalm declares in the most joyous and unmistakable terms that Yahweh is King. His is worthy of our praise, our obedience, our best, our whole lives. Our God reigns. Have you allowed him to reign over you?

---

[14] Robert D. Culver, *mālak*, TWOT #1199.
[15] Robert D. Culver, *shāpat*, TWOT #2443.

Q2. (Psalm 96) What does it mean to "ascribe" to God attributes of glory and strength? What happens when we fail to ascribe such qualities to him? In what sense is praise to God "fitting" or "worthy"?

http://www.joyfulheart.com/forums/index.php?showtopic=685

Psalm 126 – He Who Goes Out Weeping Will Return with Songs of Joy

This next psalm is a mixture of a hymn of high praise and a lament. Though we don't know the author or the exact setting of this little psalm, this "song of ascents," it seems that the first half (verses 1-3) remembers a great event of God's restoration to the people of Israel. The second half (verses 4-6) is a prayer and promise that God will "do it again," that he will restore and deliver them again.

When the Lord Brought Back the Captives (126:1a)

Before we examine this short and memorable psalm we need to observe a difference of interpretation of one word that can affect the way we interpret the psalm.

Vs.	**Captives/captivity** (NJB, cf. KJV, NASB) *shîbâ* is derived from *shābā*, "take captive"	**Fortunes** (NRSV, cf. NIV) *shîbâ* is derived from *shûb*, "(re)turn"
1a	When Yahweh brought back Zion's captives....	When the LORD restored the fortunes of Zion....
4a	Bring back, Yahweh, our people from captivity....	Restore our fortunes, O LORD....

The question is whether the noun *shîbâ* is derived from the verb *shābā*, "take captive" or from *shûb*, "(re)turn." There are good arguments for both approaches, but the translation "fortunes" is widely accepted these days. If it is translated "captives/captivity" then this psalm is probably post-exilic, while if it is translated "fortunes" then it could be from any era and of more general application.[16]

Our Mouths Were Filled with Laughter (126:1-3)

The NIV tries to have it both ways, with verse 1a referring back to the exile and verse 4a applying more generally to some current crisis Israel is facing. This approach makes sense to me. Let me explain a bit of Israel's history.

Between 604 and 587 BC there were three separate exiles from the Kingdom of Judah as the world power Babylon under King Nebuchadnezzar sought to subjugate this rebellious kingdom. From the first exile about 70 years passed until 537 BC when the Persian king Cyrus (who conquered Babylon in 539 BC) allowed a group of the Jews to return to their homeland and rebuild the temple (2 Chronicles 36:22-23; Ezra 1:2-3). The Jews who returned from Babylon to Jerusalem could hardly believe their good fortune. They were beside themselves with joy. The psalmist effectively catches the emotion in verses 1-3:

> "¹When the LORD brought back the captives to Zion,
> we were like men who dreamed.
> ²Our mouths were filled with laughter,
> our tongues with songs of joy.
> Then it was said among the nations,
> 'The LORD has done great things for them.'
> ³The LORD has done great things for us,
> and we are filled with joy." (126:1-3)

Notice the exuberance of praise – laughter, songs of joy. Other nations are amazed, too, and attribute this to Yahweh. The psalmist immediately agrees. "The LORD *has* done great things for us! A similar sentiment is expressed by David in Psalm 30:

> "You turned my wailing into dancing;
> you removed my sackcloth and clothed me with joy,
> that my heart may sing to you and not be silent.
> O LORD my God, I will give you thanks forever." (Psalm 30:11-12)

Restore Our Fortunes, O Lord (126:4)

But now the mood of the psalm turns. The psalmist uses two images in verse 4-6:

---

[16] Victor P. Hamilton (*shûb*, TWOT #2340b) cites Dahood (*Psalms III* (Anchor Bible, p. 218)) for the view that that *shîbâ* is in fact from *shûb*. Dahood offers the translation "restore the fortunes of" citing the Sefire inscription in support. He treats the word *shebût* of Psalm 126:4 also as from *shûb* offering a similar translation. This view, now widely adopted, makes it unnecessary to see in this phrase a mark of exilic literature.

1.   The quick changing desert wadi, and
2.   The slow but sure sowing and reaping of the farmer.

When the Jews returned to Jerusalem they found the walls were broken down and the beautiful Temple of Solomon completely destroyed. They had to rebuild their lives from scratch. Verse 4 is their prayer:

"Restore our fortunes, O LORD,
like streams in the Negev." (126:4)

A stream in the Negev desert is called a wadi. Like the arroyo in the American southwest, the wadi is dry most of the year, but when there are heavy rains, a flash flood can occur by which these wadis can fill to overflowing within minutes with torrents of water. Almost overnight the parched desert will be covered with a carpet of colorful wildflowers.

The psalmist is calling on the Lord to miraculously turn things around for them, to deliver them as quickly as the dry wadis can be filled with raging water. Do it like that, O Lord! he prays. Our return to Jerusalem after decades of captivity was quick and unexpected like a desert storm. You can act with the same speed in today's crisis.

Weeping Comes before Reaping (126:5-6)

But in contrast to his prayer for a sudden reversal of fortunes in verse 4, in verses 5 and 6 the psalmist advises his hearers to continue faithfully doing the right thing; God will bring the answer in due time. He uses the metaphor of sowing and reaping that would be well-known to all in this agrarian economy of subsistence farmers:

"⁵Those who sow in tears
will reap with songs of joy.
⁶He who goes out weeping,
carrying seed to sow,
will return with songs of joy,
carrying sheaves with him." (126:5-6)

The KJV translates verse 6b with the beautiful phrase, "precious seed." However, the adjective here (*meshek*) probably means "a drawing, bag, pouch," so the phrase would be rendered either "bag of seed" (NASB)[17] or perhaps "a trail of seed" (literally "a drawing-out of seed"), thus "seed for sowing" (NRSV).[18]

---

[17] So Victor P. Hamilton, *māshak*, TWOT #1257. The root *māshak*, has the idea of "to draw or drag."
[18] Kidner, *Psalms 73-150*, p. 440, footnote 2. Also Kirkpatrick, *Psalms*, p. 750.

Why the tears? Why the weeping? Is the act of planting seed usually associated with tears?[19] Not normally, though the plowing and sowing represent a great deal of labor, a labor of hope. The psalmist is writing these words as encouragement to a people who is seeking God's deliverance from a great oppression. It is a time of struggle, a time of weeping, a time of heart-wrenching trial. He is saying that later they will have cause for joy. God will answer. As David puts it in Psalm 30:

> "Weeping may remain for a night,
> but rejoicing comes in the morning." (Psalm 30:5)

The psalmist's message is that we must continue to do our part, the things we must do to achieve the final result, the difficult, day-by-day labor that is necessary. In due time the harvest will come – if we don't quit. Two passages from the Apostle Paul come to mind:

> "Let us not become weary in doing good, for at the proper time we will reap a harvest if we do not give up." (Galatians 6:9)

> "Therefore, my beloved brethren, be steadfast, immovable, always abounding in the work of the Lord, knowing that in the Lord your labor is not in vain." (1 Corinthians 15:58, RSV)

Psalm 126 gives two answers to the dilemma of struggle. First, a prayer that God will suddenly deliver as he has done in the past. and second, that if we continue our labor in faith, he will bring the inevitable harvest, and with it deliverance and joy. Come, Lord Jesus!

Q3. (Psalm 126). In this psalm, the nation is going through some kind of crisis. How does the memory of God's deliverance in verses 1-3 prepare them for the prayer of verse 4? How do you understand the two metaphors of deliverance: (1) a wadi or dry gully and (2) sowing and reaping? How do these metaphors help you in your situation?

http://www.joyfulheart.com/forums/index.php?showtopic=686

---

[19] However, it might be a time of anguish for a family that has barely enough food at planting time, since to put the seed corn in the ground for a future harvest is both an act of deprivation and of faith.

Psalm 24 – The King of Glory

Our final psalm of exultation is a gem that seems to come from the time when David brought the ark into the city of Jerusalem (2 Samuel 6). The ark, which represents the portable throne of God, is carried by Levites up the hill to the city, through the gates, and then up the hill to what would later be the temple mount. This is a psalm of royalty, celebrating the reign of Yahweh the King. It is attributed to David.

The King is the Creator (24:1-2)

The psalm begins with a bold declaration of Yahweh's sovereignty over the whole earth:

"¹The earth is the LORD's, and everything in it,
the world, and all who live in it;
²for he founded it upon the seas
and established it upon the waters." (24:1-2)

He is King and Owner of all because he is Creator of all!

The King's Requirement of Complete Loyalty (24:3-6)

As the ark is ascending to its resting place, the psalmist asks the rhetorical question:

"Who may ascend the hill of the LORD?
Who may stand in his holy place?" (24:3)

It is a similar question to the one asked in Psalm 15:

"LORD, who may dwell in your sanctuary?
Who may live on your holy hill?" (15:1)

The answer comes back:

"⁴He who has clean hands and a pure heart,
who does not lift up his soul to an idol
or swear by what is false.
⁵He will receive blessing from the LORD
and vindication from God his Savior." (24:3-5)

God requires ethical and moral purity, that is, loyalty to the King and his commands, both outwardly and inwardly. Since he is King, he demands strict allegiance, as well. "Lift up his soul to an idol" means to worship an idol. "Swear by what is false," means to take an oath by a false or bogus god, rather than by Yahweh, the only true God. The reward to the loyal follower is a promise of both blessing from the King and justice when his case is heard before the King. Blessing (*berākā*) means to be "endued with power for success, prosperity, fecundity, longevity, etc."[20] These are indeed the qualities of Yahweh's followers.

> "Such is the generation of those who seek him,
> who seek your face, O God of Jacob. *Selah*" (24:6)

We considered what it means to "seek one's face" in chapter 2 (on Psalm 27:2-8) to seek personal closeness to, a personal hearing, a relationship.

The King of Glory Shall Come In (24:7-10)

The ark and its procession have come up to the gate of the ancient fortress city of Jerusalem and entrance is called for from the gatekeeper:

> "7Lift up your heads, O you gates;
> be lifted up, you ancient doors,
> that the King of glory may come in." (24:7)

The entrance of the "King of Glory" is announced. Glory (*kābōd*) has the basic meaning of "to be heavy, weighty," but is generally used figuratively to refer to a "weighty" person in society, someone who is honorable, impressive, worthy of respect. In reference to God, *kābōd* relates to a visible manifestation of God, associated with his holiness, splendor, and blinding light.[21] So what does this title mean? It refers to the King "whose whole being and acts is glory."[22]

"Lift up" (*nāśā'*) is a strange command, for gates that defended an ancient city would swing open on hinges, projections top and bottom that fitted into sockets in the lintel and sill.[23] You would expect a command to swing open. But the speaker is commanding that the lintel of the gate be raised[24] to accommodate the King of Glory who demands entrance. Franz Delitzsch comments:

> "It is the gates of the citadel of Zion to which the cry is addressed to expand themselves in a manner worthy of the Lord who is about to enter, for whom they are too low and too straight [narrow]."[25]

The gate keeper shouts back for the King to identify himself:

---

[20] John N. Oswalt, *berākā*, TWOT #285b.

[21] John N. Oswalt, *kābēd*, TWOT #943e.

[22] Franz Delitzsch, *Psalms*, KD 5:338.

[23] Burton Scott Easton and Ralph W. Vunderink, "Gate," ISBE 2:408.

[24] So KD 5:338; Walter C. Kaiser, *nāśā'*, TWOT #1421. *Rō'sh*, "head, top, summit, upper part" is used generically for "lintel" here. The specific word for lintel is *mashqôp* (Exodus 12:7, 22-23) or *'ayil* (1 Kings 6:31).

[25] Franz Delitzsch, *Psalms*, KD 5:338.

"Who is this King of glory?" (24:8a)

The answer comes back immediately, that the King of Glory is Yahweh himself, the victorious Warrior:

"The LORD strong and mighty,
the LORD mighty in battle." (24:8b,c)

Then the call is renewed for the gates to open high and wide for the King:

"Lift up your heads, O you gates;
lift them up, you ancient doors,
that the King of glory may come in."

The final question is raised:

"Who is he, this King of glory?" (24:10a)

The answer is final and glorious:

"The LORD Almighty--
he is the King of glory. *Selah*" (24:10b,c)

Unfortunately the NIV's rendering "the LORD Almighty" misses the true import of this title, which is "Lord of hosts" (NRSV, KJV), literally, "Yahweh of the Armies!"[26] The Warrior King, head of the armies of heaven, "mighty in battle," demands entrance into his city!

Q4. (Psalm 24) How do verses 1-2 establish the Lord's right as King? What do verses 3-6 tell us about the requirements of the King? What do verses 7-10 tell us about the glory of the King? How does this psalm speak to you in your situation?
http://www.joyfulheart.com/forums/index.php?showtopic=687

The King of Glory and Our Heart's Home

This final psalm of exaltation stirs me at several levels. First, for the awesome portrait it paints of our mighty conquering God who reigns with his own might against any foe. We

---

[26] *Ṣebā'ōt* means, "armies, hosts," from the verb *ṣābā'*, "fight, serve" (John E. Hartley, *ṣābā'*, TWOT #1865b).

talk about spiritual warfare; look at the might of the one to whom we pray. Christianity is not a weak, namby-pamby religion that is a push-over for any foe:

> "You, dear children, are from God and have overcome them, because the one who is in you is greater than the one who is in the world." (1 John 4:4)

What foe can stand before our King?

> "If God is for us, who can be against us?... In all these things we are more than conquerors through him who loved us." (Romans 8:31b, 37)

Next, I think of Jesus riding a donkey down the slope from Bethany and then up to the city of Jerusalem, surrounded by a throng of followers shouting, "Son of David" and "Blessed is he who comes in the name of the Lord." He came into Jerusalem as King to die, yet his final entry shall be to reign at his Second Coming, when loud voices in heaven will shout:

> "The kingdom of the world has become
> the kingdom of our Lord and of his Christ,
> and he will reign for ever and ever." (Revelation 11:15b)

Yet at another level I am moved to tears. The King of Glory rightfully demands entrance into his city. He commands the gates to expand so that he may enter without stooping. But is he welcome in my heart? Is he King of my inner self? And now the paradox: the One who can rightfully command my heart knocks rather than battering down the door.

> "Behold, I stand at the door and knock. If anyone hears My voice and opens the door, I will come in to him and dine with him, and he with Me." (Revelation 3:20, NKJV)

Will I resist him? Will you? Or invite him into my heart's home? Will you open wide Jesus, Yahweh's King and Messiah, to enter your life, and as he does, bow at his feet? That is the question that comes to me. On how you and I answer it will hang our eternal destiny.

Exercise. For one of the psalms in this lesson – or another psalm with a similar theme – do one of the suggested exercises to help you experience the Psalms in Appendix 1. These include such things as praying a psalm, meditating, reading to a shut-in, paraphrasing, writing your own psalm, singing, preparing a liturgy, and memorizing. Then report to the forum what the exercise meant to you personally or share what you've written with others.

http://www.joyfulheart.com/forums/index.php?showtopic=688

Prayer

Almighty, glorious King, Lord of Glory. I exalt you. You are holy. You are mighty. You have all power. And yet you knock on my door, seek entrance into my heart. Do come in, Master, and live in me forever. Let your glory light my life. In Jesus' name, I pray. Amen.

Songs

- **"Be Exalted, O God,"** words and music by Brent Chambers (© 1977, Scripture in Song / Maranatha! Music). Psalm 57:9-11.
- **"Bringing in the Sheaves,"** words: Knowles Shaw (1874), music: George A. Minor (1880). Psalm 126:6
- **"Can I Ascend,"** words and music by Matt Redman (© 1995 Thankyou Music). Psalm 24:3.
- **"Clean Hands and a Pure Heart,"** words and music by Dale Garratt (© 1980, Scripture in Song). Psalm 24:3-5; 2 Chronicles 16:9.
- **"Give Us Clean Hands,"** words and music by Charlie Hall (© 2000, worshiptogether.com songs). Psalm 24:3-5.
- **"Great Is the Lord"** (and greatly to be praised), by Robert Ewing (© 1976, Robert Ewing). Psalm 48:1-2; Ephesians 4:4-5; Psalm 96:4
- **"Hallelujah! Our God Reigns,"** words and music by Dale Garratt (© 1972, Scripture in Song / Maranatha! Music). Revelation 9:6-7; Psalm 96:10
- **"He Is Exalted, the King Is Exalted on High,"** words and music by Twila Parris (© 1985, Straightway Music / Mountain Spring Music)
- **"He That Goeth Forth with Weeping,"** words: Thomas Hastings (1836), music: "Brocklesby," by Charlotte A. Barnard (1868). Psalm 126:6.
- **"I Exalt Thee"** (For Thou, Lord, art high above all the earth), words and Music by Pete Sanchez, Jr. (© 1976, Pete Sanchez, Jr.). Psalm 97:9.
- **"Lift Up Your Heads, O Ye Gates,"** #33 Chorus in "The Messiah," an Oratorio by Georg F. Handel (1741). To sing this rousing chorus as part of a choir is a wonderful and emotional experience. Psalm 24:7-10.
- **"Lift Up Your Heads to the Coming King,"** words and music by Steve Fry (© 1977, Birdwing Music). Psalm 24.
- **"My Heart Is Fixed, O God,"** words: Charles Wesley (1743), music: "Middlesex" (1875). Psalm 57:7.
- **"Our God Reigns,"** words and music by Leonard E. Smith, Jr. (© 1974, 1978, New Jerusalem Music). Isaiah 52:7; Psalm 96:10

- **"Señor, Yo Quiero Entrar"** (O God, I Want to Enter), words: anonymous, translated by David L. Edwards (1994), music: Latin American melody (20th century). Chalice Hymnal #291. Psalm 24:3-4.
- **"Sow in the Morn thy Seed,"** words: James Montgomery (1832), music: "Silver Street," by Isaac Smith (c. 1770). Psalm 126:6.
- **"The Earth Is the Lord's (Psalm 24),"** words and music by Bill Batstone and Tom Howard (© 1984, Maranatha! Music). Psalm 24.
- **"Those Who Sow in Tears,"** words and music by Tom Howard and Bill Batstone (© 1986, Maranatha! Music)
- **"Thou Hast Turned My Mourning into Dancing for Me,"** unknown. Psalm 30:11.
- **"To God Be the Glory"** (Great Things He Hath Done), words: Fanny J. Crosby, music William H. Doane.
- **"Who May Ascend to the Hill of the Lord?"** words and music by Kirk Dearman (© 1989, Maranatha Praise, Inc.). Psalm 24:3-5.
- **"You Turned My Wailing into Dancing,"** words and music by Bruce Bremner (© 1980, Scripture in Song / Maranatha! Music). Psalm 30:11-13.

9. Rejoicing in God's Character (Psalms 103, 145, 117)

One of the joys of the believer is to revel in the strong, solid character of our unchanging Father. The three psalms in this chapter explore the nature and attributes of our God.

Psalm 103 – Bless the Lord, O My Soul

Our first psalm is a familiar one, a psalm that has spawned dozens of hymns and choruses. It is attributed to David:

Bless the Lord (103:1)

The first line introduces the psalm:

Bless the Lord! Orante figure from the Catacomb of Priscilla, Cubicle of the Velata, Rome (second half of the third century). This pose of arms lifted in prayer is found in thousands of figures in the catacombs, representing a soul at peace in paradise.

> "Praise the LORD, O my soul;
> all my inmost being, praise his holy name." (103:1)

More familiar may be the Authorized Version that translates the verb as "bless":

> "Bless the LORD, O my soul:
> and all that is within me, bless his holy name."

"Bless" (KJV, NRSV, NJB) or "praise" (NIV) is *bārak*, which we examined in chapter 8, meaning "bless, praise, salute," here, "to declare God the origin of power for success, prosperity, fertility," that is, to "praise God."[1] When Aaron the high priest blessed the people, he lifted his hands toward them as an act of conferring a blessing (Leviticus 9:22). When Jesus blessed his disciples at his ascension, he lifted his hands toward them (Luke 24:50). When we bless God, we often extend our hands to him in prayer and worship, following the pattern of both the Old Testament saints and the early church.[2]

But this blessing was no mere gesture. The psalmist prays with his whole heart; he pours out his heart before God in worship. "Within me" (KJV, NRSV), "inmost being" (NIV), "depths of my being" (NJB) is *qereb*, "midst, among, inner part," denoting the internal. It is

---

[1] John N. Oswalt, *bārak*, TWOT #285; Holladay 49-50.
[2] For all the scripture references in the Bible on lifting hands, see my article, "Lifting Hands in Worship," *Paraclete*, Winter 1986, pp. 4-8. www.joyfulheart.com/scholar/hands.htm

often used as a parallel to "heart" and "soul."[3] He blesses Yahweh's "holy name," that is his holy person, his sacred being.

The psalmist calls upon his soul, himself (*nephesh*), to bless God. Sometimes our body seems tired, our spirit dull, our attitude "bummed out," depressed. Sometimes we have to tell ourselves to praise. We don't praise because we feel like it, but because God is worthy. Usually, after we've offered praise for awhile, our spirit gets in tune with God's Spirit and we begin to *feel* like worshipping. By our will we command ourselves to worship.

Forget Not All His Benefits (103:2-5)

"Praise the LORD, O my soul,
and forget not all his benefits...." (103:2)

Now David begins to enumerate all the benefits[4] that the Lord brings to us:

"[3]... who **forgives** all your sins
and **heals** all your diseases,
[4]who **redeems** your life[5] from the pit
and **crowns** you with love and compassion,
[5]who **satisfies** your desires with good things
so that your youth is renewed like the eagle's." (103:3-5)

A look at the verbs in this list tells the story, suggesting themes that are developed throughout the Bible:

- Forgiveness and pardon[6] from sin – spiritual
- Healing[7] and restoration from sickness[8] – physical
- Deliverance or redemption[9] from the grave[10]– physical

---

[3] Leonard J. Coppes, *qrb*, TWOT #2066a.

[4] "Benefits" is *gemûl*, "recompense, reward, benefit" (Jack P. Lewis, *gāmal*, TWOT #360a).

[5] "Life" is *hay*, used in the plural as a noun, "life," from *hāyā*, "to live, have life" (BDB 1092),

[6] "Forgives" is *sālah*, "forgive, pardon," always used of God's offer of pardon and forgiveness to the sinner, never of people forgiving each other (Walter C. Kaiser, *sālah*, TWOT #1505).

[7] "Heals" is *rāpā'*, "heal, make healthful." It is used a number of places in the Old Testament including Isaiah 53:5 ("with his stripes we are healed") and Exodus 15:26 ("I am the LORD who heals you") (William White, *rāpā'*, TWOT #2196). The basic idea of the word is physical healing, but it is also occasionally used in figurative sense, depending upon the context (1 Kings 18:30; 2 Kings 2:22).

[8] "Diseases" is *tahalu'îm*, used of physical ailments of one kind or another (Edwin Yamauchi, *hālā'*, TWOT #648a).

[9] "Redeems" is *gā'al*, which we've seen a number of times before, "redeem, ransom, do the part of a kinsman" to rescue or help a relative who is in need (R. Laird Harris, *gā'al*, TWOT #300).

[10] "Pit" (NIV, NRSV), "destruction" (KJV) is *shahat*, "pit, destruction, grave, corruption." There is a dispute about the derivation of *shahat*, either from *shûah* "dig a pit" or perhaps "sink down" or from *shāhat* "to go

- God's love[11] and compassion[12] as a garland on the head – physical, spiritual, emotional
- Sustenance[13] for our bodies[14] – physical

The result is:

> "... so that your youth is renewed like the eagle's." (103:5b)

The renewal[15] to one's youthful state[16] is compared to that of an eagle. References to a renewing of youth here and in Isaiah 40:31 may stem from the fact of the eagle's longevity or perhaps its fresh appearance in new plumage following moulting.[17] Kidner notes that verse 5b

> "... is not implying (as RSV's apostrophe suggests and as some ancient commentators believed) that eagles have the power of self-renewal; only that God renews us to be 'young and lusty as an eagle' (*Prayer Book Version*, 1662) – the very picture of buoyant, tireless strength which Isaiah 40:30-31 takes up."[18]

You've tasted of God's forgiveness, his healing when you've been sick, rescue from life-threatening experiences. You've felt his love, sensed his compassion, found that he supplies your physical needs. All these, the psalmist affirms, are the benefits that Yahweh bestows on us, and for all these we bless him.

The God of Righteousness and Justice (103:6)

He goes on to talk about Yahweh's moral standard of rightness and truth that stand out like a beacon of light against the backdrop of man's sleazy compromises and equivocations.

---

to ruin." The translation "grave" or "decay of the grave" fits very well in most of the passages (R. Laird Harris, *shūah*, TWOT #2343, 1c).

[11] "Love" (NIV), "lovingkindness" (KJV), "steadfast love" (NRSV) is *ḥesed*, which we've seen several times before. In our passage it appears in verse 4b, 11b, and 17b.

[12] "Compassion" (NIV), "mercy" (NRSV), "tender mercies" (KJV) is *raḥămîm*, from *reḥem/raḥam*, "womb" as the seat of one's emotions (Leonard J. Coppes, *rāḥam*, TWOT #2146b).

[13] "Satisfies" is *śābēaʿ*, basically "to be satisfied by nourishment" (Bruce K. Waltke, *śābēaʿ*, TWOT #2231).

[14] "Mouth" (KJV), "desires" (NIV), "as long as you live" (NRSV) is uncertain. The Masoretic Hebrew text reads *ʿedyēk*, "your ornament" which is taken to mean "your mouth" by the KJV. The NRSV has emended this to *ʿôdekā*, "your continuing," which they translate "as long as you live" (Kidner, *Psalms 73-150*, p. 365, footnote 1).

[15] "Renewed" is *ḥādash*, "renew, repair, rebuild" (Carl Philip Weber, *ḥādash*, TWOT #613).

[16] "Youth" is *neʿûrîm*, "youth, early life ... with a stress on the early, immature but vigorous, trainable stage of life." (Milton C. Fisher, *nʿr*, TWOT #1389d).

[17] Milton C. Fisher, *nesher*, TWOT #1437.

[18] Kidner, *Psalms 73-150*, p. 365.

"The LORD works righteousness
and justice for all the oppressed." (103:6)

If you and I are ever placed in positions of power, we dare not take advantage of the poor, for our God will be working against us. He is the one who stands up for and defends the cause of the poor, the fatherless, the prisoner, the foreigner in our midst (Deuteronomy 24:14-15; Psalm 72:4, 12; 109:31; 146:7; Proverbs 22:22-23; Isaiah 58:6-7; Jeremiah 7:6; Ezekiel 22:7). Our God is righteous and just and demands the same of his people.

The God Who Revealed Himself to Israel in the Exodus (103:7)

"He made known his ways to Moses,
his deeds to the people of Israel." (103:7)

What we know about God is not merely deduced from nature (though we can learn something about God from his creation, Romans 1:19-20; Psalm 19:1-4). The Judeo-Christian faith is a revealed faith, God speaking to and through men his truth as well as demonstrating his faithfulness in his actions.

The Gracious and Merciful God (103:8-9)

The next verses encourage us when we struggle with sin and are based on God's revelation to Moses and the Israelites in the wilderness.:

"[8]The LORD is compassionate and gracious,
slow to anger, abounding in love.
[9]He will not always accuse,
nor will he harbor his anger forever...." (103:8-9)

The "God of the Old Testament" is sometimes caricatured by unbelievers as an angry, spiteful, unforgiving God, but that is the opposite of how he actually revealed himself to his people. The definitive revelation of God's nature is found at the second giving of the Ten Commandments on Mount Sinai in Exodus, when Yahweh reveals himself to Moses with the words:

"The LORD, the LORD, the compassionate and gracious God, slow to anger, abounding in love and faithfulness, maintaining love to thousands, and forgiving wickedness, rebellion and sin. Yet he does not leave the guilty unpunished; he punishes the children and their children for the sin of the fathers to the third and fourth generation." (Exodus 34:6-7)[19]

---

[19] You can find a detailed exposition of this passage in my study on *The Names and Titles of God* (JesusWalk Publications, 1010), chapter 10, "The God of All Grace."

This passage is referred to as a summary of God's character often in both the Psalms (86:15; 103:8; 111:4; 112:4; 116:5; and 145:8) and the rest of the Old Testament (Joel 2:13; Jonah 4:2; Nahum 1:7; 2 Chronicles 30:9).

Throughout the Old and New Testaments, God is known as the merciful and compassionate God. "Compassionate" is *raḥûm*, from *reḥem/raḥam*, "womb" as the seat of one's emotions.[20] "Gracious" is *ḥannûn*, "gracious," from *ḥānan*, which depicts "a heartfelt response by someone who has something to give to someone who has a need."[21] Aren't you glad that love lies at the basic character and value system of our God?

The God Who Forgives Us Completely (103:10-13)

Now come some of the most refreshing words to the repentant sinner that one can imagine:

> "[10]He does not treat us as our sins[22] deserve
> or repay us according to our iniquities.[23]
> [11]For as high as the heavens are above the earth,
> so great is his love for those who fear him;
> [12]as far as the east is from the west,
> so far has he removed our transgressions from us." (103:10-12)

David employs two similes to illustrate the completeness of God's forgiveness:

- Height – "for as high as the heavens are above the earth...."
- Distance – "as far as the east is from the west...."

It's interesting how the graphic nature of these comparisons can help us grasp the abstract and take hold of it!

The Lord Has Compassion on Us as Children (103:13-14)

The psalmist's next simile is one of a father and his children:

> "[13]As a father has compassion on his children,
> so the LORD has compassion on those who fear him;
> [14]for he knows how we are formed,
> he remembers that we are dust." (103:13-14)

---

[20] Leonard J. Coppes, *rāḥam*, TWOT #2146c.

[21] *Ḥānan* is cognate with Akkadian *enēnu, hanānu* "to grant a favor," Ugaritic *ḥnn* "to be gracious, to favor" (Edwin Yamauchi, *ḥānan*, TWOT #694d).

[22] *Ḥēṭ'*, "sin ... the failure to hit a mark, a turning away from obedience, a lack of wholeness or of acceptance before God" (G. Herbert Livingston, *ḥāṭā'*, TWOT #638a).

[23] *'Āwōn*, "infraction, crooked behavior, perversion, iniquity, etc." (Carl Schultz, *'āwā*, TWOT #1577a).

"Has compassion" (NIV), "pitieth" (KJV) is *rāḥam*, "love deeply, have mercy, be compassionate," formed from *reḥem*, "womb," thought of as the seat of the emotions, the verb form of the adjective we saw in verse 4b above.

God has deep, heartfelt compassion because he is our Father as well as our Creator, who formed us from "the dust of the ground" (Genesis 2:7). We don't have value based on the mineral and biological content of our bodies. We have value because the Lord breathed his own breath into us, gave us life, and values us as his children, created in his own image.

The Transitory and the Eternal (103:15-18)

Now David contrasts man's tenuous, transitory existence to eternity:

> "15As for man, his days are like grass,
> he flourishes like a flower of the field;
> 16the wind blows over it and it is gone,
> and its place remembers it no more.
>
> 17But from everlasting to everlasting[24]
> the LORD's love is with those who fear him,
> and his righteousness with their children's children –
> 18with those who keep his covenant
> and remember to obey his precepts." (103:15-18)

Our time-bounded life may define us – unless we can see beyond this life to the never-ending nature of God's love for us. His love lasts beyond the grave and so do we. Yes, love is the chief of his "benefits" for which we praise him.

The Lord Is King over All (103:19)

Again and again in the Psalms we see an affirmation that Yahweh reigns! He is a "great King" above all gods (Psalm 95:3) and over all the earth (Psalm 47:2; 48:2).

> "The LORD has established his throne in heaven,
> and his kingdom rules over all." (103:19)

Jesus' proclamation that the Kingdom of God is "at hand" in his own person (Matthew 3:2; 4:17; 10:7; Luke 21:31; 17:21) follows this same theme.

Let Angels, Creation, and My Own Soul Bless the Lord (103:20-22)

The King is served by angels, heavenly hosts (armies), and servants of all kinds. They and all his works are to offer him praise.

---

[24] "Everlasting to everlasting" uses the term *'ôlām*, a word to indicate indefinite continuance into the very distant future (Allan A. MacRae, *'lm*, TWOT #1631a).

"[20]Praise the LORD, you his angels,
you mighty ones who do his bidding,
who obey his word.
[21]Praise the LORD, all his heavenly hosts,
you his servants who do his will.
[22]Praise the LORD, all his works
everywhere in his dominion."[25] (103:20-22)

All creation praises Yahweh the revealed God, the compassionate God, the Creator, and the King. The psalmist ends where he began – with his own need to praise. And so he calls his own soul – whether he feels like praising or not – to join with the chorus of heaven and earth in fulsome praise:

"Praise the LORD, O my soul." (103:22)

Q1. (Psalm 103) Which one or two aspects of God's character mentioned in this Psalm stand out to you? Why do you think the Exodus was so foundational in Israel's understanding of God? According to Psalm 103:10-12, what are the limits to God's forgiveness? http://www.joyfulheart.com/forums/index.php?showtopic=689

Psalm 145 – I Exalt You, My God the King

Our next psalm that extols God's character is also attributed to David and is titled: "a psalm of praise." In its themes it has some similarities with Psalm 103, but it is a completely different style – more didactic rather than personal.

An Acrostic Psalm

Psalm 145 is one of nine psalms (9, 10, 25, 34, 37, 111, 112, 119, 145) which are structured as an acrostic, with each verse or section beginning with a successive letter of the Hebrew alphabet. As we have observed, the intricacy of patterns in the psalms is considered part of their poetic beauty, so adding the level of complexity presented by an acrostic contributes

---

[25] "Dominion" is *memshālā*, "rule, realm, dominion, sovereignty" (Robert D. Culver, *māshal*, TWOT #1259c).

another level of aesthetic pleasure to those who used this psalm in their worship.[26] Thus verse 1 begins with a word beginning with Aleph, the first letter of the Hebrew alphabet, verse 2 begins with Beth, and so on.[27]

Beyond the acrostic structure, the psalm consists of a series of alternating calls to praise followed by grounds for praise.[28] We won't spend as much time on the details of this psalm, just enjoy it for how it extols Yahweh's nature and character.

I Extol You, My King (145:1-2)

David begins by extolling God:

"[1]I will **exalt** you, my God the King;
I will **praise** your name for ever and ever.
[2]Every day I will praise you
and **extol** your name for ever and ever." (145:1-2)

Each of these key verbs we've met before – exalt,[29] praise/bless,[30] and extol.[31] Praise is on the psalmist's lips.

Your Greatness Is Beyond Reckoning (145:3-7)

Next he meditates on how one generation will tell another of Yahweh's greatness and mighty works. He is probably thinking especially of the amazing events of the Exodus – one mighty miracle after another.

"[3]**Great** is the LORD and most worthy of praise;
his **greatness** no one can fathom.
[4]One generation will commend your **works** to another;
they will tell of your **mighty acts**.
[5]They will speak of the **glorious splendor**[32] of your **majesty**,[33]

---

[26] "The versatility of the psalmist is obvious. He took the acrostic pattern in his artistic stride and found it no obstacle to a coherent development of his message" (Allen, *Psalms 101-150*, p. 296).

[27] In the Hebrew text the letter "N" (nun) is missing, but can be found in the Dead Sea Scrolls (11QPs[a]) as well as early translations: the Septuagint, Syriac, and Vulgate. It is missing in the KJV, but included in the NKJV footnote and in most modern translations as part of verse 13b or 14a. See Allen, *Psalms 101-150*, p. 294, note 13b.

[28] Allen, *Psalms 101-150*, p. 295, cites Gunkel, *Die Psalmen*, p. 610.

[29] "Exalt" (NIV), "extol" (NRSV, KJV) is *rûm*, "to be high," here symbolic of positive notions of glory and exaltation (Andrew Bowling, *rûm*, TWOT #213).

[30] "Praise" (NIV), "bless" (NRSV, KJV) in 1b and 2a is *bārak*, "to bless," which we also saw in Psalm 103:1 at the beginning of this chapter.

[31] "Extol" (NIV), "praise" (KJV, NRSV) in 2b is *hālal*, "praise, boast," which we saw in chapter 4.

[32] "Splendor" (NIV) in verse 5a is *hādār*, "ornament, splendor, honor," which we saw in chapter 8 above, "splendor of his holiness" or "holy array." Most frequently this word is applied either to the king and his

and I will meditate[34] on your **wonderful works**.[35]
[6]They will tell of the power of your **awesome works**,[36]
and I will proclaim your **great deeds**.
[7]They will celebrate your **abundant goodness**[37]
and joyfully sing of your **righteousness**.[38]" (145:3-7)

How do we pass on our faith to the next generation? Partly through the stories we tell of God's faithfulness, both in our lives and in the history of God's people. If we keep our Christian experience to ourselves, we may well cripple the transmission of our faith to our children.

The Lord is Gracious and Compassionate (145:8-9)

As David rehearses the character of Yahweh, he repeats the characteristic description that we saw in Psalm 103:8 above and many other places in the Old Testament:

"[8]The LORD is gracious and compassionate,
slow to anger and rich in love.
[9]The LORD is good to all;
he has compassion on all he has made." (145:8-9)

All He Has Made – Yahweh the Creator (145:9b, 13b, 17b)

Notice the phrase "all he has made" in 9b. The phrase is repeated three times in Psalm 145, each with a different characteristic of God's grace.

- "He has compassion (*raḥămîm*) on **all he has made**" (9b)

---

royal majesty or to God himself. It is not only an endowment for royalty, but also an activity worthy of royalty. (Victor P. Hamilton, *hādar*, TWOT #477b).

[33] "Majesty" in verse 5a is *hôd*, which we saw in chapter 1 above in Psalm 8:1. It refers to God's "splendor, majesty, vigor, glory, honor" (Victor P. Hamilton, *hwd*, TWOT #482a).

[34] "Meditate" (NIV, NRSV) in verse 5b is *śîaḥ*, "meditate, muse, commune, speak, complain" The "basic meaning of this verb seems to be 'rehearse,' 'repent,' or 'go over a matter in one's mind.'" (Gary G. Cohen, *śîaḥ*, TWOT #2255). This is a different word than *hāgā*, "meditate, utter, mutter," which we saw in chapter 3 above in Psalm 1:2b.

[35] "Wonderful / wondrous works" in verse 5b is *pālā'*, "be marvelous, wonderful," usually referring to the acts of God beyond human capabilities, either cosmic wonders or historical achievements on behalf of Israel (Victor P. Hamilton, *pālā'*, TWOT #1768).

[36] "Awesome works / deeds" (NIV, NRSV), "terrible acts" (KJV) in verse 6a is a substantive from *yārē'*, "fear, be afraid, revere" (Andrew Bowling, *yārē'*, TWOT #907). We might use the phrase "awe inspiring."

[37] "Goodness" in verse 7a is *ṭûb*, "good things, goodness, fairness, graciousness." Here it refers to God's moral goodness (Andrew Bowling, *ṭôb*, TWOT #793b).

[38] "Righteousness" or "saving justice" (NJB) in verse 7b is *ṣĕdāqā*, "justice, righteousness," which we've seen many times (Harold G. Stigers, *ṣādēq*, TWOT #1879b).

- "The LORD is ... loving toward **all he has made**"[39] (13b)
- "The LORD is ... loving (*ḥāsîd*[40]) toward **all he has made**" (17b)

The phrase "all he has made" is the noun *ma'ăseh*, "deed, act, workmanship ... that which is done or made." This noun is derived from the verb *'āśā*, "do, fashion, accomplish," often used in the creation accounts.[41]

The Glory of Yahweh's Kingdom (145:10-13a)

The same word, "All you have made" (*ma'ăseh*) is picked up in verse 10 as well. This passage praises the Kingdom of God. Note how many times kingdom and dominion occur:

"¹⁰All you have made will praise you, O LORD;
your saints will extol you.
¹¹They will tell of the glory of your kingdom
and speak of your might,
¹²so that all men may know of your mighty acts
and the glorious splendor of your kingdom.
¹³Your kingdom is an everlasting kingdom,
and your dominion endures through all generations." (145:10-13)

Yahweh is King over an everlasting kingdom. And when Messiah Jesus began his ministry, he proclaimed the coming of just this Kingdom of God.

The Faithful Character of Our God (145:13b-16)

The next group of verses describe Yahweh's graciousness and benevolence. If you were to consider this in the same way as "all his benefits" in Psalm 103:2, you would have quite a list. Behold the character of our God:

"¹³ᵇThe LORD is **faithful** to all his promises
and **loving** toward all he has made.
¹⁴The LORD **upholds** all those who fall
and **lifts up** all who are bowed down.
¹⁵The eyes of all look to you,
and you **give them their food** at the proper time.
¹⁶You **open your hand**
and **satisfy** the desires of every living thing.

---

[39] "One manuscript of the Masoretic text, Dead Sea scrolls, and Syriac (see also Septuagint). Most manuscripts of the Masoretic text do not have the last two lines of verse 13" (NIV footnote).

[40] *Ḥāsîd*, an adjective from the same root as *ḥesed*, "love, lovingkindness" (R. Laird Harris, *ḥsd*, TWOT #698b). The Septuagint translates it as *hosios*, "holy," both in verse 13b and 17b.

[41] Thomas E. McComiskey, *'āśā*, TWOT #1708a.

> [17]The LORD is **righteous** in all his ways
> and **loving** toward all he has made.
> [18]The LORD is **near** to all who call on him,
> to all who call on him in truth.
> [19]He **fulfills the desires** of those who fear him;
> he **hears their cry and saves** them.
> [20]The LORD **watches over** all who love him,
> but all the wicked he **will destroy**. (145:13b-20)

We've seen nearly all these verbs and adjectives scattered throughout the psalms we've explored so far. Here they are all together in a paean of praise of God's character.

The Lord Is Near (145:18-20)

I especially like the promise in verses 18-20:

> "The LORD is **near** to all who call on him,
> to all who call on him in truth.
> He fulfills the desires of those who fear him;
> he hears their cry and **saves** them.
> The LORD **watches over** all who love him,
> but all the wicked he will destroy." (145:18-20)

Do you feel far away from God? Here is a promise for you. The operative words are:

- **"Near"** or "nigh," the adjective *qārōb*, from the verb *qārab*, "come near, approach ... coming into the most near and intimate proximity...." *Qārōb* is used like a noun describing one who is near – a kinsman or neighbor.[42]
- **"Saves"** is *yāsha'*, "save, deliver, give victory, help," the root from which the names Joshua and Jesus are derived.

Call on him in full sincerity and surrender (that is, "in truth") and he promises to be near you and deliver you from whatever trouble you find yourself in. He also promises in verse 20a to "watch over" (NIV, NRSV), "guard" (NJB) or "preserve" (KJV) you. The verb is *shāmar*, "keep, guard," with the root meaning, "to exercise great care over."[43] We examined this word in chapter 6 in Psalm 121:3-8

---

[42] Leonard J. Coppes, *qārab*, TWOT #2065d.
[43] *Shāmar*, TWOT #2414.

My Mouth Will Speak in Praise of the Lord (145:21)

The psalm ends in praise (*tehillâ*[44]) as it began – personally ("my mouth") and universally ("every creature"). It is a declaration of praise and a call for "every creature" (NIV) or "all flesh" (literally, KJV, NRSV) to bless (*bārak*) Yahweh's name forever.

"**My mouth** will speak in **praise** of the LORD.
Let **every creature praise** his holy name
for ever and ever." (145:21)

This call is fulfilled in the Book of Revelation where we read:

"Day and night they never stop saying:

'Holy, holy, holy
is the Lord God Almighty,
who was, and is, and is to come.'

Whenever the living creatures give glory, honor and thanks to him who sits on the throne and who lives for ever." (Revelation 4:8-9)

Q2. (Psalm 145) Which aspects of God's character mentioned in Psalm 145 stand out to you in particular? Why is it important for "every creature," every human being, to praise him? What are you doing to help that happen?
http://www.joyfulheart.com/forums/index.php?showtopic=690

---

[44] *Tehillâ*, "praise, praiseworthy deeds," is derived from *hālal*, which we first encountered in chapter 4 and Psalm 150 (Leonard J. Coppes, *hālal*, TWOT #500c)

Psalm 117 – The Faithfulness of the Lord Endures Forever

The final psalm to consider in this chapter is Psalm 117, the shortest psalm in the Psalter – all of two verses. There is no title or author indicated, just a call to praise from "all nations" and then the reason for that praise:

"¹Praise (*hālal*) the LORD, all you nations;
extol (*shābah*) him, all you peoples.
²For great is his love toward us,
and the faithfulness of the LORD endures forever.
Praise (*hālal*) the LORD." (117:1-2)

I'm struck, as I've studied the Psalms, how many times the "nations" or "Gentiles" are called upon to praise Yahweh. Faith in him is not just a national religion of Israel – or of Christians. It is a call for all the peoples of the earth to know and praise him as Yahweh, I AM THAT I AM, the everlasting God! As I mentioned in a previous chapter, full praise to God *requires* evangelism, telling all nations – and our neighbors – of the greatness of our God.

In verse 1b, "extol" (NIV, NRSV) or "praise" (KJV) is a relatively rare praise word, *shābah*, meaning "praise, glorify," here in the Hithpael stem with a reflexive connotation, "glory in." In most cases it is used to praise God for his mighty acts and deeds (Psalms 63:3; 106:47; 117:1; 145:4; 147:12; and 1 Chronicles 16:35).[45]

The second verse contains two aspects of God's character which are given as the reason for our praise:

* The greatness of his **love and mercy** (*ḥesed*) toward us, and
* The everlasting nature of his **faithfulness and truth** (*'ĕmet*).

Of course, we've seen these character anchors lauded in other psalms, but as we revisit them in this short psalm don't pass them over lightly. His love and faithfulness are the bedrock of our faith: (1) God is love. (2) God can be trusted. Praise God!

Notice the adjectival expressions that qualify these words: "great" and "everlasting" – bigger than we can imagine and for as long as we need them and longer still. I can't help but think of a couple of lines from Jeremiah's Lamentations that lie at the root of some of the great hymns of the Church:

---

[45] *Shābah*, Holladay, p. 358a. "Praise, commend" (Gary G. Cohen, *shābah*, TWOT #2313).

"[22]Because of the LORD's **great love** we are not consumed,
for his **compassions** never fail.
[23]They are new every morning;
great is your faithfulness.
[24]I say to myself, "The LORD is my portion;
therefore I will wait for him.'" (Lamentations 3:22-24)

If you've been tracking with the Hebrew words used in the psalms we've studied, you'll observe that we've seen them again and again in psalm after psalm.

- Steadfast, enduring, constant, lovingkindness, merciful love (*ḥesed*)
- Compassion, tender mercy, deep, tender love (*raḥămîm*, derived from *reḥem*, "womb," as the seat of the emotions)[46]
- Steadfastness, faithfulness, fidelity, dependability (*'emûnâ*, closely related to *'ĕmet* that appears in our psalm).[47]

Q3. (Psalm 117 and Lamentations 3:22-23). Why are love and trustworthiness so important as the bedrock of the Old Testament faith? What kinds of terms does the New Testament use to talk about these characteristics? Can you think of any New Testament verses that speak of these themes?
http://www.joyfulheart.com/forums/index.php?showtopic=691

Our God is so good! How can we ever doubt him? How can we neglect to praise him for the qualities of his core being that allow all us poor, sinful creatures to relate to him – what's more, to be loved and desired by such a majestic God? We are blessed, brothers and sisters. We are blessed beyond all measure to be loved by such a God.

As we learn from the Psalms to vocalize with our own mouths, to praise the character of our holy God, we'll be fitted both to endure the struggles of this life and to enjoy the glories of the next.

---

[46] Leonard J. Coppes, *rāḥam*, TWOT #2146b.
[47] Jack B. Scott, *'āman*, TWOT #116e.

> Exercise. For one of the psalms in this lesson – or another psalm with a similar theme – do one of the suggested exercises to help you experience the Psalms in Appendix 1. These include such things as praying a psalm, meditating, reading to a shut-in, paraphrasing, writing your own psalm, singing, preparing a liturgy, and memorizing. Then report to the forum what the exercise meant to you personally or share what you've written with others.
>
> http://www.joyfulheart.com/forums/index.php?showtopic=692

Prayer

Father, let my soul, my mouth give praise to you. Let my words tell the stories of your greatness to my children and my grandchildren. Let my deeds reflect your justice and righteousness. Let my heart soak in your love and compassion and dependability. Let me be like You, like Jesus. In His holy name, I pray. Amen.

Songs

- **"Before the Lord We Bow,"** by Francis Scott Key (1832), music: "Darwall's 148th," by John Darwall (1770). Psalm 145:1.
- **"Behold, Bless Ye the Lord,"** words and music by Bob Probert (© 1979, Maranatha! Music), may be sung as a two-part round. Psalm 103:20-22.
- **"Bless His Holy Name,"** words and music by Andrae Crouch (© 1973, Lexicon Music, Inc.). Psalm 103:1.
- **"Bless the Lord, Oh My Soul,"** author unknown. (arrangement © 1972, Youth With a Mission), Psalm 103:1-3.
- **"God My King, Thy Might Confessing,"** words: Richard Mant (1824), music: "Stuttgart," by Christian F. Witt (1715). Psalm 145:1.
- **"God of Our Life,"** words: Hugh T. Kerr (1916), music: "Sandon," by Charles H. Purday (1857). Lamentations 3:21-22.
- **"Great Is Thy Faithfulness,"** words by Thomas O. Chisholm (1923), music by William M. Runyan (1923). Lamentations 3:21-22.
- **"I Will Bless Thee, O Lord,"** words and music by Esther Watanabe (© 1970, Esther Watanabe). Psalm 103:1.
- **"I Will Sing of the Mercies of the Lord Forever,"** words and music by J. H. Fillmore (public domain). Psalm 89:1
- **"O Bless the Lord, My Soul,"** words: James Montgomery (1819), music: "St. Thomas" by Aaron Williams (1770). Psalm 103:1

- **O Bless the Lord, My Soul,"** words: Isaac Watts (1819), music: "St. Michael" by Louis Bourgeois (1551), adapted by William Crotch (1836). Psalm 103.
- **"O Lord, Thou Art My God and King,"** words: *The Psalter* (1912), music: "Duke Street," attributed to John Hatton (1793). Psalm 145:1.
- **"O Magnify the Lord with Me!"** (I Will Bless the Lord at All Times), unknown author and composer. Psalms 34:1.
- **"O My Soul, Bless God the Father,"** words: United Presbyterian *Book of Psalms* (1871), music, "Stuttgart," by Christian F. Witt (1715), adapted by Henry J. Gauntlett (1805-1876). Psalm 103.
- **"Praise, My Soul, the King of Heaven,"** words by Henry F. Lyte (1834), music: "Lauda Anima," by John Goss (1869). Psalm 103:1.
- **"Psalm 145:1-7,"** words and music by M. Warrington (© 1972, Youth With a Mission, Inc.). Psalm 145:1-7.
- **"Savior, Again to Thy Dear Name We Raise,"** words: John Ellerton (1886), music: "Ellers," by Edward J. Hopkins (1869). Psalm 145:1.
- **"The Steadfast Love"** (of the Lord never ceases)," words and music by Edith McNeill (1974, 1975, Celebration). Lamentations 3:21-22.
- **"The Tender Love a Father Has,"** words: *The Psalter* (1912), music: "Avondale," Charles H. Gabriel (1856-1932). Psalm 103:13.
- **"We Will Exalt You, Our God the King,"** words and music by Mitch Cervinka (1998). Psalm 145:1
- **"Ye Servants of God"** (your Master proclaim), words: Charles Wesley (1744), music, "Lyons," attributed to Johann M. Haydn (1737-1806). Psalm 103:21.

10. Looking Forward to the Messiah (Psalms 2, 110, 22)

An expectancy of God's deliverance through the coming Messiah is interwoven through a number of psalms, in fact, the Psalms is the Old Testament book most quoted in the New Testament. In many cases these passages find their ultimate fulfillment in Christ Jesus our Savior.[1]

Messianic Psalms and the Nature of Prophecy

Before we begin, however, we need to define what we mean by a "Messianic Psalm." There are two alternatives:

1. **Narrow sense**. This view sees a messianic psalm as prophetic and having no direct message of significance to the Old Testament period; they only predict the coming Messiah.
2. **General sense**. Psalms that anticipate the Messiah but also have meaning in a contemporary context of the writer.[2]

I think I find myself finding common ground with both definitions. I believe that some psalms *are* prophetic of the Messiah Jesus. Given under

Psalm 22 speaks rather explicitly of the crucifixion. Diego Velázquez (Spanish painter, 1599-1660) "Christ Crucified / Cristo Crucificado" (1632), 248x169 cm, Oli sobre tela, Museo del Prado (Madrid).

---

[1] See Appendix 4. "New Testament Quotations from the Psalms."

[2] Longman, *How to Read the Psalms,* pp. 67-68. But also see the discussion by Victor P. Hamilton (*māshah,* TWOT #1255c) where he contends that some Old Testament passages cannot be understood as referring to merely some contemporary figure.

the inspiration of the Spirit, they sometimes speak about concepts and persons beyond the author's knowledge and understanding.

In my study of prophecy,[3] I conclude that true prophets – Old Testament, New Testament, or today – don't necessarily understand all that they are saying to the degree that they could expound on their prophecies and interpret them accurately in advance. They may not even know that they are speaking in prophecy. They are given the words from the Holy Spirit and speak or write those words. The fulfillment and interpretation are usually far beyond them, to be revealed by God in his own good time.

In chapter 7 we looked at Psalm 16 where David speaks prophetically (I believe) of Jesus:

> "You will not abandon me to the grave,
> nor will you let your Holy One see decay." (Psalm 16:10)

David probably spoke of his confidence that in a particular instance God would deliver him rather than letting him be killed by his enemies. But as the apostles boldly declared, his words find their ultimate fulfillment in the resurrection of Jesus Christ from the dead (Acts 2:25-28; 13:35).

In this chapter we'll consider three additional psalms which, to Christians, clearly point to Christ. They formed part of the core of the early church's apologetic to Judaism that ultimately won tens of thousands of Jews to the Christian faith in the first century.

Psalm 2 – You Are My Son, Today I Have Begotten You

Psalm 2 has no author given nor title to explain its context or use, though it was doubtless used in ancient Judaism to refer to the Davidic king, perhaps at the enthronement of a new king. However, the New Testament reads it as speaking far beyond any earthly monarch. The relationship to the Messiah and Yahweh described in this psalm is far closer than could be said of any Davidic king prior to Christ.

The Nations Conspire Against Yahweh and His Messiah (2:1-6)

> "[1]Why do the nations conspire
> and the peoples plot in vain?
> [2]The kings of the earth take their stand
> and the rulers gather together
> against the LORD

---

[3] See my articles, "Is Preaching Prophecy?", "The Purpose of Prophecy Today," and "Beginning to Prophesy," from *The Holy Spirit as the Agent of Renewal*, unpublished doctoral dissertation, Fuller Theological Seminary (1984). www.joyfulheart.com/scholar/

and against his Anointed One.
[3]'Let us break their chains,' they say,
'and throw off their fetters.'

[4]The One enthroned in heaven laughs;
the Lord scoffs at them.
[5]Then he rebukes them in his anger
and terrifies them in his wrath, saying,
[6]'I have installed my King
on Zion, my holy hill.'" (2:1-6)

The psalmist is speaking about an international conspiracy against Yahweh and his King. While its first readers saw this in terms of the nations that surrounded Israel and the descendent of David who ruled in Jerusalem (until 587 BC), the passage is framed with a cosmic dimension. In Revelation this spiritual rebellion against God and his Messiah is couched in terms of the woman and her male child (Revelation 12:1-6), the battle between the archangel Michael and the dragon (Revelation 12:7-17), the Antichrist and the False Prophet (Revelation 13), and the Whore of Babylon (Revelation 17). It is a spiritual battle fought in heavenly places.

The term "Anointed One" (NIV) or "anointed" (KJV, NRSV) is *māshīah*, from the verb *māshah*, "to anoint, spread a liquid."[4] Anointing was used in a ritual sense to apply oil to set apart to God religious items (Exodus 40:9-11) and especially people to divine service – priests (Exodus 29:7; Leviticus 21:10; Numbers 35:25), kings (1 Samuel 10:1; 15:17; 16:13; 2 Samuel 12:7; Psalm 18:50), and finally Yahweh's ultimate King, the Messiah (Isaiah 61:1; Daniel 9:24-26).

The Apostle Peter preached that Psalm 2:1-2 are prophetic of the conspiracy of Herod and Pontius Pilate that resulted in Christ's crucifixion (Acts 4:25-26). The "nations" refer to the Gentiles (the Romans), and "kings of the earth" and "rulers" to Herod, Pontius Pilate, and the Sanhedrin.

You Are My Son (2:7-8)

The psalmist may have initially thought he was speaking of the Davidic king as a "son" in the figurative sense portrayed in the Davidic Covenant:

"I will be his father, and he will be my son.[5] When he does wrong, I will punish him with the rod of men, with floggings inflicted by men." (2 Samuel 7:14-15)

---

[4] Victor P. Hamilton, *māshah*, TWOT #1255c.
[5] Israel is referred to as "my son" in Exodus 4:22.

But Psalm 2:7-9 goes far beyond this sense. Verse 7 speaks of an especially close relationship between the Father and Son, Yahweh and his Messiah, that is difficult to interpret as speaking of a merely human king. Verse 8 seems to speak of a king that rules over the whole earth, not just the nations that surround Israel itself:

"7I will proclaim the decree of the LORD:
He said to me, 'You are my Son;
today I have become your Father.'
8Ask of me,
and I will make the nations your inheritance,
the ends of the earth your possession.
9You will rule them with an iron scepter;
you will dash them to pieces like pottery." (2:7-9)

God uses this Father-Son terminology when he speaks in a voice from heaven at both Jesus' baptism (Matthew 3:17) and at his Transfiguration (Matthew 17:5): "This is my Son, whom I love; with him I am well pleased."

In John's Gospel, Jesus used this kind of Father-Son metaphor extensively, to such an extent that the Jews believed he was applying it in the sense of claiming to be divine himself (John 8:54; 10:30-33), accused him of blasphemy, and tried to stone him.

The revealed truth of this Father-Son metaphor is so strong and important that feminist attempts in our day to remove the male, "paternalistic" overtones of the metaphor come up short and seriously shortchange our understanding. They typically fall back to Creator-Christ terminology which, though true, gut the important relational elements of the Father-Son metaphor which are clearly part of the relation of God and Christ. This Father-Son metaphor is first clearly revealed in Psalm 2:7.

The phrase "today I have begotten you" (2:7) uses the verb *yālad*, which, when used of females referring to the act of giving birth and when used of males refers to the act of begetting or insemination. Here it may have a figurative sense.[6] In Christian theology, of course, the Father-Son relationship is seen as an especially fitting metaphor to explain the relationship between God and Jesus, not as a literal, physical phenomenon, but as an irreplaceable metaphor which is essential to our understanding of the Godhead as revealed

---

[6] In the Hebrew Hiphil stem *yālad* has a causative sense, "bear, beget." In our verse the word is used in the Qal stem, which may refer figuratively to a relation of love, according to R. Laird Harris, *yālad*, TWOT #867.

by Jesus in the Bible.[7] Verse 7 is quoted as referring to Jesus in Acts 13:33 and Hebrews 1:5 and 5:5.

Today I Have Begotten You (2:7)

This verse:

"You are my Son;
today I have begotten you." (2:7)

is also the source of the "only begotten son" terminology in John's writings (John 1:14, 18; 3:16, 18; 1 John 4:9; 5:1, 18).

The *sense* in which Jesus was begotten has spawned some heresies in church history. In the days leading up to the Council of Nicea in 325 AD, the Gnostic-leaning Alexandrian priest Arius (c. 250/256 – 336 AD) claimed that since Jesus was "begotten," that there was a time that he didn't exist, and that being "begotten" meant that, in a sense, he was *created* by God. The Jehovah's Witnesses have continued this idea that "only begotten" meant that Jesus was created. The Jehovah's Witnesses' New World Translation infamously translates John 1:1 as "the word was *a god*" rather than "the Word *was* God" (all other modern translations). Some liberal theologians, seeking to deny the inherent divinity of Jesus, have suggested that Jesus was an ordinary man who was "begotten" when he received the Holy Spirit at his baptism.

It is impossible to trace all these arguments here, but orthodox Christians have always maintained Christ's essential divinity, as clearly delineated in the Nicene Creed (originally in 325 and finally in 381 AD):

"We believe in ... one Lord Jesus Christ, the only-begotten Son of God, begotten of the Father before all worlds, Light of Light, very God of very God, begotten, not made, being of one substance with the Father...."

The Nicene Creed made clear that Jesus was not some kind of divine human or lesser God, but that his divinity was on a par with that of the Father Himself – "very God of very God," that is, "true God coming from the true God." The idea of "begotten, not made" made clear that this was not an act of creation, but that Jesus had the same essence or "substance" (*hypostatis*) as the Father, he was formed of the same divine "stuff" as the Father – that is, Jesus is fully divine, not some kind of lesser divinity.

I've probably said more than you ever wanted to know about Jesus being "begotten," but since it figures so prominently in our understanding of who Jesus is, I felt that it is important for you to know.

---

[7] See Ralph F. Wilson, *Disciple Lessons from the Faith of Abraham* (JesusWalk Publications, 2004), chapter 3, and *Disciple Lessons from Hebrews* (JesusWalk Publications, 2007), chapter 6.

Kiss the Son (2:10-12)

The psalm concludes:

"¹⁰Therefore, you kings, be wise;
be warned, you rulers of the earth.
¹¹Serve the LORD with fear
and rejoice with trembling.
¹²Kiss the Son, lest he be angry
and you be destroyed in your way,
for his wrath can flare up in a moment.
Blessed are all who take refuge in him." (2:10-12)

Verse 12a has been translated variously "kiss the Son" (KJV, NIV), "kiss his feet" (NRSV, NJB), and "kiss the mighty one" (New English Bible). The Hebrew text (*bar*, "son") seems to be best translated "kiss the Son." The other translations are based on emendations or conjectures of what a "corrupted" text originally said. But whether the translation is "kiss the Son" (as seems called for by the text) or "kiss his feet," the point is that the kings and rulers of the earth need to submit to Yahweh's anointed Son with the kiss of homage *before* he comes with might to put down their rebellion towards him.

Q1. (Psalm 2) What does Psalm 2 teach us about Yahweh's "anointed" king? Why do you think the apostles saw this passage as referring to Jesus the Messiah? What does the passage teach about the importance of submission to Jesus the Christ before it is too late?
http://www.joyfulheart.com/forums/index.php?showtopic=693

Psalm 110 – The Messiah as Priest and King

Psalm 110 is attributed to David and referred to as "a psalm," which probably means an accompanied song.

The Messiah Is Greater than David (110:1)

It is Jesus himself who pointed to this psalm as one that refers to the Messiah:

> "The LORD says to my Lord:
> 'Sit at my right hand
> until I make your enemies
> a footstool for your feet.'" (110:1)

Matthew records:

> "⁴¹While the Pharisees were gathered together, Jesus asked them, ⁴²'What do you think about the Christ ? Whose son is he?'
> 'The son of David,' they replied.
> ⁴³He said to them, "'How is it then that David, speaking by the Spirit, calls him "Lord"? For he says,
> ⁴⁴"The Lord said to my Lord:
> 'Sit at my right hand
> until I put your enemies under your feet.'"
> ⁴⁵If then David calls him "Lord," how can he be his son?' ⁴⁶No one could say a word in reply, and from that day on no one dared to ask him any more questions." (Matthew 22:41-46)

Though the Jews of Jesus' time saw Psalm 110 as Messianic, they saw the Messiah in purely human terms, as a physical descendent of David, and thus inferior to David. Jesus' question, based on his careful understanding of this psalm, revealed the "greater than David" nature of the Messiah.

A Universal Messianic Rule (110:2-3)

Now the psalmist declares that Yahweh will extend the Messiah's kingdom far beyond the boundaries of Israel:

> "²The LORD will extend your mighty scepter from Zion;
> you will rule in the midst of your enemies.
> ³Your troops will be willing
> on your day of battle.
> Arrayed in holy majesty,
> from the womb of the dawn
> you will receive the dew of your youth." (110:2-3)

Messiah's rule will be resisted by his enemies (as in Psalm 2), but will be extended by force with the Messiah at the head of a mighty army (verse 3; see Revelation 19:11-21).

Throughout the Psalms is the image of Yahweh as the Mighty Warrior. Yahweh's Messiah, the one that reigns for him and extends his rule, is the Mighty Warrior *par excellence*!

The Eternal Priest from Melchizedek's Order (110:4)

The Jews of Jesus' day understood Messiah coming as a *conquering king* who would set up Yahweh's kingdom on earth, reviving the glory days of David's rule. What they did *not* understand was the Messiah as a *priest*. Verse 4 presents a cryptic image:

> "The LORD has sworn
> and will not change his mind:
> 'You are a priest forever,
> in the order of Melchizedek.'" (110:4)

Melchizedek was a contemporary of Abraham. He was both king of Jerusalem and priest of the Most High God. Because of his position as a priest of the God that Abraham served, Abraham presented him with one tenth of the spoils of battle (Genesis 14:18-20).

The writer of Hebrews, in an extensive exposition of Psalm 110:4 (Hebrews 5:6-10; 6:20-7:28), clearly sees Melchizedek as a *type* of Christ our High Priest (though not as an actual *appearance* of Christ himself, as some hold).[8]

Psalm 110 combines the roles of king and priest in a way that is unheard of elsewhere in the Old Testament.[9] This King and Priest of Psalm 110 not only rules for Yahweh, he acts as a mediator between man and God to atone for man's sins. Only when we understand Jesus as the Suffering Servant of Isaiah 53, who in himself bore our sins and carried our iniquities, can we understand how Jesus served as a priest to bring us to God. The Apostle Paul put it this way:

> "For there is one God and one mediator between God and men, the man Christ Jesus, who gave himself as a ransom for all men...." (1 Timothy 2:5-6; also Hebrews 8:6; 9:15; and Mark 10:45)

Messiah Will Subdue and Judge the Nations (110:5-7)

Psalm 110 concludes with a poetic prophecy of how the Messiah will exert his rule over all his enemies, fulfilled ultimately at the Battle of Armageddon and the final battle at the end of days spoken of in Revelation:

> "5The Lord is at your right hand;
> he will crush kings on the day of his wrath.

---

[8] I have discussed Melchizedek extensively in my studies on Abraham and the Book of Hebrews

[9] With the possible exception of Joshua the high priest, son of Jehozadak (Zechariah 6:11-13), who may also be a type of the Messiah, "the Branch."

⁶He will judge the nations, heaping up the dead
and crushing the rulers of the whole earth.
⁷He will drink from a brook beside the way;
therefore he will lift up his head." (110:5-7)

Verse 7 concludes the psalm with the Warrior-Messiah pausing to refresh himself at a brook as he is in pursuit of his enemy, and then continuing on, like Gideon at the Jordan, "faint yet pursuing." The final promise, "Therefore he will lift up his head" (7b) looks forward to his final victory over his enemy.

Q2. (Psalm 110) Why do you think that Jesus asked the Pharisees about verse 1, "If then David calls him 'Lord,' how can he be his son?" What point was Jesus making? How does Jesus combine the roles of Warrior-King and Priest in his ministry to us and to this world? How do you reconcile the violence suggested in verses 5-6 with Jesus as "Prince of Peace"?

http://www.joyfulheart.com/forums/index.php?showtopic=694

Psalm 22 – My God, Why Have You Forsaken Me?

Psalm 22 is a remarkable psalm indeed. In the context of the Old Testament, it can be seen as a lament followed by a hymn of praise. But in the context of the New Testament, it must be clearly seen as a psalm pointing again and again to the crucifixion of Christ. Frost went so far as to call this psalm the "Fifth Gospel" account of the crucifixion.[10] Kidner titles it, "The Psalm of the Cross."[11] It is quite clear that Psalm 22 and Isaiah 53 together formed the core of Jesus' and the early church's understanding of the crucifixion.

---

[10] Craigie (*Psalms 1-50*, p. 202) cites Stanley Brice Frost, "Psalm 22: an Exposition," *Canadian Journal of Theology* 8 (1962) 102-115.
[11] Kidner, *Psalms 1-72*, p. 105.

Peter notes that David was a prophet (Acts 2:30-31). Indeed he was filled with the Spirit at his anointing. But did David know what he was saying? I doubt it. When he wrote the first part of the psalm, he probably was expressing his own deep lament in highly figurative terms – figures that were brought to his mind by the Holy Spirit. This side of the cross, however, those figures speak to us strongly of Jesus' crucifixion. Were they intended by David to refer to the cross? No. Were they intended by the Spirit to speak of Jesus' crucifixion. Of that I have no doubt. But I'm getting ahead of myself.

Why Have You Forsaken Me? (22:1-2)

Verse 1 was on Jesus' lips during his crucifixion:

"¹My God, my God, why have you forsaken me?
Why are you so far from saving me,
so far from the words of my groaning?
²O my God, I cry out by day, but you do not answer,
by night, and am not silent." (22:1-2)

Before the Psalms were numbered, a particular psalm would be referred to by its first line. In speaking the first line of Psalm 22, Jesus pointed not to just the first verse, but to the whole psalm.

However, his quoting the first line may be significant as well. Though we are probing here beyond the explicit teaching of scripture, when Jesus was on the cross bearing our sins, he may have felt spiritual separation from the holy God because of our sin he was bearing. He felt alone because he took our sin and guilt upon himself.

Q3. (Psalm 22:1) Why do you think Jesus spoke the words of Psalm 22:1? What was he seeking to express? What was he feeling? How did God answer his plea?
http://www.joyfulheart.com/forums/index.php?showtopic=695

God Is Enthroned on Our Praises (22:3)

A phrase commonly cited by worship leaders comes from the KJV of Psalm 22:3:

"But thou art holy,
O thou that inhabitest the praises of Israel." (KJV)

"Yet you are holy,
enthroned on the praises of Israel." (NRSV)

"Yet you are enthroned as the Holy One;
you are the praise of Israel." (NIV)

The keyword to understand clearly is "inhabitest" (KJV), "enthroned" (NIV, NRSV), "make your home" (NJB). It is the verb *yāshab*, "sit, remain, dwell." The word's meaning is based on the context. In the Qal stem it can mean (1) "to sit on anything, (2) "to remain, stay, linger," (3) "to dwell in a house, city, territory," and (4) of a place, city, or country being inhabited.[12] Could the idea of "inhabit, dwell" be intended here? Yes. But because of the context of the first assertion, "You are holy," I believe *yāshab* refers to Yahweh's splendor and majesty, an idea conveyed by the concept of enthronement better than by that of habitation. God is everywhere; there is nowhere we can go where he is not (Psalm 139:7-10). But from our human perspective, when we worship and praise God we can certainly *sense* his presence much more easily. By our praise, we declare him King, exalt him, and thus "enthrone" him before us.

Comparisons to the Crucifixion (22:6-18)

Rather than try to provide an exposition of the entire psalm, for the purposes of considering the messianic aspects of the psalm, I will focus on the verses that have the greatest correspondence with Jesus' crucifixion. While I have no doubt that the actual events of Jesus' crucifixion took place as recorded in the Gospels, it is probable that the terminology by which they were communicated was influenced by the words of this startling psalm that we are studying:

"But I am a worm and not a man,
scorned by men
and **despised** by the people." (22:6)

"He was **despised**
and **rejected** by men,
a man of sorrows,
and familiar with suffering.
Like one from whom men
hide their faces
he was **despised**,
and we **esteemed him not**."
(Isaiah 53:3)

---

[12] Walter C. Kaiser, *yāshab*, TWOT #922.

"All who see me **mock** me;
they hurl **insults**, shaking their heads:
'He **trusts** in the LORD;
let the LORD rescue him.
Let him deliver him,
since he delights in him.'" (22:7-8)

"Many **bulls** surround me;
strong bulls of Bashan encircle me.
Roaring lions tearing their prey
open their mouths wide against me."
(22:12-13)

"I am **poured out** like water,
and all my bones are out of joint.
My heart has turned to wax;
it has melted away within me." (22:14)

"My strength is dried up
like a potsherd,
and my **tongue sticks**
to the roof of my mouth;
you lay me in the dust of death."
(22:15)

"He will be handed over to the Gentiles. They will **mock** him, **insult** him, spit on him, flog him and kill him." (Luke 18:32-33)

"The people stood watching, and the rulers even sneered at him. They said, 'He saved others; **let him save himself** if he is the Christ of God, the Chosen One.'" (Luke 23:35)

"Indeed **Herod and Pontius Pilate** met together with the Gentiles and the people of Israel in this city to conspire against your holy servant Jesus, whom you anointed." (Acts 4:27)

"Then he said to them, "My soul is **overwhelmed with sorrow** to the point of death.'" (Matthew 26:38a).

"And being in **anguish**, he prayed more earnestly, and his sweat was like drops of blood falling to the ground." (Luke 22:44)

"Later, knowing that all was now completed, and so that the Scripture would be fulfilled, Jesus said, '**I am thirsty.**'" (John 19:28)

"Dogs have surrounded me;
a band of evil men has encircled me,
they have **pierced my hands and my feet**."
(22:16)

"And they **crucified** him." (Mark 15:25)

"They will look on me, the one they have **pierced**, and they will mourn for him as one mourns for an only child, and grieve bitterly for him as one grieves for a firstborn son." (Zechariah 12:10)

"I can count all my bones;
people stare and gloat over me.
They **divide my garments** among them
and **cast lots for my clothing**." (22:17-18)

"And they **divided up his clothes** by **casting lots**." (Luke 23:34)

"When the soldiers crucified Jesus, they took his clothes, dividing them into four shares, one for each of them, with the undergarment remaining. This garment was seamless, woven in one piece from top to bottom. 'Let's not tear it,' they said to one another. 'Let's **decide by lot** who will get it.'" (John 19:23-24)

David's lament seemed to be about his own sorrow, but in reality he was relating the lament of the Son of David, the Messiah himself.

The Conclusion of Praise (22:19-31)

This remarkable psalm begins with a lament but ends with a hymn of praise in verses 19-31. Most of the verses in this praise section seem more general, not specific to Jesus the Messiah. However, the author of Hebrews quotes verse 22 in reference to Jesus (Hebrews 2:12). And the final verses seem to point again to the Messiah that God would send:

"Posterity will serve him;
future generations will be told about the Lord.
They will proclaim his righteousness
to a people yet unborn –
for he has done it." (22:30-31)

His people would finally appreciate the depths to which the Son of God and Son of Man went to redeem us. We *do* declare his righteousness! And we will pass on the "Greatest Story Ever Told" to our children's children, "to a people yet unborn – for He has done it!"

Q4. (Psalm 22) What similarities do you see between the words of Psalm 22 and the events of Jesus' crucifixion? Do you think Jesus understood Psalm 22 as referring to himself? Why do you think the Spirit inspired David to pen these words? http://www.joyfulheart.com/forums/index.php?showtopic=696

Exercise. For one of the psalms in this lesson – or another psalm with a similar theme – do one of the suggested exercises to help you experience the Psalms in Appendix 1. These include such things as praying a psalm, meditating, reading to a shut-in, paraphrasing, writing your own psalm, singing, preparing a liturgy, and memorizing. Then report to the forum what the exercise meant to you personally or share what you've written with others. http://www.joyfulheart.com/forums/index.php?showtopic=697

Prayer

Father, your ways are above our ways. Here in the Psalms, thousands of years before Jesus, you have set the stage, given the clues, and set in motion the plan. We come to you with reverent and awed hearts, O God. Thank you for your love expressed in Jesus our Messiah! In his mighty name, we pray. Amen.

Songs

None of these three psalms seem to have become the theme of many popular hymns or praise choruses:

- **"Every Time that We Are Gathered,"** words and music by Denise Graves (© 1993, 1995, Maranatha Praise, Inc.). Reference to Psalm 22:6.

- **"Here Am I"** ("Ask of Me and I will give the nations, an inheritance for you"), words and music by Bob Kilpatrick (© 1987, Bob Kilpatrick Ministries, assigned to Lorenz Publishing Company 1998). Psalm 28; Psalm 2:8.
- **"Let There Be Praise,"** words and music by Dick and Melodie Tunney (© 1985, BMG songs, Inc.). Reference to Psalm 22:6.
- **"My God, My God, I Cry to Thee,"** words: paraphrase author unknown, music: "Hebron," by Lowell Mason (1830)
- **"The Day of Thy Power,"** words and music by Jack W. Hayford (© 1976, Rocksmith Music). Psalm 110:3.
- **"Why Did the Nations Join to Slay,"** words: Isaac Watts (1719); music: "Manoah," arranged from Gioachino A. Rosini by Henry W. Greatorex (1851). Paraphrase of Psalm 2.

11. Finding Forgiveness and Restoration (Psalms 32 and 51)

We can come away from the defeat and shame of sin feeling like a prizefighter who has been battered and humiliated. These psalms deal with repentance and God's forgiveness and restoration. How is it that a man or woman can love God at one moment and then commit a sin in the next? When we sin against one we love, there is a wound in our soul – that is why sin is such a struggle for a Christian. It's not something that we can just shrug off – that is if we truly love God.

We've seen the joy and extent of God's forgiveness in Psalm 103. However, the psalms in this chapter focus on the anguish of sin. What should we do when we sin? David was a great lover of God but also a great sinner. Let's examine two of his psalms.

Psalm 32 – Blessed Is the One Whose Sin Is Forgiven

Psalm 32 is attributed to David, though we're not told the circumstances. It could relate to the Bathsheba-Uriah incident that Psalm 51 clearly references, or to another time in David's life when he struggled with sin. It is termed "a maskil." The root of the word denotes insight or wisdom, so this may be a psalm of wisdom, though we're not sure. What we are sure of

Dante Gabriel Rosetti (1828-1882), "King David" (1858-1864), watercolor on paper, 279 x 127 mm, from "The Seed of David," Tate Gallery, London.

is that in this psalm is a good deal of insight into the human psyche and the workings of self-deception and guilt within the soul.

Structure

The structure of the psalm seems to be:

- Blessedness of the forgiven person (1-2)
- The weight of guilt (3-4)

- The relief of confession and forgiveness (5)
- The protection of God for those who seek him (6-7)
- An admonition from God to be pliable and not stubborn (8-10)
- A concluding praise (11)

Blessed Is the Forgiven Person (32:1-2)

David begins his sonnet of guilt and forgiveness with a comment on how fortunate the forgiven person really is:

"[1]Blessed is he
whose transgressions (*pesha'*) are forgiven,
whose sins (*hattā't*) are covered.
[2]Blessed is the man
whose sin (*'āwōn*) the LORD does not count against him
and in whose spirit is no deceit." (32:1-2)

David uses several synonyms for sin and guilt in Psalms 32 and 51, each with its own flavor:

- **"Transgression"** (*pesha'*) means "rebellion, revolt," designating those who reject God's authority.[1]
- **"Sin"** (*hattā't* and *hēt'*) from the root *hātā'* that means to miss a mark or miss the way.[2]
- **"Iniquity"** (*'āwōn*), is "infraction, crooked behavior, perversion, iniquity, etc." from a root that means "to bend, twist, distort."[3]
- **"Deceit"** (NIV, NRSV) or "guile" (KJV) is *remiyyâ*, "deceit, fraud."[4]

We sometimes try to rationalize and minimize our "weaknesses" and "mistakes." But David calls them for what they are – rebellion, revolt, iniquity. David also uses a pair of synonyms for forgiveness in verse 1:

- **Forgiven** (*nāśā'*), "lift, carry, take." Here the emphasis is on "taking away, forgiveness, or pardon of sin, iniquity and transgression." Sin can be forgiven and forgotten because it is taken up and carried away.[5]
- **Covered** (*kāsā*), "cover, conceal, hide." It is probably the meaning "hide" that leads to the sense "forgive."[6]

---

[1] G. Herbert Livingston, *pāsha'*, TWOT #1846a.
[2] G. Herbert Livingston, *hātā'*, TWOT #638e.
[3] Carl Schultz, *'āwā*, TWOT #1577a.
[4] William White, *rāmā*, TWOT #2169a. Holladay sees two derivatives and thus two meanings for this word (I) "slackness, looseness" and (II) "deceit" (340b).
[5] Walter C. Kaiser, *nāśā'*, TWOT #1421.

Given how sinful we can sometimes be, David is reflecting upon God's grace, his willingness to forgive. The Apostle Paul cites these verses as speaking "of the blessedness of the man to whom God credits righteousness apart from works" (Romans 4:6-8). Is there genuine grace in the Old Testament? Oh, yes!

The Agony of Guilt (32:3-4)

How miserable we are when we try to wriggle away from our sins and avoid dealing with them:

> "³When I kept silent,
> my bones wasted away
> through my groaning all day long.
> ⁴For day and night
> your hand was heavy upon me;
> my strength was sapped
> as in the heat of summer. *Selah*." (32:3-4)

Why do we do this? The clue is found in verse 2:

> "Blessed is the man ... in whose spirit is no deceit." (32:2b)

It is this self-deceit in our inner person that is so self-destructive. We might know deep down that we've done something wrong, but at the surface level we rationalize our actions, refusing to admit the depth of our guilt. The result David describes from personal experience in verses 3 and 4 – a physical and emotional drain that takes its toll on the life. The key is to apply truth to the self-deceit. That is what the Word does for us, what pastors and counselors do in public exhortation and private counsel. When we apply lies to mask our sin, the result is ultimately unsatisfying. There is no secular substitute for forgiveness. The inner soul of a human being cries out for relief from guilt at some level.

The Freedom of Confession (32:5)

If this was the incident with Bathsheba and Uriah, then Nathan the prophet was the one God used to pierce David's wall of self-deceit with the truth (2 Samuel 12:3-15), like you might lance an infected boil. Whatever sin and guilt it was that was causing David inner turmoil, he finally found release through confession.

> "Then I acknowledged my sin to you
> and did not cover up my iniquity.
> I said, 'I will confess
> my transgressions to the LORD' –

---

[6] R. Laird Harris, *kāsā*, TWOT #1008.

and you forgave
the guilt of my sin. *Selah*." (32:5)

David uses three synonyms for confession:

- **"Acknowledge"** is *yāda'*, "notice, observe." In the Hiphil stem this word has the causative connotation, "let someone know something, inform, announce, make known."[7]
- **"Not cover up,"** that is, *not* to pretend it didn't happen or wasn't important.
- **"Confess"** is *yādā*, "to acknowledge or confess sin." We've seen this verb often in our studies of praise psalms, since it is translated "praise, give thanks, thank," in the sense of to acknowledge or confess God's character and works.[8]

In a reaction to the Catholic practice of confession and absolution, many Protestants have let the pendulum swing far in the other direction, imagining that they have no need of confession or a confessor. Yes, we can and should confess our sins to God. But confessing our sins to a godly Christian leader can also help bring healing to the soul:

"Therefore confess your sins to each other and pray for each other so that you may be healed. The prayer of a righteous man is powerful and effective." (James 5:16)

Q1. (Psalm 32:2-5) How does self-deceit operate with sin to enslave us? How does confession enable us to get free from sin? Why do we sometimes resist the truth about ourselves? What does it take to get us to see truth sometimes?
http://www.joyfulheart.com/forums/index.php?showtopic=698

You Are My Hiding Place (32:6-7)

Now that sin is confessed and dealt with, the tenor of the psalm turns to an acknowledgement of God as Savior and Protector:

---

[7] *Yāda'*, Holladay 129b.
[8] Ralph H. Alexander, *yādā*, TWOT #847.

"Therefore let everyone who is godly pray to you
while you may be found." (32:6a)

David urges praying to the Lord "while you may be found," implying that there are
definite times when God is near and accessible to us, and times when because of our sin or
hardness we just are unable or unwilling to come to him. We must take advantage of the
opportunity to draw close to him. A few centuries later, Isaiah wrote:

"Seek the LORD while he may be found;
call on him while he is near.
Let the wicked forsake his way
and the evil man his thoughts.
Let him turn to the LORD, and he will have mercy on him,
and to our God, for he will freely pardon." (Isaiah 55:6-7)

When we do make peace with God, then we have his promise of protection:

"6bSurely when the mighty waters rise,
they will not reach him.
7You are my hiding place;
you will protect me from trouble
and surround me with songs of deliverance. *Selah*. " (Psalm 32:6b-7)

I've heard skeptics disparage the concept of God as a Protector as a crutch for the weak.
But this comes from an arrogance that has never faced the "mighty waters" of life, the
overwhelming enemies. In chapter 6 we examined psalms of protection, especially Psalm
91:1 that addresses, "He who dwells in the shelter of the Most High." Here "shelter, secret
place" (*sēter*) is the same word as "hiding place" in 32:7, from *sātar*, "hide, conceal," with the
idea of protection.[9]

The shouts or "songs of deliverance" in verse 7 that surround us are what you would
expect in the camp of the victorious army, not in a fear-filled hovel. God both protects us and
encourages our faith.

A Call to Teachability rather than Stubbornness (32:8-11)

We have heard the psalmist's voice. But now God speaks through David a promise and
an admonition:

"8I will instruct you and teach you in the way you should go;
I will counsel you and watch over you.
9Do not be like the horse or the mule,
which have no understanding

[9] R. D. Patterson, *sātar*, TWOT #1551a.

but must be controlled by bit and bridle
or they will not come to you.
[10]Many are the woes of the wicked,
but the LORD's unfailing love
surrounds the man who trusts in him." (32:8-10)

Once the Lord has cleansed us from guilt and sin, and brought us into his protective care, he wants to teach us and instruct us. He uses the metaphor of a stubborn horse or mule that will only come to their master when forced to by a bit and bridle. Don't be like that, the Lord says, let me teach you. Let my "unfailing love" (ḥesed) surround you. Don't resist me. Sin causes us to run away from God, to "kick against the goads" (Acts 26:14). Relax, let your rebellion and sin go, and hear his words of instruction in a safe place. The psalm concludes with a call to praise:

"Rejoice in the LORD and be glad, you righteous;
sing, all you who are upright in heart!" (32:11)

Psalm 51 – Create in Me a Clean Heart, O Lord

Now we come to the classic psalm of repentance, confession, and plea for pardon.

Setting the Scene (2 Samuel 11-12)

The ascription to Psalm 51 reads,

"For the director of music. A psalm of David. When the prophet Nathan came to him after David had committed adultery with Bathsheba,"

a story of humble origins, a rise to glory, self-indulgence, moral corruption, and finally David's restoration to the God that he loved.

When David's nemesis King Saul finally dies and David is crowned king, he begins as a righteous ruler. But power and wealth take their toll on his moral compass. One day from the height of his palace, he watches as Bathsheba, wife of Uriah, one of his loyal warriors, bathes on her rooftop. In lust he calls her to the palace and she becomes pregnant. When he can't blame her pregnancy on her husband, he has her husband killed.

One day God sends Nathan the prophet who tells him the simple story of a poor man being cheated by a rich man out of the little ewe lamb that he loves. Enraged, David says, "The man deserves to die."

Nathan lifts a bony finger, points directly at the corrupt King, says with an even voice, "You are that man," and pronounces the Lord's judgment upon him. This shocks David out his denial and cover-up.

Then David said to Nathan, "I have sinned against the LORD."

Nathan replied, "The LORD has taken away your sin. You are not going to die. But because by doing this you have made the enemies of the LORD show utter contempt, the son born to you will die." (2 Samuel 12:13-14)

The Lord punishes David for his sin, a Father's stern discipline you might call it, but he forgives the sin that had become a wedge between David and his God and restores him to fellowship. The Lord draws him close and David, now chastened, responds.

Structure

Here is the structure of Psalm 51:

1. Pleading for God's mercy (1-2)
2. Confessing and acknowledging sin (3-5)
3. Hungering for a pure heart once more (6-12)
4. Resolving to declare God's grace (13-15)
5. Offering the sacrifice of a contrite heart (16-17)
6. Praying for Jerusalem's prosperity (18-19)

Pleading for God's Mercy (51:1-2)

"¹Have mercy on me, O God,
according to your unfailing love;
according to your great compassion
blot out my transgressions.
²Wash away all my iniquity
and cleanse me from my sin." (51:1-2)

David begins by calling out for mercy. Why? Because he recognizes that God's revealed character is one of love and compassion. From the time of Moses, God has revealed himself as:

"The LORD, the LORD,
the compassionate and gracious God,
slow to anger,
abounding in love and faithfulness,
maintaining love to thousands,
and forgiving wickedness, rebellion and sin." (Exodus 34:6)

God owes David no favors; David realizes he is bankrupt. So he begins his prayer:

"Have mercy on me, O God,
according to your unfailing love;
according to your great compassion." (51:1)

We've seen most of these words before:

- **"Have mercy"** (*ḥānan*) means "be gracious, pity … a heartfelt response by someone who has something to give to one who has a need." Here it is a plea to Yahweh to "be gracious to me."[10] David asks for this mercy in accordance with (that is, on the basis of) God's well-known character qualities of steadfast love and compassion.
- **"Unfailing love"** (NIV), "lovingkindness" (KJV), and "steadfast love" (NRSV) translate the common Hebrew noun *ḥesed*, which includes the ideas love, faithfulness, good-heartedness, kindness.[11]
- **"Compassion"** (NIV), "tender mercies" (KJV), and "mercy" (NRSV) represent the Hebrew noun *raḥămîm*, "tender mercy, compassion, deep love."[12]

David knows he doesn't deserve forgiveness, so he calls on God's character of mercy. He knows God is like this, so he prays with faith. Here is David's request:

"… Blot out my transgressions.
Wash away all my iniquity
and cleanse me from my sin." (51:1b-2)

This is Spirit-inspired poetry, so in keeping with Hebrew poetic style of synoptic parallelism where two or more lines repeat the same idea, David makes his request with three synonyms for forgiveness and three synonyms for sin.

Blot out	transgressions
Wash away	iniquity
Cleanse	sin

We looked at synonyms for sin in Psalm 32:1-2 above. Now let's examine the synonyms for pardon.

- **"Blot out"** (*māḥā*) means "wipe, wipe out."[13] The word is used for blotting out the inhabitants of the earth in the flood and erasures in ancient leather scrolls made by

[10] Edwin Yamauchi, *ḥānan*, TWOT #694.
[11] R. Laird Harris, *ḥesed*, TWOT #698.
[12] Leonard J. Coppes, *rāḥam*, TWOT #2146a.
[13] Walter C. Kaiser, *māḥā*, TWOT #1178.

washing or expunging. Here and in verse 9 the word seems to suggest "removing a
stain."

- **"Wash away"** (NIV, *kābas*) or "wash thoroughly" (KJV, NRSV) means "wash, be
  washed, perform the work of a fuller," that is "to make stuffs clean and soft by tread-
  ing, kneading and beating them in cold water."[14] The same verb is found in verse 7b:
  "Wash me and I will be whiter than snow." The stain of sin is deep and David recognizes his need for radical and deep washing.
- **"Cleanse"** (*ṭāhēr*) means "be pure, be clean." The word is used of wind sweeping the
  skies clear and the purifying of silver. It is used of moral purity as well as the ritual
  purity of the Levites and of holy vessels in the tabernacle.[15] The adjective formed
  from this verb is used in verse 10 where David asks for a "pure heart" or a "clean
  heart."

David asks God for a full pardon – and cleansing of his character – based on God's
merciful nature. It is a bold and very hopeful prayer prayed by a desperately wounded
sinner longing to be restored to fellowship with his God.

Confessing and Acknowledging Sin (51:3-5)

We've considered the importance of repentance and confession in Psalm 32 above. Here
in Psalm 51, David does not hide or minimize his sin.

> "³For I know my transgressions,
> and my sin is always before me.
> ⁴Against you, you only, have I sinned
> and done what is evil[16] in your sight,
> so that you are proved right when you speak
> and justified when you judge.
>
> ⁵Surely I was sinful (*'āwōn*) at birth,
> sinful (*hēt'*) from the time my mother conceived me.
> ⁶Surely you desire truth in the inner parts;
> you teach me wisdom in the inmost place." (51:3-6)

Notice verse 4:

---

[14] KB, p. 422, cited in John N. Oswalt, *kābas*, TWOT #946.

[15] Edwin Yamauchi, *ṭāhēr*, TWOT #792.

[16] (Do) evil (*ra'*), "evil, distress, wickedness," the opposite of good (G. Herbert Livingston, *rā'a'*, TWOT
#2191a).

"Against you, you only, have I sinned
and done what is evil in your sight."

Does this mean that David's sins against Bathsheba and her husband Uriah were meaningless, inconsequential? No, not at all. But David recognizes that the greatest sin of all is against the Lord that he purports to love. When he sins, he is flaunting his rebellion in God's face. Yes, we can sin against people and need to make these sins right (Matthew 5:23). But our sin is even more against our heavenly Father. It is *that* breach that must be healed at all costs.

In verses 5 and 6 when David talks about being sinful from before birth, is David claiming that Original Sin made him do it? Is he excusing himself in that he just can't help sinning because he is "only human." I don't think so. Rather, he is affirming that he is sinful through and through. He is acknowledging the awfulness of his sin in the clearest possible way by using these various synonyms of sin that describe its convolutions of rebellion, twistedness, missing the way, and wickedness.

Q2. (Psalm 51:3-6) When David says, "Against you only I have sinned" (4a) is he minimizing his sin against Bathsheba and Uriah? What does he mean by this? When he mentions his sinfulness from before birth is he excusing himself or blaming Original Sin? What does he mean by this?

http://www.joyfulheart.com/forums/index.php?showtopic=699

Hungering for Fellowship Once More (51:6-12)

David has painted his iniquity in clear colors. Now he begins to contrast his own sinfulness with what God desires. He looks within. Sinfulness is not primarily in one's actions, but in one's heart.

"Surely you desire truth in the inner parts;
you teach me wisdom in the inmost place." (51:6)

198 Experiencing the Psalms

In verse 6 David speaks of "the inner parts" (NIV), "the inward parts" (KJV), "the inward being" (NRSV).[17] It is this inner person who must be converted and cleansed and discipled. Our actions (when we are not putting on an act for others) flow from this inner person, from our heart of hearts. Jesus taught:

"For out of the overflow of the heart the mouth speaks." (Matthew 12:34)

"For out of the heart come evil thoughts, murder, adultery, sexual immorality, theft, false testimony, slander." (Matthew 15:19)

Remember the danger of "deceit" hiding in the spirit in Psalm 32:2? Now sadder and wiser, David calls on God for "truth in the inner parts" and "wisdom in the inmost place" (51:6).

He offers a prayer for deep cleansing:

"Cleanse me with hyssop, and I will be clean;
wash me, and I will be whiter than snow." (51:7)

"Cleanse" (NIV) or "purge" (KJV) translate a word that denotes a cleansing or purifying ceremony during which sin is done away with.[18] Hyssop is a small plant that grows on walls, probably marjoram in the mint family. It was used in purification ceremonies to apply blood and water.[19] David is calling upon God himself, not just a priest, to cleanse him through and through to remove his deeply ingrained sin. If God cleanses him, if God washes him, then he will be "whiter than snow."

While he has been separated from God he has withered. Now he longs for the joy of the Lord once again:

"Let me hear joy and gladness;
let the bones you have crushed rejoice." (51:8)

"Restore to me the joy of your salvation." (51:12a)

---

[17] The noun *ṭūḥōt* describes an object "covered over, hidden, or concealed," carrying the idea of the inner being of a person covered up by the body (Ralph H. Alexander, *tûaḥ*, TWOT #795b). The parallel idea in 6b is of an "inmost place" (NIV), "hidden part" (KJV), "secret heart" (NRSV), from the word *sātam*, "stop up, shut up, keep close" (*sātam*, TWOT #1550). In the New Testament Paul talks about the "inner being" (Romans 7:22), the "new self" (Ephesians 4:24; Colossians 3:9). Peter uses the expression of "the inner self" (NIV, 1 Peter 3:4) or "the hidden man of the heart" (KJV).

[18] The verb *ḥāṭā'* which means "sin, miss the way" in the Qal stem, means in the Piel and Hithpael stems "to make a sin offering" or a cleansing or purifying ceremony during which sin is done away with (G. Herbert Livingston, *ḥāṭā'*, TWOT #638). See Exodus 12:22; Leviticus 14:4-6, 49-52; Numbers 19:6, 17-19; Hebrews 9:19; John 19:29.

[19] Herbert Wolf, *'ēzōb*, TWOT #55.

Contrary to those who cynically perceive Christianity as a guilt-driven religion, God doesn't desire us to live with guilt, but to enjoy forgiveness and full fellowship with him. Here David prays for joy to replace his misery and "the bones you have crushed" (51:8b).

In verse 12a, the word "restore" (shûb), "turn back, return," carries the idea of "give back, restore."[20] David has known the joy of God's salvation and rescue before. Now he longs for this joy in fellowship to be restored to him once more. It is his earnest prayer.

Have you lost the "joy" of your salvation? Have you become somewhat distant from God? Have you taken God for granted? Or perhaps have you never really gotten to know him. God wants to restore the joy to you that is your birthright as a Christian. Joy is a fruit of the Holy Spirit's work in your life (Galatians 5:22-23). Call out to him in repentance and receive the joy God desires for you.

The Longing for a Pure Heart (51:10, 12)

David also prays for a pure heart and a willing spirit.

> "**Create** in me a **pure** heart, O God,
> and renew a steadfast spirit within me." (51:10)

> "and grant me a **willing spirit**, to sustain me." (51:12b)

David uses two interesting words in his prayer in verse 10 – "create" and "pure." "Create" (bārā') in this verse carries the connotation of "to initiate something new."[21] "Pure" (NIV) or "clean" (KJV) comes from ṭāhēr which we saw in 51:2, "to cleanse," used of ritual or moral purity and of the pureness of the unalloyed gold of the temple furniture.[22] Now the word describes the heart David longs for.

But isn't he asking for too much? David has been a slave to lust, drunk with power, stained by murder. How can he now pray for a pure heart? Isn't it too late? No. Can we be pure again once we've been corrupted? Yes.

Jesus taught us, "Blessed are the pure in heart, for they will see God" (Matthew 5:8). Peter observed, "He made no distinction between us and them, for he purified their hearts by faith" (Acts 15:9). God spoke to Peter, "Do not call anything impure that God has made clean" (Acts 10:15). God is in the heart purification business. The author of Hebrews wrote:

> "How much more, then, will the blood of Christ, who through the eternal Spirit offered himself unblemished to God, cleanse our consciences from acts that lead to death, so that we may serve the living God!" (Hebrews 9:14)

---

[20] Shûb, BDB 999, Hiphil 1d.
[21] Thomas E. McComiskey, bārā', TWOT #278. A different synonym for "create," is yāsar, which suggests "to fashion, to shape something new."
[22] Edwin Yamauchi, ṭāhēr, TWOT #792.

Do you feel unforgiven? Unforgivable? Jesus died for your sins and he desires to forgive you, no matter what you have done. Pray this prayer with David:

> "Create in me a pure heart, O God,
>   and **renew** a **steadfast spirit** within me." (51:10)

The second part of verse 10 is a prayer for God to renew (*ḥādash*, "repair, renew, rebuild"[23]) a "right" (KJV, NRSV, *kûn*) or "steadfast" (NIV) spirit, "established, prepared, made ready, fixed, certain, right."[24]

In verse 12b he prays for a "willing spirit" (NIV, NRSV) or to be upheld by God's "free spirit" (KJV). The adjective *nādîb*, "noble, willing, inclined," is from the root *nādab*, "make willing, incite, an uncompelled and free movement of the will unto divine service or sacrifice."[25] Oh, for a spirit that longs to serve God, a heart that is inclined to him!

Q3. (Psalm 51:10-12) How is it possible to have a "pure heart" after great sin? What does a "pure heart" consist of? What is the relationship between a "pure heart" (Psalm 51:10) and a "united" or "undivided heart" (Psalm 86:11)? Who purifies the heart? What is the process?

http://www.joyfulheart.com/forums/index.php?showtopic=700

Do Not Take Your Holy Spirit from Me (51:11)

Now David prays against his great fear:

> "Do not cast me from your presence
>   or take your Holy Spirit from me." (51:11)

When David was just a boy, King Saul had sinned and rebelled against God. Shortly after this, the Prophet Samuel had come to his father's farm, directing that all Jesse's sons appear before him:

---

[23] Carl Philip Weber, *ḥādash*, TWOT #613.

[24] John N. Oswalt, *kûh*, TWOT #964. "The root meaning is to bring something into being with the consequence that its existence is a certainty."

[25] Leonard J. Coppes, *nādab*, TWOT #1299b.

"So Samuel took the horn of oil and anointed him in the presence of his brothers, and from that day on the Spirit of the LORD came upon David in power.... Now the Spirit of the LORD had departed from Saul...." (1 Samuel 16:13-14)

The Spirit of God had left Saul and come upon David. So David is terrified that in his sin this would happen to him as well, that God's Spirit will desert him. But he repents and trusts God for the answer to his prayer.

Resolving to Declare God's Grace (51:13-15)

Now David looks forward to the answer to his prayer and how he will serve God.

"13Then I will teach transgressors your ways,
and sinners will turn back to you.
14Save me from bloodguilt,26 O God,
the God who saves me,
and my tongue will sing of your righteousness.
15O Lord, open my lips,
and my mouth will declare your praise." (51:13-15)

Restored and forgiven, he sees himself once again serving the Lord – teaching, singing, praising. Note that he is not bargaining with God, but anticipating and promising to God what he will do. I don't see this so much as a vow as a vision of the future.

Offering the Sacrifice of a Contrite Heart (51:16-17)

Now David compares true repentance to ritual sacrifice.

"You do not delight in sacrifice, or I would bring it;
you do not take pleasure in burnt offerings." (51:16-17)

Though Israel had a well-developed sacrificial system designed to atone for sin, too often people just went through the motions of religion without real repentance, without a genuine desire for change, without a real love for God. Across the Old Testament you see a recognition that it is an inner obedience and submissive spirit that God desires, not the outward rituals (1 Samuel 15:22; Isaiah 1:11; Micah 6:6-9).

We Christians also have developed rituals through which we can be absolved from sin. It may be formal confession and absolution by a priest or pastor, or by praying a particular prayer. Confession is important in this process (James 5:16). But whatever shape it takes, God is not looking for outward religious action but for heart repentance and change. In Psalm 51, David fully realizes and celebrates this fact.

---

26 Bloodguilt (*dām*, "blood") was the sin of shedding innocent blood, considered a mortal sin. In David's case, he had ordered the death of Uriah, Bathsheba's husband. TWOT #436; BDB 197, g.

"The sacrifices of God are a **broken spirit**;
a broken and contrite heart,
O God, you will not despise." (51:17)

"The sacrifices of God" (NIV, KJV) or "the sacrifice acceptable to God" (NRSV) could also be translated, "My sacrifice, O God" (NIV, NRSV footnote). "Broken" (*shābar*) is used figuratively here of a broken heart.

"Contrite" is *dākă*, a by-form of the verb *dk'*, which also means "to crush," and of *dûk*, "to pound, beat." The verb is consistently used of one who is physically and emotionally crushed because of sin or the onslaught of an enemy.[27] Together, the broken and contrite heart of verse 17 "describe the condition of profound contrition and awe experienced by a sinful person who becomes aware of the divine presence."[28]

Until our hearts break with sorrow at our sin, we are not quite ready for forgiveness. So often we are sad at being caught or exposed, but not sad at hurting the God who loves us or injuring his reputation by our sins. Nathan had told David that his sin had "made the enemies of the LORD show utter contempt" (2 Samuel 12:14). Many conversions these days seem to lack the deep repentance that rends the heart (Joel 2:13). It is not religion, but a relationship that has been injured and must be restored. "Against you, you only, have I sinned and done what is evil in your sight, " David cries (51:4). Oh, that our sins would break our hearts!

Q4. (Psalm 51:17) How does one achieve a "broken and contrite heart"? What are the earmarks of this condition? How does this differ from "being sorry" for a sin? How does humility relate to this condition?
http://www.joyfulheart.com/forums/index.php?showtopic=701

Praying for Jerusalem's Prosperity (51:18-19)

The psalm concludes with a prayer for Jerusalem.

[27] Herbert Wolf, *dākă*, TWOT #428.
[28] Marvin E. Tate, *Psalms 51-100* (Word Biblical Commentary, Vol. 20; Word, 1990), pp. 28.

"In your good pleasure make Zion prosper;
build up the walls of Jerusalem.
Then there will be righteous sacrifices,
whole burnt offerings to delight you;
then bulls will be offered on your altar." (51:18-19)

Assuming that the earlier part of the psalm was penned by David, these last two verses could have been added after the fall of Jerusalem, as a prayer for the restoration of the city and temple worship that had been destroyed because of the sin of the nation, recognizing the value of the psalm as a corporate confession as well as a personal prayer for mercy.[29]

Exercise. For one of the psalms in this lesson – or another psalm with a similar theme – do one of the suggested exercises to help you experience the Psalms in Appendix 1. These include such things as praying a psalm, meditating, reading to a shut-in, paraphrasing, writing your own psalm, singing, preparing a liturgy, and memorizing. Then report to the forum what the exercise meant to you personally or share what you've written with others.

http://www.joyfulheart.com/forums/index.php?showtopic=702

Prayer

O Lord, we have sinned. We have struggled with temptation. Teach us how to confess our sins before you. Teach us a broken and contrite heart, a humble spirit. Help us to walk before you in humility and find the protection of your presence around us. In Jesus' name, we pray. Amen.

Songs

- **"A Broken Spirit,"** words and music by Don Harris and Martin Nystrom (© 1993, Integrity's Hosanna! Music). Psalm 51:17.
- **"Change My Heart, O God,"** words and music by Eddie Espinosa (© 1982, Mercy Publishing). Psalm 51:10
- **"Create in Me a Clean Heart,"** author unknown. Psalm 51:10-12.

---

[29] So Derek Kidner, *Psalms 1-72* (Tyndale Old Testament Commentaries; InterVarsity Press, 1973), p. 194; and Tate, *Psalms 51-100*, pp. 29-30. Franz Delitzsch (Keil and Delitzsch 5:141-143) defends Davidic authorship of these verses.

- **"Create in Me a Clean Heart,"** words and music by Brown Bannister (© 1982, Bases Loaded Music). Psalm 51:10-12.
- **"Create in Me,"** words and music by Mary Rice Hopkins (© 1989, Big Steps 4 U, Maranatha! Music. Psalm 51:10.
- **"Freely Forgiven,"** words and music by Bill Batstone (© 1984, Maranatha! Music). Psalm 32:1-6.
- **"Give Me a Clean Heart,"** words and music by Margaret J. Douroux (n.d.). Psalm 51:10.
- **"God Be Merciful to Me"** (On thy grace I rest my plea), words and music by Christopher Miner and Richard Redhead (© 1998, Christopher Miner). Psalm 51.
- **"He Is Faithful,"** words and music by Walt Harrah (© 1986, Maranatha! Music). Psalm 32:1.
- **"Jesus, the Very Thought of Thee"** (O hope of every contrite heart), words: Bernard of Clairvaux (12th century), *Jesu dulcis memoria*, translated by Edward Caswall (1849). Music: "St. Agnes," by John B. Dykes (1866).
- **"O Blessed Souls Are They,"** words: Isaac Watts (1719), music: "Pekin" arranged from a German carol by J.E. Kingsley (1847). Psalm 32.
- **"Precious Promise"** (I Will Guide Thee), words: Nathaniel Niles (1873), music: Philip P. Bliss. Psalm 32:8.
- **"Refiner's Fire"** (Purify my heart), words and music by Brian Doerksen (© 1990, Vineyard Songs Canada, ION Publishing). Psalm 51.
- **"Refresh My Heart,"** words and music by Geoff Bullock (© 1992, Word Music, LLC, Maranatha! Music). Psalm 51:10.
- **"Search Me, Know Me,"** words and music by Kathryn Scott and Mildred Rainey (© 2003, Vertical Worship Songs). Psalm 51:10
- **"Search Me, O God"** (Cleanse Me), words by J. Edwin Orr (1936). Music: Maori tune. Psalm 52.1-2.
- **"Whiter than Snow,"** words: James Nicholson (1872), music: William G. Fischer (1872). Psalm 51:7.
- **"You Are My Hiding Place,"** words and music by Michael Ledner (© 1981 Maranatha! Music, Admin. by The Copyright Company). Psalm 32:7.

12. Giving Thanks to Our Faithful God (Psalms 100, 107, 118, 34)

We've looked at all kinds of psalms on our journey through the Psalter. Perhaps a fitting conclusion will be psalms of thanksgiving and praise. They bear close resemblance to other psalms we've studied. Two in particular are gems with a character all their own that has made them beloved through the centuries. They have inspired countless hymns and choruses – Psalm 100 ("Old Hundredth") and Psalm 34. First we'll examine three psalms of thanksgiving (100, 107, and 118). Then we'll conclude with a psalm of deliverance (34).

Peter Paul Rubens and Jan Boeckhorst, "King David Playing the Harp" (c. 1616, finished 1640s), oil on wood panel, Städel Museum, Frankfurt am Main, Germany.

Psalm 100 – Enter His Gates with Thanksgiving

The key idea found again and again in this short psalm is giving thanks.

Title   "A psalm of **thanksgiving** (*tôdâ*)" (NRSV)

Verse 4   "Enter his gates with **thanksgiving** (*tôdâ*)
and his courts with praise;
give thanks (*yādā*) to him
and praise his name."

The primary meaning of the root verb *yādā* is "to acknowledge or confess," here, to acknowledge and confess God's character and works. While *hālal*, "praise," stresses "acclaim of, boasting of, glorying in" God, the verb *yādā*, emphasizes "recognition, declaration" of a fact. The noun in the title, *tôdâ*, "confession, praise," was employed uniquely in reference to a type of sacrifice, usually translated a "thank-offering." The sacrifice was accompanied with praise or confession of God as a time of joy.[1] Psalm 100 pairs with another verse from the Psalter:

> "He who sacrifices thank offerings (*tôdâ*) honors me,
> and he prepares the way
> so that I may show him the salvation of God." (Psalm 50:23)

Psalm 100 is clearly in the "hymn" genre. One of the most beloved psalms in the Bible, it has quite a history. It was closely identified with the "thank-offering" in the temple, probably sung when thank-offerings were offered on the altar. In Jewish piety Psalm 100 is a regular part of morning prayers, included among the *Pesukei D'Zimrah* ("verses of praise"). "Old Hundredth," based on this psalm, is one of the great hymns of the Protestant Christian churches.

Psalm 100 breathes thanksgiving and praise. Let's consider it briefly.

Giving Thanks with Joy (100:1-2)

This psalm has no author, but is identified as "a psalm," probably with an instrumental accompaniment. As mentioned, the title: "A psalm of thanksgiving" identifies it with the temple thank-offering. Many of the key words in these verses we've already looked at in previous psalms. For the first three verses I've put the NIV and KJV translations side by side, since many of us are familiar with the more traditional translation. Notice the abundance of praise words in the first two verses.

"**¹Shout for joy** to the LORD, all the earth. ²**Worship** the LORD with **gladness**; come before him with **joyful songs**." (100:1-2, NIV)	"**¹Make a joyful noise** unto the LORD, all ye lands. ²**Serve** the LORD with **gladness**: come before his presence with **singing**." (100:1-2, KJV)

Let's review some of the praise words:

- **"Shout for joy"** (NIV), "make a joyful noise" (KJV, NRSV) *rûa'*, "shout, raise a sound, cry out." It is a jubilant word, a spontaneous shout of praise to Yahweh.[2]
- **"Worship"** (NIV, NRSV), "serve" (KJV, NJB) is *'ābad*, "work, serve," here "serve, worship" God, more properly, "perform the proper rites for,"[3] "serving Yahweh with the Levitical service."[4]

---

[1] Ralph H. Alexander, *yādā*, TWOT #847.
[2] William White, *rûa'*, TWOT #2135.

- **"Gladness"** is *śimḥâ*, "joy, mirth." The root denotes being glad or joyful with the whole disposition.[5]
- **"Joyful songs"** (NIV), "singing" (KJV, NRSV) is *renānā*, "cry of joy." This noun is only found in three other poetic passages (Psalm 63:5; Job 3:7; 20:5). The verb is widely used as a shout of jubilation, joy at God's saving acts, holy joy.[6]

We Are the Sheep of His Pasture (100:3)

Verses 1 and 2 are a call to joyful thanksgiving. Verse 3 gives the reason for the jubilation – Yahweh is our Creator, King, and Shepherd. Verse 3 presents a minor difficulty. See how the NIV and KJV translations differ from each other:

"Know that the LORD is God.	"Know ye that the LORD he is God:
It is he who made us,	it is he that hath made us,
and we are his ;	**and not we ourselves**;
we are his people,	we are his people,
the sheep of his pasture." (NIV)	and the sheep of his pasture." (KJV)

Verse 3b can be rendered "we are his" (NIV, NRSV, NJB) or "not we ourselves" (KJV, NASB). Here's why. The Hebrew word for "not" (*lō'*) and "his" (*lô*) sound alike. Both wordings have manuscript support. Either of the words could be used appropriately here. But the sentence goes more smoothly as "and we are his." I think it also seems to fit the context better – creation and belonging to God that is carried out in verse 3c.

Notice the warm sense of belonging that verse 3 creates in us. Why should we worship? (verse 1-2). Because Yahweh is God who created us. We belong to him, like a king with his people, like a shepherd and his flock. We are not alone! We belong to the family of God and are tenderly cared for as sheep. God takes responsibility for us!

Enter His Gates with Thanksgiving (100:4-5)

And so we praise him. The psalmist calls us into the temple to present a joyful thanksgiving offering, to praise him in the courts of the temple.

"Enter his gates with thanksgiving
and his courts with praise;
give thanks to him and praise his name." (100:4)

---

[3] *'Ābad*, Holladay, 261.
[4] Walter C. Kaiser, *'ābad*, TWOT #1553.
[5] Bruce K. Waltke, *śāmah*, TWOT #2268b.
[6] William White, *rānan*, TWOT #2179b.

I'm always curious about the praise words, since they instruct us in praise. We've seen them all before. The noun "thanksgiving" (*tôdâ*) and related verb "give thanks" (*yādā*) we discussed above. The noun "praise" in verse 4b is *tehillâ*, "renown, praise, glory," from the verb *hālal*, "praise, boast."[7]. The verb "praise" (NIV), "bless" (KJV, NRSV) in 4c is *bārak*, which we discussed on Psalm 103:1. This is both an invitation to enter his presence and gentle command to praise. Why should we praise?

> "For the LORD is good and his love endures forever;
> his faithfulness continues through all generations." (100:5)

Verse 5 gives the reasons for our jubilant praise – God's character. These are qualities that we've seen throughout the psalms, especially in chapter 9 of our study – his goodness and righteousness (*tôb*[8]), his steadfast love (*hesed*), and his faithfulness (*'emûnâ*[9]).

Q1. (Psalm 100) What is the predominant emotion in Psalm 100? How does this psalm make you feel emotionally about God? What are the reasons for praise given in verses 3 and 5? What are the commands in this psalm?

http://www.joyfulheart.com/forums/index.php?showtopic=703

Psalm 107 – Give Thanks to the Lord for His Unfailing Love

Another thanksgiving psalm is Psalm 107, that stands without any title or ascription in our Psalter. I wish we could give it more time, but read it on your own.

> "[1]Give thanks (*yādā*) to the LORD, for he is good;
> his love endures forever.
> [2]Let the redeemed of the LORD say this –
> those he redeemed from the hand of the foe,

---

[7] *Tehillâ*, Holladay, 387. The word is used as a technical term for "song of praise" in Psalm 145:1, Isaiah 63:7.
[8] "Good" is *tôb*, "good" or "goodness," here "moral goodness" (Andrew Bowling, *tôb*, TWOT #793a).
[9] *'Emûnâ* means "firmness, faithfulness, fidelity" (Jack B. Scott, *'āman*, TWOT #116e).

> ³those he gathered from the lands,
> from east and west, from north and south." (107:1-3)

This psalm consists of a number of verses outlining Israel's woes, followed by a refrain, probably sung by a chorus:

> "Let them give thanks to the LORD for his unfailing love
> and his wonderful deeds for men" (verses 8, 15, 21, and 31)

Following each refrain is a reason for the thanksgiving:

> "... For he satisfies the thirsty
> and fills the hungry with good things." (107:9)

> "... For he breaks down gates of bronze
> and cuts through bars of iron." (107:16)

Or a desired response:

> "Let them sacrifice thank offerings
> and tell of his works with songs of joy." (107:22)

> "Let them exalt him in the assembly of the people
> and praise him in the council of the elders." (107:32)

It is a wonderful psalm of praise, detailing the appropriateness of our thanksgiving. It could also easily lend itself to corporate worship, with the congregation saying or singing the refrain and various readers taking the narrative portions.

Psalm 118 – His Love Endures Forever

Another wonderful thanksgiving psalm is Psalm 118, also without title or author. Let's examine a few choice verses:

> "Give thanks (*yādā*) to the LORD, for he is good;
> his love endures forever." (118:1)

The next verses almost beg for a choral response after each call:

> "²Let Israel say:
> *'His love endures forever.'*
> ³Let the house of Aaron say:
> *'His love endures forever.'*
> ⁴Let those who fear the LORD say:
> *'His love endures forever.'* " (118:2-4)

Now the psalmist begins to talk about how he has faced various perils, but has found God's help:

"The LORD is with me; I will not be afraid.
What can man do to me?
The LORD is with me; he is my helper.
I will look in triumph on my enemies." (118:6-7)

Verse 6 is quoted in Hebrews 13:6. Throughout the psalm there are wonderful outbreaks of praise, such as:

"The LORD is my strength and my song;
he has become my salvation.
Shouts of joy and victory
resound in the tents of the righteous..." (118:14-15)

"Open for me the gates of righteousness;
I will enter and give thanks to the LORD.
This is the gate of the LORD
through which the righteous may enter.
I will give you thanks, for you answered me;
you have become my salvation." (118:19-21)

The Stone that the Builders Rejected (118:22-23)

Now comes a famous verse that the New Testament designates as speaking of Jesus the Messiah:

"The stone the builders rejected
has become the capstone;
the LORD has done this,
and it is marvelous in our eyes." (118:22-23)

It is quoted by Jesus (Matthew 21:42; Mark 12:10, 11; Luke 20:17) and the Apostle Peter (Acts 4:11; 1 Peter 2:4, 7). The imagery is from building construction, masonry. Houses of the poor were typically built from blocks of sun-dried clay, then whitewashed. Wealthier people would construct houses of stone (*'eben*) that was dressed to square it up using a hammer and chisel, sometimes a stone saw.[10] Before placement in the building the mason would inspect each block for quality, trueness, squareness, and fit. Once he personally approved the cut stone, it would be incorporated into the building.

The "chief cornerstone" (NRSV, NJB), "capstone" (NIV), "head stone of the corner" (KJV), is the stone that crowns the building, the most prominent and important stone of the entire

---

[10] Adrianus van Selms, "Build," ISBE 1:553-555

structure.[11] Jesus and Peter interpret the builders as the leaders of Israel – the chief priests, scribes, and Pharisees. They rejected the Messiah, "the stone," while Yahweh has designated him the Capstone, Keystone, Cornerstone (depending on your translation of the word). Another verse refers to Messiah in this way (quoted in 1 Peter 2:6; Romans 9:33; 10:11; and referred to in 1 Corinthians 3:11 and Ephesians 2:20):

> "See, I lay a stone in Zion,
> a tested stone,
> a precious cornerstone for a sure foundation;
> the one who trusts will never be dismayed." (Isaiah 28:16)

Jesus is also referred to as the "a stone that causes men to stumble and a rock that makes them fall" (Isaiah 8:14; Romans 9:32-33; 1 Peter 2:8).

This Is the Day which the Lord Has Made (118:24)

One of our most common antiphons or calls to worship is found in verse 24:

> "This is the day the LORD has made;
> let us rejoice and be glad in it." (118:24)

"Rejoice" is *gîl*, "rejoice, be glad." The root meaning is "to circle around," from which such ideas as "to circle in joy" and "dance for joy" are readily derived. The root meaning is applicable to vigorous, enthusiastic expressions of joy."[12]

Hosanna! (118:25-27)

The next two verses are found on the lips of worshippers during Jesus' Triumphal Entry on Palm Sunday:

> "O LORD, save us;
> O LORD, grant us success.
> **Blessed is he who comes in the name of the LORD.**
> From the house of the LORD we bless you." (118:25-26)

The cry *hōsanna* is usually taken as a Greek transliteration of the cry for help "Save us" in verse 25.[13] John records of the great crowds that:

> "They took palm branches and went out to meet him, shouting,
> **'Hosanna!**

---

[11] This phrase is made up of two words, *rō'sh*, "head, top, chief," and *pinnâ*, "corner." Hamilton notes that in Isaiah 28:16 it refers to a foundation stone, but in Psalm 118:22 to the stone which crowns the building (Victor P. Hamilton, *pnn*, TWOT #1783a).

[12] Jack P. Lewis, *gîl*, TWOT 346.

[13] Eduard Lohse, *hōsanna*, TDNT 9:682-684.

> **Blessed is he who comes in the name of the Lord!**
> Blessed is the King of Israel!'" (John 12:13; also see Matthew 21:9-11)

In that light look at the next verse in Psalm 118:

> "The LORD is God,
> and he has made his light shine upon us.
> **With boughs in hand, join in the festal procession**
> up to the horns of the altar." (118:27)

With the words of this psalm the crowds welcomed Jesus as the Messianic King into Jerusalem riding on a donkey, while throwing palm branches on the road before him. But the leaders rejected him and had him crucified. Just before his crucifixion Jesus addresses the city with great sadness:

> "O Jerusalem, Jerusalem, you who kill the prophets and stone those sent to you, how often I have longed to gather your children together, as a hen gathers her chicks under her wings, but you were not willing. Look, your house is left to you desolate. **For I tell you, you will not see me again until you say, 'Blessed is he who comes in the name of the Lord.'"** (Matthew 23:37-39)

Just as Jerusalem's leaders rejected him, Jesus cannot enter and reign in our hearts either until we acknowledge him for who he is: "The one who comes in the name of the Lord Yahweh."

Q2. (Psalm 118) What does "the stone the builders rejected" (verses 22-23) have to do with the Messiah? What do verses 25-27 have to do with the Messiah?
http://www.joyfulheart.com/forums/index.php?showtopic=704

I Will Give You Thanks (118:28-29)

> "You are my God, and I will give you thanks;
> you are my God, and I will exalt you.
> Give thanks to the LORD, for he is good;
> his love endures forever." (118:28-29)

The psalm concludes as it began, with thanksgiving. The final verse repeats the first: "Give thanks!"

This concludes our look at psalms of thanksgiving.

Psalm 34 – Taste and See that the Lord Is Good

However, there is one final psalm I'd like us to consider as we conclude our study of the psalms. It is a psalm of deliverance – Psalm 34, one of the favorite psalms of all time. Its main structural element is an acrostic, with each verse beginning with a successive letter of the Hebrew alphabet. This structure seems to limit the psalmist's poetic themes to couplets in single verses. However, you can see a clear division between the early part of the psalm and the latter part.

1. **Rejoice with Me** (verses 1-10). In a hymn of praise, the psalmist calls his hearers to rejoice along with him because of the wonderful deliverance he experienced from fear and trouble.
2. **Learn from Me** (verses 11-22). Now the psalmist assumes the teacher's role, and the genre shifts to a wisdom psalm with instructions reminiscent of wisdom literature such as Proverbs.

The psalmist is identified in the title as David. The occasion is also given: "When he pretended to be insane before Abimelech, who drove him away, and he left." This points to an incident described in 1 Samuel 21:10-22:1. David suddenly becomes aware that Saul is serious about killing him. So that Saul can't capture him, David flees to the Philistine city of Gath, an arch enemy of Israel. The king is named Achish. (The psalmist's designation "Abimelech" probably refers to the name of a dynasty of kings of Gath. Abimelech means "son of the king."). When Achish's servants remind him of David's military prowess exercised against the Philistines, David gets worried. After all, Goliath whom David slew as a young man was from Gath. Out of fear that he will be executed, David feigns insanity. Achish concludes he is harmless and lets him go. David doesn't stick around. But once free from danger from both enemies – the Philistines and Saul – he composes this psalm of praise and exhortation.

I Will Bless the Lord at All Times (34:1-2)

The psalm begins with David's praise and then a call for others to join him.

"¹I will extol the LORD at all times;
his praise will always be on my lips.

²My soul will boast in the LORD;
    let the afflicted hear and rejoice." (34:1-2)

Here again we find the familiar praise words. "Extol" (NIV) or "bless" is *bārak*, that we found in Psalm 103:1 – "kneel, bless, praise, salute" (chapter 9).[14] The noun "praise" is *tehillâ*, "renown, praise, glory," which we discussed above in Psalm 100:4b (from the verb *hālal*). "Boast" (verse 2) is the verb *hālal*, the root of "Hallelujah," which we first explored in Psalm 150:1 (chapter 4). Literally verse 2 reads, "In Yahweh shall glory my soul." *Hālal* means to "praise, hail, acclaim," but also to brag or boast in someone.[15] "Rejoice" (NIV) or "be glad" is *śāmēah*, " being glad or joyful with the whole disposition,"[16] which we saw above in Psalm 100:2a.

How often are we to bring praise to God? "at all times" (verse 1a) and "always" (verse 1b). This is something like Paul's admonitions:

> **Be joyful always; pray continually; give thanks in all circumstances**, for this is God's will for you in Christ Jesus." (1 Thessalonians 5:16-18)

> "... **Always giving thanks** to God the Father for everything, in the name of our Lord Jesus Christ." (Ephesians 5:20)

So often we reserve praise for Sunday morning worship. During the rest of the week we might read the Bible and pray, but is praise on our lips always? This is a matter of training, of habit. Write yourself a note where you can read it often: "Have I praised God in the last hour?" You'll fail often at first, but as you begin to remind yourself to praise, it will eventually come naturally to you. This is a part of being "transformed by the renewing of your mind" that God wants to do in your life (Romans 12:2).

Magnifying and Exalting (34:3)

Verse 3 has a pair of verbs and a command to praise:

> "O **magnify** the LORD with me,
>   and let us **exalt** his name together." (34:3, NRSV)

"Magnify" (NRSV, KJV), "glorify" (NIV) is the verb *gādal*, "to become great or important, promote, praise." In the Piel stem as here it has a causative connotation, "magnify, consider great," calling worshippers to ascribe greatness to the Lord and to his name (Psalm 35:27; 40:16; 70:4).[17]

[14] John N. Oswalt, *bārak*, TWOT #285.
[15] Leonard J. Coppes, *hālal*, TWOT #50.
[16] Bruce K. Waltke, *śāmēah*, TWOT #2268.
[17] Elmer B. Smick, *gādal*, TWOT #315.

"Exalt" is *rûm*, "be high, lofty." A frequent idiom is the expression of God "being high" or "exalted," representing God's high rank.[18] In the polel stem it means "to lift someone high, exalt, extol God."[19]

Can mere man make God any higher than he already is? No, but he can make God's reputation more exalted by his testimony of God's deliverance. And that is what David does in verses 4 and 6.

Q3. (Psalm 34:1-3) Why should we praise God continually? What are barriers to continual praise? What does continual praise do to our spirit? How are you training yourself to praise continually?
http://www.joyfulheart.com/forums/index.php?showtopic=705

I Sought the Lord and He Delivered Me (34:4-7)

David gives his testimony:

"[4]I sought the LORD, and he answered me;
he delivered (*yāsha'*) me from all my fears.
[5]Those who look to him are radiant;
their faces are never covered with shame.
[6]This poor man called, and the LORD heard him;
he saved (*yāsha'*) him out of all his troubles.
[7]The angel of the LORD encamps around those who fear him,
and **he delivers** (*ḥālas*) them." (34:4-7)

No doubt the fears and troubles that David is recalling relate to the close call he had in the Philistine city of Gath. The term "delivered" (NIV), "saved" (KJV, NRSV) in verses 4b and 6b is *yāsha'*, in the Hiphil stem, "save, deliver, give victory, help."[20] A synonym is found in verse 7b translated "delivers," *ḥālas*, in the Piel stem, "rescue, deliver, save." The root idea

---

[18] Andrew Bowling, *rûm*, TWOT #213.
[19] *Rûm*, Holladay 334-335.
[20] John E. Hartley, *yāsha'*, TWOT #929.

is "to draw off," so here David testifies that God "pulls him out" of his distress.[21] Those who seek Yahweh, who look to him, are radiant[22] with joy (5a) rather than "covered" with shame and sorrow (5b).

David "sought the LORD" (4a) and "called" (6a); Yahweh answered. How did he answer? David suggests that his deliverance was the work of "the angel of the LORD," a phrase which suggests Yahweh himself. "Encamp," ḥānā, has the root idea, "to bend, curve," suggesting that the ancient Semitic camp was circular in layout, or perhaps that the lines of a besieging force were circular.[23] If Yahweh and his host of angelic armies sets up their military encampment around believers, nothing can get through to harm them. That is the image here.

Angels rescued Lot and his family from Sodom (Genesis 19:1-22). An angel shut the mouths of lions to deliver Daniel (Daniel 6:22). Twelve legions of angels could have been instantly at Jesus' disposal in the Garden of Gethsemane (Matthew 26:53). An angel woke Peter up in the middle of the night, released his shackles, and opened the doors of Herod's maximum security prison (Acts 12:6-10). Perhaps David had a similar experience of angelic intervention that allowed him to escape from the city of Gath in one piece.

Taste and See that the Lord is Good (34:8-10)

Now David invites his hearers to trust in the Lord also, so that they can experience his trustworthiness and abundant provision:

> "Taste and see that the LORD is good;
> blessed is the man who takes refuge in him." (34:8)

With the incident in Gath, God has been stretching David, teaching him to trust in, to rely on, to "take refuge" in the Lord. And God came through! Now David is excited to share this experience, to encourage others that they too can trust in God. He calls out across the centuries to you and me: "Taste and see that the LORD is good." "Taste" is ṭā'am, "taste, eat, perceive," with the primary meaning, "to try, or to evaluate with the tongue, normally with a view to consumption if the flavor is suitable."[24] Have you tasted? Have you found that you can take refuge in the Lord? If not, step out in trust at your next opportunity, your next trial. You will find the blessing of the person who "takes refuge" in the Lord.

---

[21] Elmer B. Smick, ḥālas, TWOT #667; Holladay 106b, piel 3.
[22] Nāhar, metaphorical, "shine, be radiant (with joy)" Holladay 230b, II.
[23] Victor P. Hamilton, ḥānā, TWOT #690.
[24] Ralph H. Alexander, ṭā'am, TWOT #815.

David also exhorts us trust God for our provision, much like Jesus did for his disciples: "But seek first his kingdom and his righteousness, and all these things will be given to you as well" (Matthew 6:33). David tells us:

> "⁹Fear the LORD, you his saints,
> for those who fear him lack nothing.
> ¹⁰The lions may grow weak and hungry,
> but those who seek the LORD lack no good thing." (34:9-10)

Lions are "king of the jungle," the top of the food chain. But when even lions are hungry, God will supply those who trust in God. That is the promise of these verses. We are told to do two things:

- **"Fear the LORD,"** that is, reverence him, put our confidence in him even when others around us don't take God seriously.
- **"Seek the LORD,"** that is, make a concerted effort to connect with him, even when our first efforts seem to fail. (See more on "seeking the Lord" in chapter 2 on Psalm 27:8.)

I Will Teach You the Fear of Yahweh (34:11-14)

Now David turns to a teaching mode. He has exhorted us to "fear the LORD" in verse 9. Now he spells out what this entails, the practicalities of serving Yahweh in a world that doesn't take Him seriously:

> "¹¹Come, my children, listen to me;
> I will teach you the fear of the LORD.
> ¹²Whoever of you loves life
> and desires to see many good days,
> ¹³keep your tongue from evil
> and your lips from speaking lies.
> ¹⁴Turn from evil and do good;
> seek peace and pursue it." (34:11-14)

Notice the strong ethical instruction about evil speaking, lies, unrighteous. Verse 13 spells it out in a *negative* format; verse 14 looks at it from a *positive* point of view.

I am particularly interested in verse 14: "Seek peace and pursue it." What does that mean? "Peace" is *shālōm*. It is not merely the absence of strife, though that is part of it. *Shālōm* is something much broader. The general meaning behind the root is of completion and fulfillment, of entering into a state of wholeness, unity, harmony, a restored relationship. Implicit in *shālōm* is the idea of unimpaired relationships with others and fulfillment in one's undertakings.[25] Seeking *shālōm*, moreover, is a state of fulfillment in God's presence, with God's help.

So we are told to fear God, seek God. The same idea is found here. We are to both seek after God's wholeness and pursue it with all our strength. We are to chase peace and not quit until we have achieved it. A zeal for peace, a zeal for God. This is what Jesus was talking about when he said, "Seek first the kingdom of God and his righteousness..." (Matthew 6:33). Lord, give me a passion for You that doesn't quit!

His Ears Are Attentive to the Cry of the Righteous (34:15-16)

Sometimes we may feel like our prayers are imposing on God. Not so, says David:

""¹⁵The **eyes of the Lord are on the righteous**
and **his ears are attentive to their cry**;
¹⁶the face of the Lord is against those who do evil,
to cut off the memory of them from the earth." (34:15-16)

God has his channel always open to hear you when you pray to him and he listens attentively.

Many Are the Afflictions of the Righteous, but the Lord Delivers (34:17-20)

In verses 4-7 David talked about God's deliverance in his time of need. Now he generalizes it for all believers. I called out and the Lord delivered me. You can call out, too, and he'll hear you as well:

"¹⁷The righteous cry out, and the Lord hears them;
he **delivers** (*nāṣal*) them from all their troubles.
¹⁸The Lord is close to the brokenhearted
and **saves** (*yāsha'*) those who are crushed in spirit.
¹⁹A righteous man may have many troubles,
but the Lord **delivers** (*nāṣal*) him from them all;
²⁰he protects all his bones,
not one of them will be broken." (34:17-20)

Verse 20 is referred to in John 19:36 as referring to the Messiah. Two verses pop out for me:

"The Lord is close to the **brokenhearted**
and saves those who are **crushed in spirit**." (34:18)

I've been there. My heart has been broken. My spirit has been crushed. Yet I've experienced God there with me. He's there with you, too. When your troubles seem to crash down upon

---

[25] G. Lloyd Carr, *shālōm*, TWOT #2401a.

you and you nearly lose hope, he is with you. Call out, seek him in your lowest time. You'll find him close, nearby. Reach out.

The other verse that I call to mind I remember best from the RSV:

"Many are the afflictions of the righteous;
but the LORD delivers him out of them all." (34:19)

We are not immune to the troubles common to this life. We even face death, sooner often than we would like. The psalmist who lived on the far side of the cross, believed in the Lord's ultimate deliverance from trouble. On this side of the cross we see that the Lord ultimately delivers from death itself. Resurrection is our promise. The message here is: Don't give up hope. Don't quit. The Lord is with you and he will bring you through even this!

The Lord Redeems His Servants, Does Not Condemn Them (34:21-22)

David, fresh from deliverance from Gath, concludes his psalm of deliverance with a word of hope. In the end, God will come through:

"²¹Evil will slay the wicked;
the foes of the righteous will be condemned.
²²The LORD redeems his servants;
no one will be condemned who takes refuge in him." (34:21-22)

In verse 22 there are two very precious promises containing images pregnant with meaning:

1. Redeemer of Servants (34:22a)

"The LORD redeems his servants." (34:22a)

We've come to the concept of "redeem" several times. We've seen the "Kinsman-Redeemer" (*gāʾal*) who does not desert his own kin, but does what it takes to pay their debts, buy back their land, pay whatever ransom is necessary to secure their freedom.[26] This word "redeem" here is similar, *pādā*, but focuses on the financial part of redemption, "to transfer ownership from one to another through payment of a price."[27] In verse 22a, Yahweh values his servants so much that he will pay whatever is necessary to secure their freedom.

This is fulfilled on the cross, where the Father gave his best, his only Son. And the Son's love and obedience met the piercing of the nails through his hands and our sins through his soul. He redeemed us at highest cost. We are worth an infinite amount to God.

2. Faithful Judge (22b)

"No one will be condemned who takes refuge in him." (34:22b)

[26] R. Laird Harris, *gāʾal*, TWOT #300.
[27] William B. Coker, *pādâ*, TWOT #1734.

Have you ever felt so oppressed by your guilt that you didn't think God could – or should – forgive you? That you were hopeless in your sin? I have a marvelous promise for you. If you take refuge in the Lord and his Messiah, Jesus, you don't have to worry about your sins. We are hidden in God's refuge. The Apostle Paul puts it this way:

> "For you died, and your life is now hidden with Christ in God. When Christ, who is your life, appears, then you also will appear with him in glory." (Colossians 3:3-4)

If you are wounded, God is close. If you are brokenhearted, he is near. Reach out. If you feel trapped he'll redeem you – *has* redeemed you through Christ. If you feel guilty, he has given you an amazing promise: take refuge in him and your condemnation goes away.

> "Therefore, there is now no condemnation for those who are in Christ Jesus, because through Christ Jesus the law of the Spirit of life set me free from the law of sin and death." (Romans 8:1-2)

There it is, Psalm 34, a wonderful acrostic psalm of deliverance. It speaks across the ages from a miraculous deliverance from a Philistine city in 1000 BC, to the needs of believers in the twenty-first century AD. Our everlasting God is present to thank, to praise, to enjoy, and to deliver!

Q4. (Psalm 34:18-22) What encouragement does David give to the brokenhearted? What does it mean that God "redeems" you? How can we avoid condemnation according to Psalm 34:22?
http://www.joyfulheart.com/forums/index.php?showtopic=706

Exercise. For one of the psalms in this lesson – or another psalm with a similar theme – do one of the suggested exercises to help you experience the Psalms in Appendix 1. These include such things as praying a psalm, meditating, reading to a shut-in, paraphrasing, writing your own psalm, singing, preparing a liturgy, and memorizing. Then report to the forum what the exercise meant to you personally or share what you've written with others.
http://www.joyfulheart.com/forums/index.php?showtopic=707

Prayer

Lord, thank you for your great blessings in Christ Jesus. Teach us to always have thanksgiving on our lips. Teach us to take refuge in you when we are in trouble. Soothe our troubled souls when we are wounded and broken. And give us hope, joy, and *shalom* in You. In Jesus' holy name, we pray. Amen.

Songs

- **"All People that on Earth Do Dwell"** (Old Hundredth), words attributed to William Keth (1561), music attributed to Louis Bourgeois (1551).
- **"Bless His Holy Name,"** words and music by Andrae Crouch (© 1973, Lexicon Music, Inc.). Psalm 34:1, 3.
- **"For the Lord Is Good,"** words and music by Gary Sadler and Lynn DeShazo (© 1997, Integrity's Hosanna! Music). Psalm 100:5.
- **"God Is Good"** (all the time), words and music by Morris Chapman (© 1992, Maranatha Praise, Inc.). Psalm 100:5
- **"He Has Made Me Glad"** ("I Will Enter His Gates with Thanksgiving in My Heart"), words and music by Leona Von Brethorst (© 1976, Maranatha Praise, Inc.). Psalm 100:4.
- **"I Will Bless the Lord at All Times,"** author unknown. Psalm 34:1-4.
- **"I Will Magnify,"** words and music by Scott Palazzo (© 1985, Mercy Publishing). Psalm 34:3.
- **"Lovely Noise,"** words and music by Greg Sparks and Rebecca Ed Sparks (© 1997, worshiptogether.com songs). Psalm 107:8-9.
- **"Redeemed, How I Love to Proclaim It,"** words by Fanny Crosby (1882), music by William J. Kirkpatrick. Psalm 107:2.
- **"Shout to the Lord,"** words and music by Darlene Zschench (© 1993, Hillsong Publishing). Psalm 100:1.
- **"Sing to the Lord,"** words and music by Bill Bastone and Tom Howard (© 1984, Maranatha Music). Psalm 100.
- **"The Lord Is Good,"** words and music by Dan Marks (© 1982, Maranatha! Music). Psalm 34:8.
- **"The Haven of Rest,"** words: Henry L. Gilmour (1890), music: George D. Moore. Psalm 107:29-30.
- **"This Is the Day the Lord Hath Made,"** words: Isaac Watts (1719), music, "Arlington" by Thomas A. Arne (1762). Psalm 118:24.

- **"This Is the Day,"** words and music by Les Garrett (© 1967, 1980, Scripture in Song / Maranatha! Music). Psalm 118:24.
- **"Through All the Changing Scenes of Life,"** words by Nahum Tate and Nicholas Brady (1698), music: "Irish" melody from *A Collection of Hymns and Sacred Poems* (1749). Psalm 34.3.
- **"Thou Art My God,"** words and music by Tony Hopkins (© 1972, Scripture in Song / Maranatha! Music), Psalm 118:28-28.

Epilogue (Psalms 47 and 119)

We've come to the end and I am sad. I am sad because I have so enjoyed an immersion in the Psalms and I hope you have, but now it is over. I'm also sad that I haven't had a chance to share with you others of my favorite psalms. I love Psalms 18, 86, and 89, for example, but they're too long to treat adequately in the space we have.

Psalm 47 – Clap Your Hands All Nations

Here's a short one:

"¹Clap your hands, all you nations;
shout to God with cries of joy.
²How awesome is the LORD Most High,
the great King over all the earth!"
(Psalm 47:1-2)

Detail of Pieter de Grebber (Dutch painter, ca. 1600-1653), "King David in Prayer" (1635-40), oil on canvas, 94x84 cm, Museum Catharijneconvent, Utrecht..

Here the psalmist calls all nations to worship Yahweh and acknowledge that he not just a national God. He is the ultimate King over the whole earth. What does it mean in Hebrew culture to clap one's hands? In western cultures clapping means to applaud and bring honor to a person. In the Old Testament clapping can be a sign of joy (here, Psalm 98:8, and Isaiah 55:12) or triumph (Nahum 3:19). A king is applauded at his coronation (2 Kings 11:12). In a business relationship clapping the hands signifies pledging oneself as collateral, but clapping can also be a sign of mocking.[1] Interesting!

You see, it is difficult for me to quit.

---

[1] *Tāqa'*, "blow, clap, strike, sound." In Nahum 3:19 clapping signifies triumph over an enemy (Ronald F. Youngblood, *tāqa'*, TWOT #2541). *Māḥā'*, "strike" is used of clapping in joy in Psalm 98:8 and Isaiah 55:12, but negatively in Ezekiel 25:6. Another word used for clapping is *nākā*, "smite strike, hit" in 2 Kings 11:12, clapping hands before the king (Marvin R. Wilson, *nākā*, TWOT #1364). The verb *śāpaq* is used in the sense of clapping as mocking and scorn in Job 27:23; 34:37; Lamentations 2:15.

Psalm 119 – Delight in the Law of the Lord

How can we leave the Psalms without experiencing Psalm 119, the longest psalm in the Bible, all of 176 verses? It is organized as an acrostic psalm. This time eight couplets all begin with Aleph, then eight couplets begin with Beth, and so on. It is a written as a meditation on the "law of the LORD" in all its different facets. It contains many memorable verses, such as:

"How can a young man keep his way pure?
By living according to your word." (119:9)

"I have hidden your word in my heart
that I might not sin against you." (119:10)

"Open my eyes that I may see
wonderful things in your law." (119:18)

"Before I was afflicted I went astray,
but now I obey your word." (119:67)

"It was good for me to be afflicted
so that I might learn your decrees." (119:71)

"I know, O LORD, that your laws are righteous,
and in faithfulness you have afflicted me." (119:75)

"Your word is a lamp to my feet
and a light for my path." (119:105)

"The unfolding of your words gives light;
it gives understanding to the simple." (119:130)

"Your promises have been thoroughly tested,
and your servant loves them." (119:140)

"Great peace have they who love your law,
and nothing can make them stumble." (119:165)

I must stop. There are still more psalms I'd love to share with you. But though this is an end of our study, my prayer is that it is a new beginning of your exploration of the wonderful Word of God contained in the Psalms. It is rich! It is soul-food! It is sweet!

"How sweet are your words to my taste,
sweeter than honey to my mouth!" (119:103)

If you haven't already, why don't you plan now to read a psalm every day. Revel in the Psalms. Enjoy them for a lifetime. They are God's wonderful gift to his people and a song-book for our souls.

Prayer

Father, thank you for the wonderful time we've had experiencing the Psalms. Thank you for your blessing, your goodness, your love. Help me, help us to praise you to highest heaven, and when we have laments to turn our hearts toward You who alone can heal us. Thank you. In Jesus' wonderful name, we pray. Amen.

Songs

- **"Clap Your Hands"** (all you people), may be sung as a round. Words and music by Jimmy Owens (© 1972, Bud John Songs, Inc., admin by EMI Christian Music Publishing). Psalm 47:1.

- **"More Precious Than Silver"** (LORD, You are...), words and music by Lynn DeShazo (© 1979, Hosanna! Music). Psalm 119:72.

- **"O Word of God Incarnate,"** words: William W. How (1867), music "Munich," from *Neuvermehrtes Gesangbuch* (1663), adapted by Felix Mendelssohn (1847). Psalm 119:105.

- **"Teach Me Thy Way,"** words and music by Tom Howard and Bill Batstone (© 1986, Maranatha! Music). Psalm 119:35-41.

- **"Thy Word"** (is a Lamp unto my feet, and a Light unto my path), words by Amy Grant, music by Michael W. Smith (© 1984 Meadowgreen Music Co., Word Music LLC. Psalm 119:105

- **"You Are the Mighty King,"** words and music by Eddie Espinosa (© 1982, Mercy / Vineyard Publishing). Psalm 47:2.

Appendix 1: Exercises to Help You Experience the Psalms

A study of the Psalms should never be merely an academic or cognitive exercise, as important as that may be. The psalms were written as poetry and song to be experienced, to touch the heart and emotions.

In order to encourage you to truly experience the psalms and make them your own, **I'm asking you to complete one of the following exercises for each of the lessons in this study.** These aren't designed to create busywork, but to stretch you spiritually. When you finish, report back on the Forum how the exercise worked for you. Ideally, you'll vary the exercises from lesson to lesson to allow the Psalms to become part of you in new ways.

1. **Pray a Psalm**. Select one of the psalms along the theme of the lesson. Then, using the ideas and as many of the words as seem to fit your situation, pray that prayer to God, inserting your own struggles and needs within the prayer. Go through the entire psalm, paraphrasing it as you pray it sincerely to God. Many people have exercised this kind of prayer – they pray through every Scripture passage they read. Why don't you start this practice with one of the psalms?

2. **Meditate on a Psalm**. To meditate means to think deeply about something and mull it over in your mind over a period of time. You might read it several times in different translations. Say it over to yourself to feel the words on your lips. Write it out longhand. Consider the meaning of each important word. Memorization is another exercise, but memorizing is a good way to meditate on a verse or a passage.

3. **Read a Psalm to a Shut-in**. People who are home-bound or in hospitals, nursing homes, jails, etc. need encouragement. As your exercise, read a psalm from this week's theme to a shut-in. If you read more than one you'll be doubly blessed!

4. **Paraphrase a Psalm**. Write out a paraphrase of the psalm of your choosing in your own words. Try to find modern-day synonyms and thoughts that correspond to the thoughts in the psalm. Don't be afraid to be creative. If you need ideas, try reading a few psalms from *The Message* to see how Eugene Peterson creatively paraphrased the Psalms.

5. **Write Your Own Psalm**. Write your own psalm based on the theme of this lesson. You're entirely free in how you do this. Some approaches include:

- Write in the style of Hebrew poetry using thought parallelism and imagery. This will be fun, though you may find it challenging. Consult my Introduction to Psalms in the section on Hebrew Poetry before beginning.
- Write a psalm with lines that rhyme like traditional Western poetry.
- Write a psalm in free verse, not bothering to make the lines rhyme. Just express yourself to God.
- Write a psalm in Haiku style.

Write a psalm in any style you wish. The idea here is to learn to express yourself to God more freely.

6. **Sing a Psalm**. Find a song, hymn, or praise chorus that relates to the theme of this chapter – and that is based on a psalm. Then sing it or lead it for your group. If you like, write your own song, or find a melody that you can use to sing the words of the song from a translation you prefer. Be creative here.

7. **Prepare a Liturgy, Responsive Reading, or Choral Reading from a Psalm**. Psalms are at the core of the liturgy of Catholic, Orthodox, and Anglican branches of the Church. Explore adapting a psalm for public worship. You might enjoy writing the script for a choral reading of a psalm or portion of a psalm creating parts for 3 or 4 readers. Then try it out during a worship service or in your small group or class. For an example of how this might look, see my Reader's Theater Script on Psalm 19 (Appendix 6)

8. **Teach or Preach a Psalm**. It's hard to prepare a message for people without really getting inside the text. Teach a psalm to a class of children, youth, or adults, or preach a psalm to your congregation.

9. **Memorize a Psalm**. "My mind is too old to memorize!" Hogwash! Try it, but perhaps start with a short psalm, or one you've already partially memorized. It's work, but you can do it and you'll find it very spiritually enriching. In ancient days many Hebrew boys memorized the entire Psalter. In his 90s, Billy Graham put it this way: "Over the years I've memorized many passages from the Bible, and I'm especially thankful now that I did this. I wish we gave more attention to Bible memorization in our churches today."[1] Memorize one psalm that relates to the theme of the lesson.

---

[1] Billy Graham in "Quotation Marks," *Christianity Today*, June 2007, p. 19.

Once you've completed the exercise you've chosen for this lesson, share it with someone else or report it in the section of the online Forum designated for that purpose. You can share the words if your exercise is written. Or share what doing this exercise meant to you personally. Or complain about being forced to memorize. Whatever. As you are accountable someone else, it will help stretch you to be more than you are today.

Appendix 2. Psalms in Worship throughout the Centuries

For thousands of years the Psalter has been a wonderful resource to enrich a person's spirit, both in public worship and in the believer's private devotional life.

Beginning with David

Though Hebrew poetry predates the time of David, he is the first person we know to use psalms devotionally. Seventy-three psalms are attributed to David, an extremely prolific poet and musician. He is known as "the sweet psalmist of Israel" (2 Samuel 23:1). I have no doubt that under the inspiration and guidance of the Spirit he composed psalms as a shepherd, on the run from Saul, and later as king. Throughout his life he would sing and compose, and in the process rejoice in his God.

Psalms in Temple Worship

David established orders of musicians and singers to bring regular organized worship before the tent in Jerusalem which David had pitched for the ark of God. First Chronicles tells us:

Simeon Solomon (1840-1905), "Hosanna" (1881), engraved by the Brothers Dalziel..

"Kenaniah the head Levite was in charge of the singing; that was his responsibility because he was skillful at it...." (1 Chronicles 15:22)

"He appointed some of the Levites to minister before the ark of the LORD, to make petition, to give thanks, and to praise the LORD, the God of Israel: Asaph was the chief, Zechariah second, then Jeiel .... They were to play the lyres and harps, Asaph was to sound the cymbals, and Benaiah and Jahaziel the priests were to blow the trumpets regularly before the ark of the covenant of God. That day David first committed to Asaph and his associates this psalm of thanks to the LORD...." (1 Chronicles 16:4-7)

This passage is followed by a psalm that presumably David had written for the occasion (1 Chronicles 16:8-36), parts of which are found in our Psalter – Psalm 105:1-15; Psalm 94 and Psalm 106:1, 47, and 48).

> "David left Asaph and his associates before the ark of the covenant of the LORD to minister there regularly, according to each day's requirements. He also left Obed-Edom and his sixty-eight associates to minister with them." (1 Chronicles 16:37-38)

Temple Singers. J.J. Tissot, "The Choristers" (1896-1900), watercolor.

By Jesus' day, Alfred Edersheim explains how psalm-singing in the Second Temple services followed the morning sacrifice:

> "The Levites, accompanied by instrumental music, began the Psalm of the day. It was sustained by no less than twelve voices, with which mingled the delicious treble from selected voices of young sons of the Levites, who, standing by their fathers, might take part in this service alone....

> The psalm of the day was always sung in three sections. At the close of each the priests drew three blasts from their silver trumpets and the people bowed down and worshipped. This closed the morning service."[1]

---

[1] Alfred Edersheim, *The Temple: Its Ministry and Services As They Were at the Time of Christ* (Eerdmans, reprinted 1960, from the original facsimile published in 1874), p. 172.

Psalms were sung in a particular pattern in the daily temple service:[2]

Sunday:	Psalm 24	Thursday:	Psalm 81
Monday:	Psalm 48	Friday:	Psalm 93
Tuesday:	Psalm 82	Saturday:	Psalm 92
Wednesday:	Psalm 94		

Special psalms were prepared for the new month, and other occasions, the Hallel during major Jewish holidays, and psalms for special sacrifices such as the "Psalm for the Thanksgiving Offering" (Psalm 100).

Psalms in the Synagogue

Though evidence is scanty, scholars believe that the institution of the Jewish synagogue developed during the exile, when worship at the temple was no longer possible. Even after the temple was built following the exile – and rebuilt by Herod – synagogues flourished, even in Jerusalem, the city of the temple itself (Acts 6:9). At the destruction of Jerusalem, some 400 to 500 synagogues were found in the city.[3] A synagogue could be formed by as few as ten males. The synagogue was the local house of worship. Jesus attended the synagogue regularly (Luke 4:16) and taught in synagogues up and down Galilee.

What was worship like in the synagogues of this era? They were devoted to prayer and the reading of the scripture. We have a number of indications that the Jews used psalms regularly on feast days as well as in their synagogue worship. George Foot Moore postulates:

> "It would seem natural that with other features of the temple worship, the songs of the Levites at the morning and evening sacrifices should be imitated in the synagogue. The first group of psalms to be so employed was Psalms 145-150; but it appears that in the middle of the second century AD, the daily repetition of the psalms was a pious practice of individuals rather than a regular observance of the congregation."[4]

The Passover ritual, too, drew heavily on the Psalms. The "hymn" sung by Jesus and the apostles at the conclusion of the Lord's Supper (Matthew 26:30) on the night of Passover was

---

[2] Edersheim, *Temple*, p. 172, footnote 2, cites Tamid, sec. 7, and Maimonides in Tamid.

[3] According to one legend, there were 394 synagogues at Jerusalem when the city was destroyed by Titus (*Ket.* 105), while a second tradition gives the number as 480 (*Yer. Meg.* 73d et al.). Cited by Wilhelm Bacher and Lewis N. Dembitz, "Synagogue," *Jewish Encyclopedia* (1906).

[4] George Foot Moore, *Judaism in the First Centuries of the Christian Era: The Age of Tannaim* (Hendrickson Publishers; reprinted 1997 from Harvard University Press edition, 1927), vol. 1, p. 296.

doubtless one the psalms prescribed for the occasion – the second half of the Hallel (Psalms 114-118 or 115-118).[5]

From Synagogue to House Church

Early Christianity was practiced in the temple and in the homes of believers (Acts 2:46). When the Apostle Paul would take the Gospel to a new city, he would typically begin by attending the local synagogue and teaching there about Jesus. Eventually, the Christians would be driven out of the synagogues and formed their own congregations, which were essentially Christian synagogues governed by elders (Acts 14:23). We have several passages of scripture, which indicate that psalms were part of the worship in these early house churches:

> "When you come together, everyone has a **hymn**, or a word of instruction, a revelation, a tongue or an interpretation. All of these must be done for the strengthening of the church." (1 Corinthians 14:26)

> "Be filled with the Spirit. Speak to one another with **psalms**, hymns and spiritual songs." (Ephesians 5:18b-19a)

> "Let the word of Christ dwell in you richly as you teach and admonish one another with all wisdom, and as you sing **psalms**, hymns and spiritual songs with gratitude in your hearts to God." (Colossians 3:16)

> "Is any one of you in trouble? He should pray. Is anyone happy? Let him sing **songs of praise**." (James 5:13)

The Post-Apostolic Church

After the original apostles died, psalms continued as part of the worship of the church. Tertullian (c. 160-225 AD) mentions singing songs from the scripture as part of the Lord's Supper celebration.[6] Church historian Arthur McGiffert notes,

> "In the church of Rome nothing except the Psalms and New Testament hymns (such as the *Gloria in Excelsis*, the *Magnificat*, the *Nunc Dimittis*, etc.) was, as a rule, sung in public worship before the fourth century."[7]

---

[5] Joachim Jeremias, *The Eucharistic Words of Jesus* (Oxford: Basil Blackwood, 1955), pp. 30-31, especially fn. 1 on page 31.

[6] Tertullian, *Apology*, 39.16. "Each is asked to stand forth and sing, as he can, a hymn to God, either one from the holy Scriptures or one of his own composing...."

[7] Arthur Cushman McGiffert, *The Church History of Eusebius*, p. 247, footnote 14, commenting on Eusebius, *Church History*, 28,5, in *A Select Library of Nicene and Post-Nicene Fathers of the Christian Church* (Second Series), Philip Schaff and Henry Wace (editors), vol. 1 (1890).

St. Jerome (c. 348-420 AD) shares something of the primitive monastic life that was beginning to develop within Christianity:

> "In the cottage of Christ [the monastery] all is simple and rustic: and except for the chanting of psalms there is complete silence. Wherever one turns the laborer at his plow sings Alleluia, the toiling mower cheers himself with psalms, and the vine-dresser while he prunes his vine sings one of the songs of David."[8]

The Liturgy of the Hours

Fra Angelico, detail of St. Benedict (1439-1445), fresco, Monastery of San Marco, Florence

While psalms were used in worship services in churches, in the growing monastic movement, the practice of reciting the Psalter formed the core of the devotional practice of the community. St. Benedict (c. 480-543) developed a widely-copied rule for monasteries known as The Rule of St. Benedict (c. 530-540 AD). Among other practices it outlined the *Opus Dei*, the Divine Office of prayers and psalms. This liturgy consisted of gatherings of the community at eight times during the day and night with the purpose to "sanctify" the day with prayer. At these various times they would say or chant together the set of prayers and psalms designated for that day and time. In time, the Divine Office involved reciting the entire Psalter through in a single week and would require several hours each day to complete. Clergy and most religious orders in both the Roman Catholic Church as well as Eastern Orthodox were – and are – required to recite the Divine Office. The best-known example of this is the beautiful Gregorian Chant practiced in certain orders, going back perhaps as far as Pope Gregory (c. 540-604 AD), for which it was named.

At Vatican II in the 1960s, the Roman Church revised the Liturgy of the Hours so that it now goes through the entire Psalter in one month rather than in one week, and reduced the number of required times of prayer each day. Those in the Roman Church that practice this discipline use the *Breviary*, a set of four volumes that contain the one-month Psalter plus the prayers for each day and each feast day.[9] Those living as part of a community, such as in a

---

[8] Jerome, *Epistle* 46.12.

[9] Univarsalis (www.universalis.com) contains the Breviary online with all the readings for the Liturgy of the Hours, based on the Roman Breviary 1985 edition, in a four-week cycle of the psalms. Scripture readings are from the Jerusalem Bible. Psalm translations are specially commissioned.

monastery or convent, recite their psalms and prayers together ("in choir") for at least some of services, such as morning and evening prayer. Clergy living alone recite these psalms and prayers by themselves privately.

Other churches with a liturgical tradition, such as Anglican, Episcopal, Lutheran, Presbyterian, Methodist, often have in their prayer book or book of discipline a calendar to guide the faithful in Morning Prayer and Evening Prayer (Vespers).

The effect of those practicing a discipline of the Liturgy of the Hours has been an immersion in the psalms and regular prayer. While it can be seen as a burden, for those who have entered into it wholeheartedly, it can be a lifetime of blessing.

Singing the Psalter

Protestant Churches, too, have a strong tradition of singing the Psalms. The Church of England, under heavy Puritan influence, sought to bring about reform by publishing a metrical psalmody that could be sung by a congregation. In 1562 John Day printed the Book of Psalms with psalm text translated by Thomas Sternhold, John Hopkins, and others. Standard metrical patterns were developed that could adapt each of the psalms to a common metrical pattern – which would then allow the psalm to be sung to one of several standard tunes. Patterns included: Common Meter (8.6.8.6), Short Meter (6.6.8.6), and Long Meter (8.8.8.8). Various adaptations were made in Scotland, New England, etc., but the psalms were the primary focus of singing in many Protestant congregations for hundreds of years.

Detail of Isaac Watts, hymn writer (1674-1748) by an unknown artist (1720-1735), National Portrait Gallery, London.

Isaac Watts (1674-1748) set a new direction for independent or congregational churches when he published his *Psalms of David* in 1719. Instead of close fitting translations, these hymns were poetic paraphrases of the biblical psalms. The best known of these today are probably "Our God, Our Help in Ages Past" (Psalm 90) and "Joy to the World, the Lord Is Come" (Psalm 98).

The nineteenth and twentieth centuries saw a near eclipse of psalm singing in most Protestant churches in North America, replaced by devotional lyrics and gospel songs with a more emotional and subjective bent.

Late Twentieth Century Psalm Singing

A liturgical renewal following World War II saw a revival of psalm-singing in some churches. Vatican II (1962-65) encouraged the use of psalms in worship and fostered a wealth of "responsorial psalms."

The Charismatic Renewal also brought about a huge surge of Christian music. During the 1970s and 1980s especially, singing the scriptures was common in some groups, though contemporary Christian music seems to have moved past that as a whole by the turn of the twenty-first century.

Throughout history the Psalms have often been central in both corporate worship and personal devotional practice. As the psalms have remained strong, the church has been revived and personal spiritual life has been enriched. Isn't it about time to renew the ancient practice of the Psalms in your congregation and in your life?

Appendix 3. How Should We Understand the Imprecatory Psalms in which Enemies Are Cursed?

The psalmists write of terrible injustices done to the righteous at the hands of enemies – slandering them, hunting them down, and slaying them. Many of the laments are evidence of the pain of injustice, the fruit of unrighteousness. Indeed, the whole creation groans in eager expectation for God to usher in the age of the Messiah when all wrongs are righted, all injustices judged, where righteousness reigns.

Imprecations and Curses

But along side that longing for justice to finally come, we occasionally hear the psalmists utter terrible curses against their enemies. These words are called imprecations, from "imprecate," "to invoke evil on, curse." Psalms that contain such passages are called imprecatory psalms. Let me give you a sampling of these curses:

Passage	Excerpt
7:6-16	"O righteous God, who searches minds and hearts, bring to an end the violence of the wicked and make the righteous secure." (7:9) Pretty mild so far.
35:4-10	"May those who seek my life be disgraced and put to shame; may those who plot my ruin be turned back in dismay. May they be like chaff before the wind, with the angel of the LORD driving them away." (35:4-5)
59:10-13	"But do not kill them, O Lord our shield, or my people will forget. In your might make them wander about, and bring them down. For the sins of their mouths, for the words of their lips, let them be caught in their pride. For the curses and lies they utter, consume them in wrath, consume them till they are no more." (59:11-13a)
69:22-28	"May their eyes be darkened so they cannot see, and their backs be bent forever. Pour out your wrath on them; let your fierce anger overtake them..... Charge them with crime upon crime; do not let them share in your salvation. May they be blotted out of the book of life and not be listed with the righteous." (69:23-24, 27-28)

83:9-18	"Make them like tumbleweed, O my God, like chaff before the wind. As fire consumes the forest or a flame sets the mountains ablaze, so pursue them with your tempest and terrify them with your storm." (83:13-15)
109:6-20	"May his children be fatherless and his wife a widow. May his children be wandering beggars; may they be driven from their ruined homes. May a creditor seize all he has; may strangers plunder the fruits of his labor. May no one extend kindness to him or take pity on his fatherless children. May his descendants be cut off, their names blotted out from the next generation." (109:9-13)
137:7-9	"O Daughter of Babylon, doomed to destruction, happy is he who repays you for what you have done to us – he who seizes your infants and dashes them against the rocks" (137:8-9)
139:19-22	"Do I not hate those who hate you, O LORD, and abhor those who rise up against you? I have nothing but hatred for them; I count them my enemies. (139:21-22)

Some of these are pretty terrible indeed! How do we understand them?

A Story of Persecution and Hatred

When I was a young pastor I had an elderly couple in my congregation from Czechoslovakia. The husband had been a Baptist pastor, first in Czechoslovakia and later in Chicago. But now they were retired. I would visit them and bring them the Lord's Supper as their health failed.

And I would ask them about their life and ministry. When they spoke of their time as leaders of a Protestant congregation in Eastern Europe you could almost sense them begin to tighten up in anger. They and their flock had suffered terrible persecution from Roman Catholics in their district. And though their tormenters had probably died by this time, the hate that evil had engendered lived on in this couple – especially in the wife.

If she were a psalmist, I could almost imagine the kinds of poetic curses she would hurl at her enemies. What a tragedy! What a tragedy that this hatred was between people who both name the name of Christ. What a tragedy that this otherwise sweet couple was so very bitter! Christ came to end the hatred.

A Longing for Justice and Judgment

When it comes to the Psalms, first we need to see what is "right" and "righteous" about these psalm invectives against one's enemies. Three attitudes are quite appropriate:

1. **Hating evil and injustice**. We need to be very clear about our position against evil. The world waffles and excuses. We must be sure that our desire to be tolerant doesn't water down our own value system.

2. **Desiring that justice be executed** to end the tyranny of sin. Our justice system has terrible consequences for criminals, but it is very important for our society that justice is actually done and, where appropriate, criminal behavior is punished.

3. **A zeal that God's good name not be discredited** by evil continuing to be allowed. This zeal goes hand in hand with the shame that God's people feel when sin is exalted and righteousness is condemned.

So far, so good. But the psalmists sometimes cross the line.

The Fine Line between Justice and Revenge

There is a very fine line between (1) a desire for justice to prevail over unrighteousness and (2) a *personalization* of that unrighteousness. It's easy to say, "Hate the sin, love the sinner," but this is easier said than done. If we are not careful – and empowered by God's Spirit – we very easily begin to hate both the sin *and* the sinner, especially if the sinner is intent on destroying us.

That's what happened to my retired pastor couple. Their bitterness set in and they justified it. They became blind to their own passionate hatred for their persecutors because they despised oppression and injustice so keenly.

This is tricky stuff. Before we condemn David and the other psalmists to harshly, let's examine our own hearts, too. We may be a bit more sophisticated about our unforgiveness, but so long as we hold unforgiveness towards our persecutors, we too stand under the same judgment that we would render towards the psalmists.

Christ Our Exemplar and Judge

Of course, the one who will judge us is Christ himself. Oppression had borne fruit in hatred for millennia before the Messiah came. David and his descendents were but types and shadows of the true King, who would usher in the Kingdom of God. When Messiah Jesus came, he instituted in himself a new era of love. He taught us what it is like to truly love our neighbor.

> "Blessed are those who are persecuted because of righteousness, for theirs is the kingdom of heaven. Blessed are you when people insult you, persecute you and falsely say

all kinds of evil against you because of me. Rejoice and be glad, because great is your reward in heaven, for in the same way they persecuted the prophets who were before you." (Matthew 5:10-12)

"You have heard that it was said, 'Love your neighbor and hate your enemy.' But I tell you: Love your enemies and pray for those who persecute you, that you may be sons of your Father in heaven. He causes his sun to rise on the evil and the good, and sends rain on the righteous and the unrighteous. If you love those who love you, what reward will you get? Are not even the tax collectors doing that? And if you greet only your brothers, what are you doing more than others? Do not even pagans do that? Be perfect, therefore, as your heavenly Father is perfect." (Matthew 5:43-48)

That is what Messiah taught us in his words. Then he completed his teaching by demonstrating what this meant. They slandered him at his trial. They brutally scourged him. They mocked him. And finally they crucified him, inflicting on the Son of the Living God, their Savior, the most cruel and prolonged of punishments. And he said:

"Father, forgive them, for they do not know what they are doing." (Luke 23:34)

He, the Righteous One, died for the unrighteous who were killing him, in order to bear their sins and iniquities away. Forgiveness did not come cheap to Jesus. Nor is forgiving our enemies easy for us.

Progressive Revelation

So while recognizing that hating our enemies and wishing horrible things to happen to them isn't Christian, let's give them a break. The psalmists were *pre*-Christian. They hadn't heard Christ's teaching. They hadn't witnessed Christ's forgiveness at his death.

We believe in "progressive revelation" – that all the truth is not understood or unwrapped in the Old Testament. Some revelation awaited the coming of the Messiah to bring it. The Old Testament saints understood faith pretty well. But they sometimes came up short when it came to love. They lived according to the light they had. But "the true Light that gives light to every man was coming into the world" (John 1:9).

How to Respond to the Psalmists' Terrible Curses

When you come to an imprecatory psalm where the writer curses his enemies, here's how I recommend you handle it:

1. Recognize the rightness of hating sin and unrighteousness.
2. Acknowledge that the psalmist's curses are an example of pre-Christian attitudes. They are understandable. They are human. But they are not to be examples for our lives as Christians.

3. Examine your own heart to see if that same kind of bitterness and hatred is lurking deep within. And if the Lord allows you to see it there, repent and forgive. Let it go, and claim the higher road of Christ and his cross.

To study this matter further I recommend that you read:

*   Derek Kidner, *Psalms 1-72* (InterVarsity Press, 1973), pp. 25-32. Kidner offers a carefully nuanced examination of curses in the Psalms and in the New Testament. Well worth reading!
*   C.S. Lewis, *Reflections on the Psalms* (Harcourt, Brace and Company, 1958), chapter 3, pp. 20-33. Lewis offers an essay, a thoughtful reflection on the sin of cursing one's enemies. While not excusing the curses, he concludes that the moral indignation behind such curses is better than the amorality that isn't upset about injustice.

Appendix 4. New Testament Quotations from the Psalms

Copied from the appendix in A. F. Kirkpatrick, *The Book of Psalms* (The Cambridge Bible; Cambridge University Press, 1902)

2:1, 2	Acts 4:25, 26
2:7	Acts 13:33; Hebrews 1:5 ; 5:5
2:8, 9	Revelation 2:26, 27; 12:5; 19:15
4:4	Ephesians 4:26
5:9	Romans 3:13
6:3a	John 12:27
6:8	Matthew 7:23; Luke 13:27
8:2	Matthew 21:16
8:4-6	Hebrews 2:6-8
8:6	1 Corinthians 15:27; Ephesians 1:22
10:7	Romans 3:14
14:1c, 2b, 3	Romans 3:10-12
16:8-11	Acts 2:25-28
16:10b	Acts 13:35
18:2b	Hebrews 2:13
18:49	Romans 15:9
19:4	Romans 10:18
22:1	Matthew 27:46; Mark 15:34
22:7	Matthew 27:39; Mark 15:29; Luke 23:35

22:8	Matthew 27:43
22:18	John 19:24; compare Matthew 27:35; Mark 15:24; Luke 23:34
22:22	Hebrews 2:12
24:1	1 Corinthians 10:26 [28]
31:5a	Luke 23:46
32:1, 2	Romans 4:7, 8
34:8	1 Peter 2:3
34:12-16	1 Peter 3:10-12
34:20	John 19:36
35:19b	John 15:25
36:1b	Romans 3:18
37:11a	Matthew 5:5
38:11	Luke 23:49
40:6-8	Hebrews 10:5-7
41:9	John 13:18
41:13	Luke 1:68
42:5	Matthew 26:38; Mark 14:34
44:22	Romans 8:36
45:6, 7	Hebrews 1:8, 9
48:2	Matthew 5:35
51:4	Romans 3:4
53:1-3	Romans 3:10-12
55:22	1 Peter 5:7
62:12	Matthew 16:27; Romans 2:6

68:18	Ephesians 4:8
69:4	John 15:25
69:9a	John 2:17
69:9b	Romans 15:3
69:21	Matthew 27:34, 48; Mark 15:36; Luke 23:36; John 19:28, 29
69:22, 23	Romans 11:9, 10
69:25	Acts 1:20
72:18	Luke 1:68
78:2	Matthew 13:35
78:24	John 6:31
82:6	John 10:34
86:9	Revelation 15:4
88:8	Luke 23:49
89:10	Luke 1:51
89:20	Acts 13:22
90:4	2 Peter 3:8
91:11, 12	Matthew 4:6; Luke 4:10, 11
91:13	Luke 10:19
94:11	1 Corinthians 3:20
94:14	Romans 11:1, 2
95:7-11	Hebrews 3:7-11, 15, 18; 4:1, 3, 5, 7
97:7	Hebrews 1:6
98:3	Luke 1:54
102:25-27	Hebrews 1:10-12

103:17	Luke 1:50
104:4	Hebrews 1:7
105:8, 9	Luke 1:72, 73
106:10	Luke 1:71
106:45	Luke 1:72
106:48	Luke 1:68
107:9	Luke 1:53
109:8	Acts 1:20
109:25	Matthew 27:39
110:1	Matthew 22:44; Mark 12:36; Luke 20:42, 43; Acts 2:34, 35; Hebrews 1:13. Compare. Matthew 26:64; Mark 14:62; 16:19; Luke 22:69; 1 Corinthians 15:25; Ephesians 1:20; Colossians 3:1; Hebrews 1:3; 8:1; 10:12, 13; 12:2; 1 Peter 3:22
110:4	Hebrews 5:6; 6:20; 7:17, 21
111:9a	Luke 1:68
111:9c	Luke 1:49
112:9	2 Corinthians 9:9
116:10	2 Corinthians 4:13
117:1	Romans 15:11
118:6	Hebrews 13:6
118:22, 23	Matthew 21:42; Mark 12:10, 11; Luke 20:17; Acts 4:11; 1 Peter 2:4, 7
118:25, 26	Matthew 21:9; 23:39; Mark 11:9; Luke 13:35; 19:38; John 12:13
132:5	Acts 7:46
132:11	Acts 2:30
132:17	Luke 1:69

135:14a	Hebrews 10:30
140:3b	Romans 3:13
143:2b	Romans 3:20
146:6	Acts 4:24; 14:15

This list includes a few passages which are not formally introduced as quotations, though they are taken directly from the Psalms, but it does not attempt to collect the numerous indirect allusions and references to the thought and language of the Psalms which are to be found in the New Testament, and which are interesting and important as an indication of the writers' familiarity with the Psalter.

Appendix 5. Example of a Readers Theater Approach to the Psalms

I've found that passages of scripture can be read with profit by a team of three or four readers from a script which indicates which reader should read which portion.

It is quite possible to create a script to ready scripture just as it as written. However, I have found that repetition can often help the listeners get some of the important points of the passage. Below is an example from Psalm 19 in the NIV. Experiment on this out with several readers to see what is possible. Then try your hand at writing readers theater scripts for whatever psalms or other scriptures you'd like to read publicly.

I prepare the script in Microsoft Word and make copies for each reader. Then I use a yellow highlighter on each script to clarify which portions that reader will be reading. Then I try to get the readers together for one run-through prior to the worship service in which the reading is used.

Psalm 19 – Readers Theater

A readers theater with three voices. by Ralph F. Wilson

ALL	The heavens declare the glory of God.
READER 1	The **heavens** declare the glory of God.
READER 2	The heavens **declare** the glory of God.
READER 3	The heavens declare the **glory of God**.
ALL	The skies proclaim the work of his hands.
READER 1	Day after day they pour forth speech.
READER 2	Night after night they display knowledge.
READER 1	Day after day.
READER 2	Night after night.
READER 1	There is no speech or language where their voice is not heard.
READER 2	Their voice goes out into all the earth.

READER 3	Their words to the ends of the world.
READER 1	In the heavens he has pitched a tent for the sun.
READER 2	It is like a bridegroom coming forth from his pavilion.
READER 3	It is like a champion rejoicing to run his course.
READER 1	It rises at one end of the heavens.
READER 2	And makes its circuit to the other.
READER 3	Nothing is hidden from its heat.
ALL	The law of the LORD is perfect....
READER 1	Reviving the soul.
ALL	The statutes of the LORD are trustworthy....
READER 2	Making wise the simple.
ALL	The precepts of the LORD are right....
READER 3	Giving joy to the heart.
ALL	The commands of the LORD are radiant....
READER 1	Giving light to the eyes.
ALL	The fear of the LORD is pure....
READER 2	Enduring forever.
ALL	The ordinances of the LORD are sure
READER 1	And altogether righteous.
READER 2	Altogether righteous
READER 3	Righteous altogether.
READER 1	They are more precious than gold,
READER 2	Gold!

READER 3	Gold!
READER 2	More than much pure gold.
READER 1	They are sweeter than honey.
READER 2	Sweeter like honey.
READER 3	Sweeter than honey.
READER 2	Sweeter than honey from the honeycomb.
READER 1	By them is your servant warned.
READER 2	In keeping them there is great reward.
ALL	Who can discern his errors?
READER 2	Not I.
READER 3	Not I.
ALL	Forgive my hidden faults.
READER 3	Yes, forgive them.
READER 1	Keep your servant also from willful sins.
READER 2	May they not rule over me.
READER 3	Keep me from being a puppet of my sinful compulsions.
READER 2	Set me free from them.
READER 1	Then will I be blameless.
READER 2	Then I will be innocent of great transgression.
READER 3	Yes, innocent.
READER 1	May the words of my mouth....
READER 2	And the meditation of my heart
READER 3	Yes, my musings and thoughts.

READER 1	Be pleasing in your sight.
READER 2	Yes, may my very thoughts please you.
ALL	O LORD, my Rock and my Redeemer.
READER 1	O LORD!
READER 2	O Rock of mine!
READER 1	O Lord my Redeemer.
READER 3	O my Kinsman-Redeemer.
READER 1	May the words of my mouth
READER 2	And the meditation of my heart
READER 3	Be pleasing in your sight,
ALL	O LORD, my Rock and my Redeemer.

Appendix 6. Class or Group Handouts

If you're working with a class or small group, feel free to duplicate the handouts in this appendix at no additional charge. If you'd like to print 8-1/2" x 11" or A4 sheets, you can download the free Participant Guide handout sheets at:

www.jesuswalk.com/psalms/psalms-lesson-handouts.pdf

You'll find three to five questions for each lesson. Each question may include several sub-questions. These are designed to get group members engaged in discussion of the key points of the passage. If you're running short of time, feel free to skip questions or portions of questions.

During the first lesson, hand out the "Exercises to Help You Experience the Psalms" sheet. Then for each successive lesson, ask class members to come prepared to share how they chose to experience one of the psalms included in that lesson based on some of the suggestions given in the exercise sheet. This alone will engage members and make the class great fun – and bring great learning.

Exercises to Help You Experience the Psalms

In order to encourage you to truly experience the psalms and make them your own, **complete one of the following exercises for each of the lessons in this study.** These aren't designed to create busywork, but to stretch you spiritually. When you finish, report back to the group how the exercise worked for you. Ideally, you'll vary the exercises from lesson to lesson to allow the Psalms to become part of you in new ways.

1. **Pray a Psalm.** Select one of the psalms along the theme of the lesson. Then, using the ideas and as many of the words as seem to fit your situation, pray that prayer to God, inserting your own struggles and needs within the prayer. Go through the entire psalm, paraphrasing it as you pray it sincerely to God. Many people have exercised this kind of prayer – they pray through every Scripture passage they read. Why don't you start this practice with one of the psalms?

2. **Meditate on a Psalm.** To meditate means to think deeply about something and mull it over in your mind over a period of time. You might read it several times in different translations. Say it over to yourself to feel the words on your lips. Write it out longhand. Consider the meaning of each important word. Memorization is another exercise, but memorizing is a good way to meditate on a verse or a passage.

3. **Read a Psalm to a Shut-in.** People who are home-bound or in hospitals, nursing homes, jails, etc. need encouragement. As your exercise, read a psalm from this week's theme to a shut-in. If you read more than one you'll be doubly blessed!

4. **Paraphrase a Psalm.** Write out a paraphrase of the psalm of your choosing in your own words. Try to find modern-day synonyms and thoughts that correspond to the thoughts in the psalm. Don't be afraid to be creative. If you need ideas, try reading a few psalms from *The Message* to see how Eugene Peterson creatively paraphrased the Psalms.

5. **Write Your Own Psalm.** Write your own psalm based on the theme of this lesson. You're entirely free in how you do this. Some approaches include:
   o Write in the style of Hebrew poetry using thought parallelism and imagery. This will be fun, though you may find it challenging. Consult my Introduction to Psalms in the section on Hebrew Poetry before beginning.
   o Write a psalm with lines that rhyme like traditional Western poetry.
   o Write a psalm in free verse, not bothering to make the lines rhyme. Just express yourself to God.
   o Write a psalm in Haiku style.

Write a psalm in any style you wish. The idea here is to learn to express yourself to God more freely.

6. **Sing a Psalm**. Find a song, hymn, or praise chorus that relates to the theme of this chapter – and that is based on a psalm. Then sing it or lead it for your group. If you like, write your own song, or find a melody that you can use to sing the words of the song from a translation you prefer. Be creative here.

7. **Prepare a Liturgy, Responsive Reading, or Choral Reading from a Psalm**. Psalms are at the core of the liturgy of Catholic, Orthodox, and Anglican branches of the Church. Explore adapting a psalm for public worship. You might enjoy writing the script for a choral reading of a psalm or portion of a psalm creating parts for 3 or 4 readers. Then try it out during a worship service or in your small group or class.

8. **Teach or Preach a Psalm**. It's hard to prepare a message for people without really getting inside the text. Teach a psalm to a class of children, youth, or adults, or preach a psalm to your congregation.

9. **Memorize a Psalm**. "My mind is too old to memorize!" Hogwash! Try it, but perhaps start with a short psalm, or one you've already partially memorized. It's work, but you can do it and you'll find it very spiritually enriching. In ancient days many Hebrew boys memorized the entire Psalter. In his 90s, Billy Graham put it this way:

> "Over the years I've memorized many passages from the Bible, and I'm especially thankful now that I did this. I wish we gave more attention to Bible memorization in our churches today."[1]

Memorize one psalm that relates to the theme of the lesson.

[1] Billy Graham in "Quotation Marks," *Christianity Today*, June 2007, p. 19.

1. Marveling at God's Majesty in Creation (Psalms 8, 19, 139)

Psalm 8 – How Majestic Is Your Name in All the Earth

Q1. (Psalm 8). What does this psalm teach about God? What does it teach about human beings? What does it teach us about Christ? What does it teach about our responsibilities?

Psalm 19 – The Heavens Proclaim the Glory of God

Q2. (Psalm 19) Verses 1 to 6 seem very different from verses 7 to 13, but there is a common thread that relates the first part to the second part. What is it? In what way does the psalmist seem to bask in God's Word? Have you ever felt that way? How does the psalmist's wonder in creation seem to affect him in this psalm? In the classic prayer of verse 14, what is David asking God to do?

Psalm 139 – The Creator and Searcher of My Inmost Being

Q3. (Psalm 139). In what way does the wonder of creation in the psalm seem to affect the psalmist? In his concluding prayer in verses 23-24, what does he ask God to do?

Next Lesson

Next week we'll be looking at **Lesson 2. Thirsting for God (Psalms 27, 42-43, 63)**. In order to encourage you to truly experience the psalms and make them your own, complete one of the exercises suggested in "Exercises to Help You Experience the Psalms" for *one* of the psalms we'll study next week. This isn't designed to create busywork, but to stretch you spiritually. Next week report to the group how the exercise worked for you.

2. Thirsting for God (Psalms 27, 42-43, 63)

Psalm 27 – Your face, Lord, I Will Seek

Q1. (Psalm 24) What does it mean that David desires to "dwell in the house of the Lord"? What does it mean to "seek his face"? How does David provide hope at the end of this Psalm?

Psalm 42-43 – Combating Depression with Faith

1. **Self-talk**, words addressed to himself, of hope, that he will eventually have cause to rejoice in God again. (42:5)
2. **Deliberate remembrance,** recalling God to mind, (42:6-7)
3. **Singing and praying** to God night and day (42:8)

Q2. (Psalms 42-43). What is the psalmist feeling during this spiritual struggle? How does he combat his spiritual depression? Have you ever felt this way? How did you reach out to God at this time?

Psalm 63 – Earnestly I Seek You

Q3. (Psalm 63) Why is recognition that God loves you the basis of all faith? What does this realization bring about in your life?

Next Lesson

Next week we'll be looking at **Lesson 3. Choosing the Right Path (Psalms 1, 15, and 133)**. In order to encourage you to truly experience the psalms and make them your own, complete one of the exercises suggested in "Exercises to Help You Experience the Psalms" for *one* of the psalms we'll study next week. This isn't designed to create busywork, but to stretch you spiritually. Next week report to the group how the exercise worked for you.

3. Choosing the Right Path (Psalms 1, 15, and 133)

Psalm 1 – The Two Ways, Righteous and Unrighteousness

Q1. (Psalm 1). This short psalm seems to reaffirm what we already know: the righteous will succeed and the wicked will perish. Why do we need to be reminded of this? From an emotional standpoint, what lines in this psalm stand out to you. Why do you think you like them?

Psalm 15 – Characteristics of a Righteous Person

Q2. (Psalm 15) The Wisdom Psalms are meant to instruct us. How would you use this psalm in your family to instruct your children? What topics of right living does it cover?

Psalm 133 – The Beauty of Unity

Q3. (Psalm 133) What about this short psalm seems to attract you? Why is "dwelling together in unity" so difficult? What kinds of commitments does unity require of us? How do the principles of unity and purity seem to conflict with each other? Why are reconciliation and unity such high values in Jesus' teaching, do you think?

Next Lesson

Next week we'll be looking at **Lesson 4. Offering High Praises to God (Psalms 150, 95, and 98)**. In order to encourage you to truly experience the psalms and make them your own, complete one of the exercises suggested in "Exercises to Help You Experience the Psalms" for *one* of the psalms we'll study next week. This isn't designed to create busywork, but to stretch you spiritually. Next week report to the group how the exercise worked for you.

4. Offering High Praises to God (Psalms 150, 95, and 98)

Hallelujah mean? It is a command, an imperative, made up of three parts:

hālal	*lu*	*Yah*
Praise	you (plural)	short for Yahweh, "the LORD"

The verb *hālal* means "praise." "This root connotes being sincerely and deeply thankful for and/or satisfied in lauding a superior quality(ies) or great, great act(s) of the object." It can mean, "to brag," and be used to praise a man or woman. But its primary use in the Old Testament is directed toward God.

Psalm 150 – Let Everything that Has Breath Praise the Lord!

Q1. (Psalm 150) What does this psalm teach us about praise? Where should praise occur? With what should praise be conducted? Who should praise? What does this psalm make you feel like after reading it out loud?

Psalm 95 – Come, Let Us Worship and Bow Down

Q2. (Psalm 95) In Psalm 95 we are commanded to worship the Lord. What are the reasons *why* we should worship contained in this psalm? Why do you think the warning in verses 8-11 is included in this psalm? How does this fit with the earlier elements of the psalm?

Psalm 98 – Sing to the Lord a New Song

Q3. (Psalm 98) What are the reasons given for praise in Psalm 98? Why do you think praise is so exuberant in this psalm? How exuberant is praise in your congregation, in your life? Why or why not is it exuberant?

Next Lesson

Next week we'll be looking at **Lesson 5. Crying Out for Rescue (Psalms 69, 40, 80)**. In order to encourage you to truly experience the psalms and make them your own, complete one of the exercises suggested in "Exercises to Help You Experience the Psalms" for *one* of the psalms we'll study next week. This isn't designed to create busywork, but to stretch you spiritually. Next week report to the group how the exercise worked for you.

5. Crying Out for Rescue (Psalms 69, 40, 80)

Psalm 69 – Deep Waters and Miry Depths

Q1. (Psalm 69:12-18) How could David dare to ask anything from God after the shameful things he had done with Bathsheba and Uriah? How does God's grace and mercy function in the face of our sins?

Q2. (Psalm 69:30-32) Why does this lament (and nearly all laments in the Psalms) end with an upswing of hope and praise? What does this teach us about our own laments and prayers? Why is praise, the language of faith, so important in our prayers, especially prayers of desperate pleas for help?

Psalm 40 – O My God, Do Not Delay

Q3. (Psalm 40:5b) When you realize that God's thoughts and plans are focused on you in particular, how does that make you respond?

Q4. (Psalm 40:17) In this verse David combines both humility and faith in his prayer to God. Why are both humility and faith necessary? What happens when one of these qualities is missing?

Psalm 80 – Restore Us, O God

Q5. (Psalm 80) If you were to formulate a personal prayer for revival for your own life or for your congregation, how would you word it? What elements should be present in a prayer for personal or congregational revival? What would this prayer have in common with 2 Chronicles 7:14? How does this kind of prayer pave the way for revival and restoration to take place?

Next Lesson

Next week we'll be looking at **Lesson 6. Trusting in God's Protection (Psalms 61, 91, 121)**. In order to encourage you to truly experience the psalms and make them your own, complete one of the exercises suggested in "Exercises to Help You Experience the Psalms" for *one* of the psalms we'll study next week. This isn't designed to create busywork, but to stretch you spiritually. Next week report to the group how the exercise worked for you.

6. Trusting in God's Protection (Psalms 61, 91, 121)

Psalm 61 – Lead Me to the Rock that Is Higher than I

Q1. (Psalm 61:1-4) What images does the psalmist evoke to communicate his trust in God's protection? How do the first four verses of this psalm make you feel?

Psalm 91 – Dwelling in the Shelter of the Most High

Q2. (Psalm 91) What does this psalm teach us about God's protection when in danger? What does it teach about our authority to vanquish our enemies? What promises does Psalm 91 contain? How does this psalm make you feel?

Psalm 121 – I Will Lift Up My Eyes to the Hills

Q3. (Psalm 121). What reassurance is it to you that God keeps you and watches over you? How does Psalm 121 make you feel?

Q4. Since Christians don't seem immune to accident, persecution, and death, how are we to understand these psalms of protection? Why don't some believers seem to be protected? Does God *really* protect us? How?

Next Lesson

Next week we'll be looking at **Lesson 7. Resting in God's Care (Psalms 131, 23, 16, 3, 31, 46)**. In order to encourage you to truly experience the psalms and make them your own, complete one of the exercises suggested in "Exercises to Help You Experience the Psalms" for *one* of the psalms we'll study next week. This isn't designed to create busywork, but to stretch you spiritually. Next week report to the group how the exercise worked for you.

7. Resting in God's Care (Psalms 131, 23, 16, 3, 31, 46)

Psalm 131 – I Have Stilled and Quieted My Soul

Q1. According to Psalm 131, just *how* does David quiet his inner person before the Lord? What are the elements mentioned in this psalm?

Psalm 23 – The Lord Is My Shepherd

Q2. According to Psalm 23, how does the Lord our Shepherd quiet his sheep and give them confidence? How many ways can you find in this psalm?

Psalm 16 – You Will Not Abandon Me to the Grave

Psalm 3 – I Lie Down and Sleep

Psalm 31 – Into Your Hands I Commit My Spirit

Q3. (Psalm 31) What does it mean to say to the Lord, "Into your hands I commit my spirit" (31:5)? How does that statement bring peace to a person? How does the statement, "My times are in your hands" (31:15), bring peace to the troubled soul?

Psalm 46 – Our Ever-Present Help in Trouble

Q4. (Psalm 46) How does the imagery of the river and streams in verse 4 function in Psalm 46 to speak peace to the harassed and harried person? Verse 10 tells us: "Be still and know that I am God." How does knowledge of who He is affect our peace? How should it affect our words? Why does He command us to "be still" as a result of this knowledge?

Q5. After you've studied the psalms in this chapter, what do you think it means to "rest" in God? How do you seek God's peace when you have a dozen things coming against you?

Next Lesson

Next week we'll be looking at **Lesson 8. Exulting in God (Psalms 57, 96, 126, and 24)**. In order to encourage you to truly experience the psalms and make them your own, complete one of the exercises suggested in "Exercises to Help You Experience the Psalms" for *one* of the psalms we'll study next week. This isn't designed to create busywork, but to stretch you spiritually. Next week report to the group how the exercise worked for you.

8. Exulting in God (Psalms 57, 96, 126, and 24)

Psalm 57 – I Will Awake the Dawn!

Q1. (Psalm 57) Why is praise difficult in the midst of trying circumstances? How does praise affect our faith? Our attitude? Our motivation?

Psalm 96 – Ascribe to the Lord the Glory Due His Name

Q2. (Psalm 96) What does it mean to "ascribe" to God attributes of glory and strength? What happens when we fail to ascribe such qualities to him? In what sense is praise to God "fitting" or "worthy"?

Psalm 126 – He Who Goes Out Weeping Will Return with Songs of Joy

Q3. (Psalm 126). In this psalm, the nation is going through some kind of crisis. How does the memory of God's deliverance in verses 1-3 prepare them for the prayer of verse 4? How do you understand the two metaphors of deliverance: (1) a wadi or dry gully and (2) sowing and reaping? How do these metaphors help you in your situation?

Psalm 24 – The King of Glory

Q4. (Psalm 24) How do verses 1-2 establish the Lord's right as King? What do verses 3-6 tell us about the requirements of the King? What do verses 7-10 tell us about the glory of the King? How does this psalm speak to you in your situation?

Next Lesson

Next week we'll be looking at **Lesson 9. Rejoicing in God's Character (Psalms 103, 145, and 117)**. In order to encourage you to truly experience the psalms and make them your own, complete one of the exercises suggested in "Exercises to Help You Experience the Psalms" for *one* of the psalms we'll study next week. This isn't designed to create busywork, but to stretch you spiritually. Next week report to the group how the exercise worked for you.

9. Rejoicing in God's Character (Psalms 103, 145, and 117)

Psalm 103 – Bless the Lord, O My Soul

Q1. (Psalm 103) Which one or two aspects of God's character mentioned in this Psalm stand out to you? Why do you think the Exodus was so foundational in Israel's understanding of God? According to Psalm 103:10-12, what are the limits to God's forgiveness?

Psalm 145 – I Exalt You, My God the King

Q2. (Psalm 145) Which aspects of God's character mentioned in Psalm 145 stand out to you in particular? Why is it important for "every creature," every human being, to praise him? What are you doing to help that happen?

Psalm 117 – The Faithfulness of the Lord Endures Forever

Q3. (Psalm 117 and Lamentations 3:22-23). Why are love and trustworthiness so important as the bedrock of the Old Testament faith? What kinds of terms does the New Testament use to talk about these characteristics? Can you think of any New Testament verses that speak of these themes?

Next Lesson

Next week we'll be looking at **Lesson 10. Looking Forward to the Messiah (Psalms 2, 110, and 22)**. In order to encourage you to truly experience the psalms and make them your own, complete one of the exercises suggested in "Exercises to Help You Experience the Psalms" for *one* of the psalms we'll study next week. This isn't designed to create busywork, but to stretch you spiritually. Next week report to the group how the exercise worked for you.

10. Looking Forward to the Messiah (Psalms 2, 110, and 22)

Psalm 2 – You Are My Son, Today I Have Begotten You

Q1. (Psalm 2) What does Psalm 2 teach us about Yahweh's "anointed" king? Why do you think the apostles saw this passage as referring to Jesus the Messiah? What does the passage teach about the importance of submission to Jesus the Christ before it is too late?

Psalm 110 – The Messiah as Priest and King

Q2. (Psalm 110) Why do you think that Jesus asked the Pharisees about verse 1, "If then David calls him 'Lord,' how can he be his son?" What point was Jesus making? How does Jesus combine the roles of Warrior-King and Priest in his ministry to us and to this world? How do you reconcile the violence suggested in verses 5-6 with Jesus as "Prince of Peace"?

Psalm 22 – My God, Why Have You Forsaken Me?

Q3. (Psalm 22:1) Why do you think Jesus spoke the words of Psalm 22:1? What was he seeking to express? What was he feeling? How did God answer his plea?

Q4. (Psalm 22) What similarities do you see between the words of Psalm 22 and the events of Jesus' crucifixion? Do you think Jesus understood Psalm 22 as referring to himself? Why do you think the Spirit inspired David to pen these words?

Next Lesson

Next week we'll be looking at **Lesson 11. Finding Forgiveness and Restoration (Psalms 32 and 51)**. In order to encourage you to truly experience the psalms and make them your own, complete one of the exercises suggested in "Exercises to Help You Experience the Psalms" for *one* of the psalms we'll study next week. This isn't designed to create busywork, but to stretch you spiritually. Next week report to the group how the exercise worked for you.

11. Finding Forgiveness and Restoration (Psalms 32 and 51)

Psalm 32 – Blessed Is the One Whose Sin Is Forgiven

Q1. (Psalm 32:2-5) How does self-deceit operate with sin to enslave us? How does confession enable us to get free from sin? Why do we sometimes resist the truth about ourselves? What does it take to get us to see truth sometimes?

Psalm 51 – Create in Me a Clean Heart, O Lord

Q2. (Psalm 51:3-6) When David says, "Against you only I have sinned" (4a) is he minimizing his sin against Bathsheba and Uriah? What does he mean by this? When he mentions his sinfulness from before birth is he excusing himself or blaming Original Sin? What does he mean by this?

Q3. (Psalm 51:10-12) How is it possible to have a "pure heart" after great sin? What does a "pure heart" consist of? What is the relationship between a "pure heart" (Psalm 51:10) and a "united" or "undivided heart" (Psalm 86:11)? Who purifies the heart? What is the process?

Q4. (Psalm 51:17) How does one achieve a "broken and contrite heart"? What are the earmarks of this condition? How does this differ from "being sorry" for a sin? How does humility relate to this condition?

12. Giving Thanks to Our Faithful God (Psalms 100, 107, 118, and 34)

Psalm 100 – Enter His Gates with Thanksgiving

Q1. (Psalm 100) What is the predominant emotion in Psalm 100? How does this psalm make you feel emotionally about God? What are the reasons for praise given in verses 3 and 5? What are the commands in this psalm?

Psalm 107 – Give Thanks to the Lord for His Unfailing Love

Psalm 118 – His Love Endures Forever

Q2. (Psalm 118) What does "the stone the builders rejected" (verses 22-23) have to do with the Messiah? What do verses 25-27 have to do with the Messiah?

Psalm 34 – Taste and See that the Lord Is Good

Q3. (Psalm 34:1-3) Why should we praise God continually? What are barriers to continual praise? What does continual praise do to our spirit? How are you training yourself to praise continually?

Q4. (Psalm 34:18-22) What encouragement does David give to the brokenhearted? What does it mean that God "redeems" you? How can we avoid condemnation according to Psalm 34:22?

My Purpose

CPSIA information can be obtained
at www.ICGtesting.com
Printed in the USA
LVHW03s0521121018
593225LV00010B/625/P